PRIVATISATION OF PUBLIC SECTOR UNDERTAKINGS: EXPERIMENTATION ABROAD

PRIVATISATION OF PUBLIC SECTOR UNDERTAKINGS: EXPERIMENTATION ABROAD

JESIAH SELVAM

SERIALS PUBLICATIONS
NEW DELHI

First Published - 2018

ISBN: 978-81-8387-110-5

Published by

SERIALS PUBLICATIONS
4830/24, Prahlad Street, Ansari Road
Darya Ganj, New Delhi-110002 (India)
Phone : 23245225 Fax : 91-11-23272135
E-mail: serials@satyam.net.in

I Dedicate this Book to my Family for the Love and Care, and to the Teachers for my knowledge

Contents

Preface

India and Ethiopia have implemented privatisation programme since 1991 carrying a story of length for fifteen years. Privatisation emerged in India as a pursuit of the industrial policy, 1991, where as in Ethiopia, the same came into action at the advent of the Transitional Economic Policy, 1991. Nonetheless, privatisation as a part and parcel of economic reforms seems to be a new phenomenon to many Indians and so do Ethiopians. The reasons why it is not so popular in these countries are many. The most important reasons are the magnitude of our privatisation programme, and prevailing political scenario. As far as size and speed are concerned, these two countries showed a dismayed performance since the privatisation programme in these countries is found to be too small in per cent of GDP,—less than half a per cent, and much slow in speed. In most of the years since 1991, they even failed to cross ten per cent of the target set by the government. There are many such similarities between these two countries thanks to their richest and oldest civilization and long-standing trade relationships. Owing to these reasons, there is a dearth of review of literature and empirical evidences about privatisation.

This book is written out of an in-depth study about privatisation in Ethiopia. The book is also designed in such a way that it is comprehensive with the important issues involved in the transition of PSUs into Private ones: Processing Issues, economic and political Issues, socio-labour and Managerial Issues. The importance of this research is that it is believed to contribute significantly towards the empirical evidences and privatization literature which are indeed dearth in the Least Developed and Developing Countries (LDCs), particularly in Asia and Africa.

TARGET AUDIENCES

This book is suitable for courses directed at advanced diploma, MBA and EMBA programmes. It is also designed to target at economists, policy makers and research scholars pursuing their research on international business and developmental economics.

ORGANISATION OF THIS BOOK

The book is organised into seven chapters, of which four chapters are empirical, and the rest are assigned to the introduction, review of literature, conceptual framework and methodology for research respectively. To complement, the findings, recommendations and the future research prospects as a final chapter conclude the book.

The Chapter I: Introduction—deals with the background of the study, the historical background of privatisation, and very importantly the causes and necessities which urged the world to adopt the privatisation as a strong reforming measure. Moreover, it has given an overview of privatisation experiences from different countries of well-developed, transition, developing and under-developed countries.

The Chapter II: Review of Literature and Methodology—gives a broad review of literature and conceptual framework and methodology of the study. The review of literature in this chapter enables the researcher to find out the gap to be filled up through this research, whereas the conceptual framework and methodology outline the objectives, research design and method in which the research was executed.

Chapter III: Economic Reforms and Privatisation in Ethiopia—discusses the Ethiopian economic background, reforms and also analyses the initiative symptoms in Ethiopia, leaning towards privatisation.

Chapter IV: Processing and Mechanism Issues in Privatisation—deals with the modus-operandi in which the privatisation programme has been executed.

Chapter V: Economic and Political Issues in Privatisation—covers the economic and political issues of privatisation. It also investigates to what extent these issues are approached by privatisation.

Chapter VI: Socio-labour and Managerial Issues in Privatisation—includes the socio-labour, and managerial issues of privatisation. It also investigates to what extent these issues are approached by privatisation.

Chapter VII: Summary of Findings, Conclusion and Suggestions—concludes the research with the summary of findings, conclusion, and suggestions, leaving scope for further research.

ACKNOWLEDGEMENT

I wish to thank my research supervisors, Dr. A. Meenakshisundararajan, Reader in Economics, P.G. Department of Economics and Research Centre, S.T. Hindu College, Nagercoil and Dr. T. Iyappan, Reader in Economics, Arignar Anna College, Aralvoimozhi for their inspiring guidance and support throughout my study. I express my gratitude to Manonmaniam Sundaranar University as well as P.G. Department of Economics and Research Centre, S.T. Hindu College, Tamil Nadu for the research opportunity they provided.

Thanks also go to Mr. Netsanet Wondirad, Post Privatisation Manager, and Mr. Tafera Tesfaye, Post Privatisation Impact Analyst, Ethiopian Privatisation Agency, Federal Democratic Republic of Ethiopia for their assistance during my data collection from their offices. The hospitality they showed towards me is unforgettable, moments which indeed gave me a leap in my target.

Sincere thanks are due to the authorities of the Ethiopian Privatisation Agency (EPA), Ethiopian Investment Authority (EIA), Ministry of Finance (MoF), Ministry of Finance and Economic Development (MoFED), Ministry of Trade and Industry (MoTI), the World Bank and the International Monetary Fund (IMF), Addis Ababa, Ethiopia. Not only does my gratitude go to the officials of these institutions, but also specially to the librarians who never showed any hesitation whenever they were approached.

Not exaggerated is the tireless assistance of M/s. M. Prasanna Kumari who helped me in all my data collection work, and her moral support for which words are inadequate to express. It is my duty to acknowledge M/s. Cynthia V. Davidson, Assistant Professor, Department of Foreign Languages and Linguistics who went through the manuscript, and offered me a standard language in enriching the book.

I honestly thank Dr. T. Somasekhar, Managing Trustee—Secretary, Indian Academy Education Trust Bangalore for his moral support in publishing this book.

I also extend my sincere thanks to Dr. R. Karunakaran, Mr. Vasanth Thompson Mr. J. Thirubhuvan, Dr. Balakrishnan and Mr. Adem G/Yesus who often helped me in sharing their experiences and research mettle.

I owe a lot to my parents Mrs. and Mr. A. Jesiah, my wife A. Mary Sujatha, my children Mary Salomin and Steve Snehan and all other family members for not only for their moral support and encouragement in writing this book, but also stood in good stead in all my endeavours.

JESIAH SELVAM

Acronyms and Abbreviations

ADLI	Agricultural Development-Led Industrialisation
AGOA	African Growth and Opportunity Act
ASEAN	Association of South East Asian Nations
AU	African Union
C&AG	Comptroller and Auditor General
COMESA	Common Market for Eastern and Southern Africa
CSA	Central Statistical Authority
EAIT	Earnings After Income Tax
EEA	Ethiopian Economic Association
EIA	Ethiopian Investment Authority
EPA	Ethiopian Privatisation Agency
ESOP	Employee Stock Ownership Enterprises
ETB	Ethiopian Birr
FAG	Federal Auditor General
GDP	Gross Domestic Product
GNI	Gross National Income
GoE	Government of Ethiopia
FDI	Foreign Direct Investment
EFY	Ethiopian Fiscal Year
HDI	Human Development Index
HIPC	Highly Indebted Poor Countries
IBRD	International Bank for Reconstruction and Development
IFC	International Finance Corporations

IGE	Imperial Government of Ethiopia
IMF	International Monetary Fund
IPO	Initial Public Offering
LDCs	Least Developed Countries
LPG	Liberalisation, Privatisation and Globalisation
MEDaC	Ministry for Economic Development and Cooperation
MEBO	Management and Employees Buy Out
MoFED	Ministry of Finance & Economic Development
NAPED	New Partnership for Africa's Development
NCBG	National Commercial Bank Group Limited
OECD	Organisation for Economic Cooperation Development
OLS	Ordinary Least Square
OPEC	Organisation of Petroleum Exporting Countries
PP	Privatisation Proceeds
PSUs	Public Sector Undertakings
ROI	Return on Investment
SAL	Structural Adjustment Loan
SAP	Structural Adjustment Programme
SNA	System of National Accounts
SSA	Sub-Saharan Africa
TGE	Transitional Government of Ethiopia
UNDP	United Nations Development Programme
USAID	United States Aid for International Development
USD	United States of America Dollars
UN	United Nations
WTO	World Trade Organisation
WB	World Bank

CHAPTER - 1

Introduction

The recent upset and turmoil experienced with the functioning of public sector undertakings[1], and the two engines of economic liberalisation and democratisation have led most of the third world countries marching towards privatisation. Since the beginning of the 1980s, most of the developing world has moved unevenly, but undeniably toward liberal, market-oriented economic reforms.

The 1960s and 1970s were decades of unprecedented economic nationalism, a growing role for state interventions in the economy and experimentation with variants of socialism and self-reliance. Comprehensive development planning was widespread, and the prevailing model of development through out much of Latin America, Asia and Africa emerged then as a variant form of state intervention model which was largely inward-oriented import-substitution industrialisation. It was also socially re-distributive, at least in rhetoric. Hence, these countries were contemplating to take steps either to make PSUs as profit earned ones or simply privatise them.

In the 1980s and 1990s, by contrast, there have been major changes in the political economy of these countries. Two trends have been evident. First, a wave of democratic revolutions swept the world. In country after country, totalitarian governments collapsed, to be replaced by democratically elected governments that were typically more committed to free market capitalism than their predecessors had been. The change was most dramatic in Eastern Europe, where the collapse of Communism brought an end to the Cold War and led to the break-up of the Soviet Union, but similar changes were occurring through out the world during the same period. Second, there has been a strong move away from centrally planned and mixed economies, and toward more of a free market economic model (Hill, 1997: 62-3). Not only are these two trends but also very particularly inefficiency of public sector undertakings (PSUs) and its subsequent effect in a drainage of their capital, excessive internal and external burden of debt, and subsequently the weakening of the government's exchequer has made a great necessity for severe economic reforms including privatisation.

Looking slightly from different perspectives particularly socially, availability of public funds for PSUs in large measures represents the sacrifice made by the people of a country, especially the poor. It is obvious that the poor people have sacrificed their benefits as most of the public fund has obviously been redirected to strengthening these enterprises, but the result was in vain.

Privatisation has been adopted in a number of countries as an economic reform either as part of structural adjustment or as a measure towards greater involvement of the private sector in the growth process. It can, thus, be said that privatisation in broad terms encompasses involvement of greater market forces to ensure higher competition, and to reduce the role of the state in the economic sphere, and thus bring in greater private involvement into government activities. However, in its strict sense, privatisation refers to 'divestiture' or 'denationalisation', i.e., the transfer of ownership from state to private entity. Put in another way, it means sale or transfer of the majority portion of the shares in a public enterprise to a private entity. The major motive behind privatisation has been to ensure greater efficiency in the system as a whole. In some countries, privatisation has also emerged because of the lack of political will to bring about reforms in the public sector.

Privatisation has been exercised in many countries as part of economic reforms coincident with liberalisation and globalisation since the 1980s because these three exercises are the major pre-conditions for the better functioning of economic reforms.

ECONOMIC REFORMS AND ITS DRIVE TO LPG (LIBERALISATION, PRIVATISATION AND GLOBALISATION)

Economic reforms cover a wide range of interpretations. Some people say that economic reforms reduce government intervention in the economy raising itself to a market economy. Some others argue that economic reforms not only reduce the government intervention, but also ensure good governance (Mutebile, 1999), which entails publicly accountable institutions of government, capable of making and implementing policies in an efficient, transparent and honest manner, thereby serving a wider public interest. The latter seems to be wider than the earlier one because market economy would not become beneficial, unless the market conditions were reformed with good governance.

Indeed, economic reforms are devised in such a way that they should go even beyond the economic sphere, and bring up the nation under a comprehensive structure of reforms which includes not only an efficient and transparent system in public expenditure management and tax system (Public financial reforms), but also a fair and effective legal and regulatory frame work, political accountability in free and fair elections and observance of fundamental freedom and rights of human beings. It also requires a clear separation of powers of executive, legislature, and the judiciary, as well as recognition of the role of an independent press and media. Economic reforms, therefore, have a wide scope—inseparable from the political and social sphere—and must be seen in this way for its better functioning in any economy.

The major pre-condition for economic reform is liberalisation, followed by privatisation and globalisation. Liberalisation, which liberates the basic commodity and labour markets through the elimination of tariff and non-tariff barriers and other preferential agreements, leads to a higher degree of adherence to the norms of international trade. Privatisation as one of the structural reforms is expected to take advantage of the most liberalised market-driven environment, converting a domestic based economy to a globalised economy. It is, therefore, well understood that by functions and mechanisms, LPG are interrelated and interdependent. But in the sequence of accomplishment, liberalisation and privatisation are roads to globalisation. The forthcoming sub-headings deal with globalisation as a prelude to the discussion moves to privatisation which is discussed in detail in the latter sub-headings.

Globalisation and its Impact on Privatisation

Globalisation, which is an impetus to privatisation, began gaining momentum in the 1960s when businesses in search of larger markets expanded their reach and interests beyond national borders. Globalisation is multidimensional, affecting all aspects of life—economic, cultural, environmental, and social—as well as relations between governments and nations on the five continents. Globalisation is characterised, in particular, by an intensification of cross-border trade and increased financial and foreign investment flows, promoted by rapid liberalisation and advances in information technologies. For many countries, this global process has made the pursuit of development and maintenance of internal and external stability a very difficult and delicate task. On the other hand, globalisation holds out to participants the promise of growth in trade and international investment, and on the contrary it heightens the risks of instability and marginalisation.

Globalisation has brought forward so many impacts on governments, which unless privatised, the trade competitiveness and quality cannot be claimed at all. The private sector has already proved its brilliance pertaining to these parameters, and is encouraged by the World Bank and the developed countries. The World Bank (George, 2002) has recently launched a new development aid package called the Private Development Strategy (PSD), while the American Government has launched its own Millennium Challenge Account (MCA). More importantly, the hurdles in trade have been getting off as globalisation likes to see the world as a Global village. Nowadays, trade, the central point of globalisation, is carried out with not much of difficulty than before.

Globalisation and its Impact on African Privatisation

There are a number of reasons why many analysts advocate Africa's greater integration with the global economy. The overriding reasons are Africa's poor overall economic performance—which is due to a number of factors, including colonial history, disadvantageous geography, heavy economic dependence on exports of primary products, and macro economic policy errors—and the advantages Africa can derive from globalisation. Africa's economic marginalisation, the result of its relatively isolationist policies and closed economies, explains why economic prosperity has eluded most of the continent. The appeal for a more open economy is based on a simple but powerful premise: economic integration will improve economic performance. Additionally, globalisation will offer new opportunities—such as expanded markets and the acquisition of new technologies and ideas—all of which can yield not increased productivity but offer higher standards of living.

The first avenue of economic integration for most countries is international trade. Trade remains the main vehicle for Africa's participation in, and full integration into, the global economy. Africa's trade is, however, concentrated in a narrow range of primary commodities, and within its narrow range, Africa's market share has been shrinking. During 1960-67, Africa's average share of total work exports was 5.3 per cent. During 1990-98, however, these figures dropped to 2.3 per cent and 2.2 per cent, respectively. This decline is attributed to, among other factors, the restrictions of Africa's trade regimes, slow growth of per capita income, high transportation costs and the continent's distance from major markets.

Although Africa made substantial progress toward trade liberalisation in the 1990s, its trade policies remain, on an average more protectionist than those of most of its trading partners and competitors. With respect to capital markets, the second avenue of globalisation, it has been noted that Africa was arguably the first continent to become integrated with the world economy: a higher proportion of Africa's wealth is held internationally than of any other continent. Estimate of the ratio of capital flight from African countries to Africa's gross national product range between 24 per cent and 143 per cent. And, although the global level of private capital flows has increased, Africa has not been one of the main beneficiaries. Thus, Africa has also missed out on the benefits that usually accompany such flows, such as job creation and transfer of technology, management, and organizational skills. In 1990-94, the net return on investment in Africa was 20-30 per cent, compared with 16-18 per cent for the developing countries as a group (*Ayayi, 2001)*.

Nevertheless, Africa failed to attract the capital flows it needs because of negative perceptions of the continent's economic and political activities, its poor infrastructure, and inadequate legal framework, particularly for the enforcement of contracts. Africa gives foreign direct investment (FDI) the pride of place because of its potential to stimulate economic growth. Although the foreign direct investment in developing countries has increased in recent years,

Africa's share of the total has remained as low as three per cent. The low profile of Africa on FDI is said to be a discouraging factor for globalisation.

HISTORICAL BACKGROUND OF PRIVATISATION

The history of privatisation dates back to the dissolution of the primitive society in which primitive clan communism existed with no state as such, and where man had to conduct his struggle with nature under exceedingly difficult conditions.

The dissolution of primitive communism led to the transfer of cattle from communal to private ownership. Land and tools became private property. With the inception of private ownership, the basis was laid not only for the origin of 'privatisation' but also for the rise and growth of inequality.

Economists' Views on Privatisation

The economic case for privatisation is also not new. Three centuries ago, Adam Smith argues that

> *"In every great monarchy in Europe the sale of the crown lands would produce a very large sum of money, which, if applied to the payment of the public debts, would deliver from mortgage a much greater revenue than any which those lands have ever afforded to the crown.... When the crown lands had become private property, they would, in the course of a few years, become well improved and well cultivated".*

Privatisation, as a conceptual idea, had evolved long back, noticeably in Northern America, where private firms had contracts to clean streets of New York, as early as 1676, a hundred years before the American Revolution (Savas, 1990). Municipal governments have been contracting with the private sector for the provision of services and infrastructure ever since. Through out the history of the United States, private organisations have been heavily involved in building toll roads, turnpikes, canals, waterways, railways and airports.

Besides placing a strong base for private enterprise economics, economists of the past two centuries notably Karl Marx, Alfred Marshall and J.M. Keynes advocated government intervention, though in different degrees, in such a fashion that the government could redistribute the resources of the economy with its constituent units. It was, moreover, added that if the private sector fails to utilise the available resources and maintain full employment, the government can interfere with the functioning of the free-enterprise economy. This was the time when governments were called on to do more and more things directly, and common concern grew for the individual who couldn't take care of himself.

Marshall, as against many other economists who believed in the legitimacy of only positive economics, was deeply interested in ameliorating the conditions of the masses. His economics is a fountain head for what is now called "welfare economics". In his theory published in the late nineteenth century, he questioned against private employees, who would not find it worth their while to spend on the education and training of the workers and children. They also found it difficult to realise that higher wages would be more profitable to them on account of greater labour efficiency (Bhatia, 1989). With the theories, principles and doctrines of these ideologists, the concept of welfare state strongly emerged, and thus the government was urged to be a major participant as well as the umpire in the economy game.

Privatisation after the World War II and in the Post Colonial Period

After the Second World War, socialist governments in the Eastern Bloc countries and Asia nationalized most industrial and service enterprises and collectivised agriculture in order to centrally plan and manage their economies and to constrain or eliminate capitalist influences. However, private sector partnerships with the government were common in Europe in the first half of the twentieth century.

In the post colonial year of the 1950s and 1960s, governments in many newly independent developing countries expropriated foreign-owned companies, centralized control over natural resources, mining and some manufacturing industries, and took a strong role in managing public services and infrastructure. Through out the 1950s and the 1960s, development economists such as Rosenstein-Rodan, Nurkse and Kuznets shared the view that there was a significant role for the state in lifting an economy out of its backwardness. This consensus stemmed from the dominance of Keynesian ideas during the 1950s.

The Socialist regimes, which came to power in Africa and Latin America during the 1970s, also sought to nationalize crucial industries. The Government of the United Republic of Tanzania under Julius

Nyerere applied the concept of "African Socialism" by taking control of the agricultural and agri-business sectors, as well as industries considered to be part of national patrimony. During Allende Government in Chile from 1970 and 1973, the number of state owned or state managed companies increased from 68 to 596 (Rondinelli, 1999).

It is vital to note at this juncture that monetarism—an antagonism to the state intervention concept that also existed contemporarily—was strong during this phase of growing concern for state intervention. Monetarists view that the economy, left to itself, is more stable than when the government manages it with discretionary policy, and that the major cause of economic fluctuations lies in inappropriate government actions (Dornbusch and Fischer, 1981). But as much as failure of the 1968 tax surcharge marked the end of magic New Economics, so the failure of gradualist policies in 1969-1971 was to mark the end of the magic of monetarism. Such monetarist theories were promoted by the then economists like Milton Friedman.

But the world wide recessions of the late 1970s and the debt crisis faced by many African and Latin American countries during the early 1980s aggravated again the problems of inefficient state owned enterprises, and refocused attention on the crucial role of the private sector in economic growth and development. As a result, the role of state came under attack from the neo-classical political economy or what was called the New Institutional Economics (NIE) School. Further more, the International financial and monetary institutions such as the World Bank and the IMF towards macroeconomic adjustment, economic stabilisation and market-oriented development policies also gave an immense pressure to developing countries to adopt the same.

Privatisation during the Modern Era

Whatever the historical profile and background be given for privatisation, the credit of the great moment in privatisation goes to the Margaret Thatcher's Thatcherism as well as the Ronald Reagan's Reaganomics. Thatcherism advocated privatisation with more arguments on efficiency of private ownership through competition, whereas Reaganomics supported privatisation as a remedy for cutting down the government's budgetary deficit and debt through enhancement of improved productivity. Reaganomics also stressed on immediate cash transaction, while selling PSUs. But at the helm, Thatcherism will ever be remembered in the history of so-called 'popular new economic system'.

Although major privatisation activity in Europe is associated with the UK since 1979, there are examples of earlier sales of state assets (not exactly the systematic privatisation programme of now), such as in West Germany after 1959, in the UK in the early 1950s and early 1970s, in Ireland in the 1960s and 1970s, and in Italy in the 1950s and 1960s (Parker, 1998: 12).

In Asia, Pakistan, Malaysia and China are those countries which laid foot prints for privatisation through their economic reforms during the 1960s and 1970s. China has pursued the privatisation process with a considerable success despite the fact it got into reforms in the late 1970s. Ram Mohan (2004) says that China has proceeded cautiously in its privatisation efforts. It has privatised to private owners only the smaller PSUs. The state retains control over the larger PSUs that dominate industrial output and profits.

India, which is after 40 years of socialism, opened up its economy after ASEAN countries, in some ways in the past decade, first under the Rajiv Gandhi government in the mid-1980s and later, after the Soviet collapse, under P.V. Narasimha Rao. It meant a reduction of the fiscal deficit, as well as more openness to foreign investment and the abolition of import licenses on many goods. Nevertheless, privatization has not been implemented in parallel (Bierstelley, 1997).

At present, countries through out the world are increasingly selling off their stakes in corporations, according to a report from the OECD. A variety of factors are propelling the trend, according to the report. The value of privatization worldwide in the year 1999 was 10 per cent higher than the year before, yielding USD145 billion to governments. The world's largest sale occurred in Italy, where the government sold a 34.5 per cent stake in the country's largest electricity producer, ENEL, for USD 14 billion. Privatisation earned France about USD 10 billion a year since the 1997 legislative elections. The sale of a second slice of Deutsche Telekom yielded USD 10 billion to the German government in 1999.

The growing need toward privatization is so fast, and has been accelerated by the fact that the private sector's net long-term resource to developing countries in 2001 was USD 160 billion but official flow could record only USD 36.5 billion. This is a surprise trend within a decade. As a matter of fact, the private and official flows were almost same that is, USD 62 billion in 1991 (Keefe, 2003). Surprisingly, Africa has not been a huge beneficiary as its governments have had a lot of push and pull towards globalisation that seems unavoidable; otherwise Africa will have no chance of deriving itself from the state of isolation.

In the above theoretical discussion, the evolution of privatisation has passed different stages such as from primitive clan communism to modern society. At any stage of its evolution, the role of private enterprise economy either by itself or through privatisation has never been underestimated but the need of state intervention has intensively been debated as to whether the economy needs a interventionist state or minimalist state. In this case, socialist regimes in the U.S.S.R. and Eastern Europe were an exceptional case but they lasted not more than half the century.

Privatisation evolved as a personal impulse through the individualism and private ownership in the primitive society, and is now positioned as a vital economic and public policy throughout the world. But the question comes regarding the justifications (reasons) for privatisation when it applies particularly to the developing countries: (i) Have these countries embraced privatisation as a self-felt need; (ii) were they forced to adopt privatisation as a measure of structural adjustment programme by the international donors and financial institutions and (iii) was this policy adopted by those countries for the reasons that are unknown?

THE REASONS BEHIND PRIVATISATION

There are many points technically obvious to say against the working and setting up of public sector undertakings. Over and above, there are so many valid points and reasons outlined below as to why privatisation is widely spread, and is seen as a major activity of most of the developing states.

The Core Reason at Micro Level: Dismal Performance of PSUs

Public Sector Undertakings all around the world performed poorly, in spite of their relative monopolistic competitive advantage. Capacity utilisation was poor, labour productivity was low and overall profitability was insignificant. What is worse is the fact that their inefficiency has affected the respective economies as a whole, because of their forward and backward linkages. Sastry (1988) says,

> *"They all got vexed up with the non-performance of these state owned enterprises and started demanding improved quality of life from their respective governments".*

Shirley (1995) added to this fact that in Egypt, Peru, Senegal, and Turkey a mere five per cent reduction in PSU operating costs would reduce fiscal deficit by about one third. PSUs often capture a disproportionate share of credit, squeezing out private-sector borrowing. In Bangladesh, PSUs take about one-fifth of the domestic credit, although PSUs output accounts for less than three per cent of GDP.

In many developing countries, PSUs absorb large amounts of funds that could be better spent on basic social services. In Tanzania, central government subsidies to PSUs equal 72 per cent of central spending on education and 150 per cent of central government spending on health. Moreover, a modest improvement in PSUs efficiency would substantially reduce, and in some cases, eliminate the fiscal deficit in most developing countries.

The reasons for failure of these PSUs are so clear; their bureaucratic ways of managing business, lethargy towards modernisation and innovation, lack of professionalisms, unwanted intervention of government and politicians, and still worse the first-degree corruption vested in these enterprises. The interest in privatisation stems from both the belief and experiences that privatisation eliminates or at least minimises these inherent obstacles of PSUs.

The Core Macro Reasons

In addition to the above reasons, many empirical studies with their authentic results defend privatisation for other reasons as well which are equally important: First, privatisation is considered indispensable with a view to ensuring the exit of the government from areas in which it must not exist, since it is prone to inefficiently managing those assets, in other words, preferring private sector to government machinery in managing those PSUs. A case study done by Sampson (1999) proves this justification through National Commercial Bank Group (NCBG), the largest commercial bank in Jamaica, a real example of excellence after divestiture. In clear terms, pre-divestment earnings before tax grew by an annual average of 7.9 per cent compared to the post-divestment period, which has averaged 14 per cent. In terms of profit growth, the NCBG seems to have performed better in the post-divestment period.

Second, unburdening the government of units that are a drain on the exchequer and contribute to a fiscal crisis of the state is the second important reason to recommend privatisation. From 1979 to 1998, over 60 national governments have raised almost USD500 billion through about 600 separate public sales of stock in PSUs, which helped them in many ways to settle their fiscal crisis. (Megginson, 1998).

Third, garnering revenues that can be used to retire government debts and improve the government's finances in the medium term. It is well known from the latest observations of statistics that many governments have noticed their debt cutting down, on account of privatising their PSUs. Some Latin American governments have raised large sum from privatisation transactions, up to 15 per cent of total annual revenue (Young, 1998). For instance, such type of revenue streams has allowed Mexico to continue the macro economic stabilization efforts and repay a large portion of state debts.

Fourth, privatisation has become an important means for countries to attract foreign investment. In post communist countries, privatisation accounts for a large proportion of total foreign investment; for example, 86 per cent in Hungary and 64 per cent in Poland. In countries such as Peru, Venezuela, Argentina, and Jamaica, privatisation accounts for 30 per cent to 40 per cent of total foreign investment. Even the oily rich countries are of no exception as they receive heavy investment especially on their oil sector (Young, 1998: 6). Finally, with all these economic advantages of privatisation, it can be ensured that the government concentrates on social development such as health and education through a substantial allocation of money from the budget.

The above discussed reasons are not common causes to all privatisations in the world. It differs from one case to another case with reference to those countries' economic background such as performance of PSUs, dependency on debt, pressure from the World Bank and IMF, degree of state intervention and so on. Although, poor performance of PSUs has been conceived a main reason behind privatisation, many other reasons are not correctly justified. Many studies (Abu Shaire, 1997: 86) point out that there is a positive correlation between privatisation and dependency on loans from international organisations. African countries are victims of such kind, privatising their PSUs, even though the conditions for privatisation were not necessarily appropriate.

In Asian and Latin American countries, on the other hand, the increasing trend towards privatisation is related to their past 'overuse' of PSUs and their fast-growing private sector, whereas the cause is not so serious and urgent in many developed countries, except unburdening their economic load. These countries, however, attracted a significant amount of FDI despite the appropriateness of the cause for privatisation. For any cause, it is suggested that the government must be very clear about their objectives, and must go ahead with what best it could achieve from the privatisation.

A Cautionary Note

A cautionary note is in order, nonetheless. Recognizing the leading role of the private sector in economic development does not mean that the nature of its role is fully understood, that it can guarantee poverty reduction, or that it can be easily guided toward achieving other desirable goals, such as long-term job security for a huge segment of society. Above all, it may mislead if it is said that reforming or privatising PSUs will lead to a high degree of efficiency and performance. Efficiency and performance did not improve after the reforms in cases such as Mali and Zaire, because the privatisation process itself was poorly handled. Buyers were chosen without regard to ability to run the enterprises, or even to meet the purchase price, which was payable in instalments.

PRIVATISATION: EXPERIMENTATIONS ABROAD

Having discussed the reasons and cautionary notes, it is more important at this moment to understand the experimentations abroad towards privatisation, pertaining how far the reasons were justified and what actually happened in those pioneers of privatisation. It helps this research to adopt a comprehensive theoretical scale to measure the performance and effectiveness of privatisation in the developing and poor countries.

It has, moreover, been justified that no execution of privatisation will be fruitful, if a country's government fails to learn theories, practices, lessons, and impacts from those advanced countries and that of those economies in transition particularly post-communist countries, followed by that of Asian and other African countries.

Because of their visionary difference in privatisation, it looks important in this research to discuss at first the practices and lessons derived from these two different set-up economies. Acknowledging this view, forthcoming sub-heading deal with the privatisation practice in some of the Developed Countries, and so is in Economies of Transition.

Privatisations in the Developed Countries and Economies of Transition

The current surge in privatization has its roots in the period of deregulation in Canada and the United States in the late 1970s. The movement towards privatisation of public transport and utility companies in France and Germany, together with conservative ideologies in aid-giving Western industrial countries during the early 1980s, brought political pressure on developing countries to adopt market oriented economic reforms.

In the U.K, the privatisation programme gathered momentum from the early 1980s after the return of a Conservative government under Margaret Thatcher, who was so keen to open up markets to competition and in encouraging wider share ownership as part of the promotion of the enterprise culture.

The privatisation programme, which was geared up exactly in 1979, passed through several phases. As a result, between 1979 and 1997 almost more than two thirds of the industries under State control which were transferred to private sellers had earned the exchequer Sterling Pound 60 billion with an average Sterling Pound 5.5 billion a year planned in the mid-1990s. This expansion of the market economy has involved almost fifty major businesses in sectors as diverse as automobiles, steel, airlines, and utilities. The privatisation programme reduced the role of public sector in the sense that their share in the GDP and total investment was reduced by almost 60 per cent (Cook, 1998: 218; Hoody and Young, 1999: 253). The UK has more privatisation experience of major utilities than any other Western European economy.

When the U.K. was in full gear of privatisation in the eighties, West Germany [before unification] was not so interested in privatisation, owing to less public ownership (Bös, 1992,) the better performance of state enterprises and less ideological conservatism comparing to the U.K. and in the U.S. Nevertheless, the initiative was visible here and there when the annual economic report in 1983 of the conservative-liberal government[3] desired to work for a policy that would reduce the activities of the state to those that were appropriate.

The debate on privatisation in Germany was again reactivated in the 1990s following the collapse of communism in East Germany. Eventually, the privatisation was successfully carried out by Treuhand's (THA) (the largest industrial holding company) management, where about 15,000 firms or parts of firms with total of debts about DM256 billion and an income of DM67 billion were privatised. About 3,000 privatisations were 'Management Buy Outs' (MBO); while only 860 firms were placed in the hands of foreign owners. Eighty-five per cent of the East German industrial assets are now in the ownership of West Germans, and is best characterised as a large-scale ownership transfer from the East to the West Germany (Esser, 1998). To conclude, it may not be exaggerated to say that the privatisation in Germany is nothing but a "symbolism in the social market economy".

Privatisation in Italy is one of those economic phenomena that surprised the world by their suddenness and by the strength of the swing which took place from a view that favoured a widespread public intervention in the economy. The strong motives that were observed behind the Italian privatisation are the PSUs' increasing debt (Posner and Woolf, 1967), market and private property which are seen as the panacea to all inefficiencies and economic failures. By the end of 1995 over 25,000 billion lire (more than 1.5 per cent of 1993 GDP) were raised by the sale of share of 21 enterprises. The most widely used technique of sale was private placement. Nevertheless, MBOs,

POs (Public Offers) and IPOs (Initial Public Offerings) were used but in total with a few companies. The success of privatisation in Italy was due to both its sequencing and to the intense restructuring process which took place before selling.

Privatisation in the U.S. can be traced back to 1955, when the Bureau of the Budget issued (Nicholas, 2001) Bureau of the Budget Bulletin Number 55-4. It was a directive to the effect that government would rely on the private sector for commercial goods and services, so that it would not be competing with business.

To be clear, what is seen as privatisation [as applied in economies of transition and African countries] is not the same as privatisation seen in the U.S. Privatisation in the U.S. refers to the government's use of the private sector[both for-profit and non-profit] to deliver public policies and improve the content and implementation of pubic programmes. The heavy use by American governments of the private and quasi-private sectors to implement public policies is a phenomenon peculiar to the United States—nearly a fifth of all federal expenditure about USD 200 billion flows to private interests through contracts. It relates to some deep, underlying belief sets that may be unique to the American political culture (Nicholas, 2001: 321). In the United States, there exists a pervasive myth that 'business is better'—that private enterprises is more efficient and effective in getting the job done than is 'the incredible bulk' of government. Empirical studies indicate that the main reason behind the U.S. privatisation is risk avoidance, particularly the avoidance of political risks.

Experimentations in Economies of Transition

Post communist countries distinguish between 'small privatisation' and the privatisation of key sector enterprises. Privatisation of public utilities typically is not on the agenda. Small privatisation refers to shops, cinemas, restaurants and small hotels. Their privatisation was a relatively easy task unless problems of property rights interfered. The privatisation of key-sector enterprises refers to industry, wharfs, transportation, mining, energy, research and development printing offices and so on. Their privatisation was comparatively more difficult and time-consuming (Bös, 1992).

One of the essential programmes of the transformation of the Czech economy is privatisation of state ownership. The implementation of the transformation process was launched by auctions of small operational units in 1991 within the "small-scale" privatisation, which was completed in 1994. The first phase privatised 42.9 per cent of the slated enterprises—the fastest privatisation next to East Germany's after unification—which transacted USD24.87 billion as well as 88.25 per cent of the property scheduled for privatisation (Radomir et al., 1995). It was subsequently followed by "large-scale" privatisation in two basic waves by publicising lists of entities slated for privatisation. It is considered the ever-largest privatisation under voucher scheme, which is considered a distinct feature of privatisation programme of all most all transitional economies.

Unlike Czech privatisation, the pace of privatisation in Hungary and Poland was modest (Dhameja,1998:109-14). In Hungary, the reform of PSUs, although a continuing feature starting from its 'New Economic Mechanism' launched in 1968, its path to privatisation was really hammered out in 1985. Albeit its low pace, the transformation process (Lászl6, 1998) radically brought down the number of state owned enterprises from 1,841 to 823 at the end of 1994 i.e. it was reduced by 70 per cent, whereas the state assets on their book value had a reduction of only 36 per cent.

In Poland, from 1990 through September 1992, nearly 25 per cent of PSUs were transferred to the private sector. This accounted for 43 per cent of the total economy. Moreover, liquidation methods had been used most frequently, by mid 1992 as a measure to facilitate the privatisation process. As a matter fact, 1249 enterprises had undergone liquidation. Four methods of privatisation adopted in Poland are: Commercialisation, transformation of PSUs into corporations, which were later to be sold individually; sale of shares of corporations owned by the government; liquidation involving leasing of assets to other entities for a fee; and liquidation of an enterprise having poor financial performance. The adopted techniques were sale by auction, public offer to sell, private placement, and distribution of vouchers to citizens.

The main difference between these two set-ups of economies for privatisation: privatisation in the Developed Countries aim at rebalancing the power between the public and the private sector, whereas privatisation in economies in transition is part of a move from a centrally planned communist system to a market economy. This distinguishing statement has both a quantitative and a qualitative dimension. Quantitatively, the type privatisation in the Developed Countries implies a reduction of the public sector by only a small percentage. However, in transitional economies, privatisation aims at a reduction of the public sector by two-digit percentages. Qualitatively, privatisation in the Developed Countries is embedded in the market economic system.

In Transitional economies, privatisation signals the change of a system. The qualitative difference mentioned above is the reason why privatisation in capitalistic countries must be seen from a different perspective than privatisation in post-communist countries. In capitalistic countries, there is a given framework, endowed with a convertible currency, well-established stock exchange, technologies and skilled labour. In post communist countries, all these features must be established as part of the transition. In many cases, even skilled labour is missing (this was one of the disappointing experiences in the course of German unification). For instance, Stock exchange initiatives were done in East Germany through the West Germany's treaty on the Economic, Monetary and Social Union (July 1990) and by the subsequent treaty on German Unification signed on 3rd October 1990 (Bös, 1992).

To conclude, the privatisation in the Developed Countries is advanced and was carried out with all pre-requisites and facilities including the sophisticated capital market, stock exchange and labour market. Moreover, privatisation in those countries is not new, so that they executed privatisation with a target precision. Whereas in those transitional countries, everything was new and strange; professionalisms were missing, and transactions were mixed up of large and small, but they did a successful venture through a gradual development of the requisites for privatisation. Privatisation in most of the transitional economies took place in an environment of collapsing markets. Hence, the requirement of restructuring coupled with privatisation has been more prevalent in post-communist countries than in Western countries.

The pace at which privatisation and its immediate effect proceeded in these countries was also so admirable because it could finish almost all what was planned in its programme. The undeniable fact was that in the Eastern Europe and the countries of the former Soviet Union after the fall of communism, the average share of national GDP attributable to the private sector accounts for more than 50 per cent over the three years period 1990-1993 (Donaldson and Wagle, 1995).

The worth deriving point from those economies of transition is the minimisation of disparity through the voucher system[4] (it does not require the need for valuation) which played a vital role in distributing ownership and guarding against the danger of sale of state property at a discount to a privileged few. Another feature of privatisation in those countries was that shares were sold to mutual funds, who, in turn disposed it off later to the public. In a nutshell, privatisation in these countries is successful, whereas in the economies of transition, it was made successful which leaves a concrete lesson for those developing countries where privatisation is ongoing.

Experimentations in Asian and Pacific Countries

Many countries in the Asian region want to improve their international competitiveness and are keen to provide a more attractive business climate for private economic activity. However, East Asia and the Pacific were the only regions in Asia that showed an increase in privatisation revenues in 1993 when their transactions reached USD 7.5 billion, up from USD 5.2 billion in 1992. After a relatively slow start compared to other regions, privatisation picked up during the 1990s. As a result, the total privatisation revenues between 1988 and 1999 amounted to USD 49.2 billion, which resulted in 25 per cent of activity that took place in East Asia and the Pacific albeit the Asian financial crisis.

The most intensive privatisers in terms of revenues from sales were Malaysia, Phillippines, and China. Between 1988 and 1993, Malaysia's privatisation sales generated USD5.8 billion in revenue, more than one-third of the regions' total. The Phillippines substantially reduced state ownership, selling sixty-three enterprises for USD2.8 billion in the same period. Although the Government of China is not willing to use the term 'privatisation', which may be due to their political supremacy, it has reduced state ownership by offering shares to domestic and foreign investors on the Shenzhen, Shanghai, and

Hong Kong stock exchanges. From 1991 to 1993 the government sold shares in sixty one state owned companies and collected a total of USD 4.1 billion (Sadar, 1995: p.7).

Privatisation in South Asia declined in 1993 to a value of USD 974 million for fifty-four enterprises, compared to USD 1.6 billion from eighty-three sales during 1992. This trend, which has still been continuing, never exceeded USD 3 billion a year till 1999. India dominated the region, selling forty-seven companies for USD 2.9 billion between 1991 and 1993. Indian Petrochemicals Corporation Ltd. was amongst the first PSUs to make a public issue after the announcement of the Structural Adjustment Reforms in June 1991. The country has now foreseen its effect through the budget for 2003-04 which would provide USD 2.9 billion as revenues from privatisation.

Privatisation efforts in Pakistan began in 1988 with the floatation of minority shares of Pakistan International Airlines Corporation. Between 1991 and 1997, the Privatisation Commission carried out 92 privatisation transactions, while by the end of 2000, the number stood at 106. Gross privatisation proceeds stood at about Rs.60.9 billion equivalent to USD 1.8 billion. Telecom and power together accounted for over two-thirds of the proceeds. The privatisation was very much a home-grown programme developed in response to the dismal performance of public enterprises.

The pace of privatisation in the Gulf countries was found very steady as the drive to create greater room for the private sector in Saudi Arabia and the Gulf states (Pamela, 1999) appears to be escalating. In spite of the less urgency of scaling down the government role, the people are aware that the private sector is needed to create jobs, attract foreign investment and so on.

Privatisation has made in roads in a number of developing countries in Asia. Privatisation is slow and steady with more precautions rather than precision. These countries have still faith on PSUs. As a result, the states retain control over the larger PSUs that dominate industrial output and profits. It seems from one argument that it might be the reason why they are more successful than those countries which rushed their privatisation programme with ambiguous objectives. It is, on the other hand, argued that full blooded privatisation might have produced even better results.

PRIVATISATION IN AFRICA

Privatisation in the name of the SAP supported by the IMF and the World Bank was implemented in many African countries in the late 1980s. The word 'Privatisation', almost unknown a decade ago in Africa, is now a key to unlocking private sector-led growth. Private investment has become the most important source of finance for developing countries in this region. This boom in private investment—though Africa particularly Sub-Saharan Africa (SSA) is reportedly a least player in the total receipt of private investment—has been the result of wide spread macro economic stabilisation and liberalisation. Africa was, however, lagging behind in the privatisation activity compared to other regions. On an average, African states privatised a smaller percentage—about 40 per cent—of their PSUs than other regions, far less than in Latin America or the transition economies. Much of the African divestiture taken place was of smaller, less valuable, often moribund manufacturing, industrial and service concerns.

Of the roughly 2300 privatisations in Sub-Saharan Africa in the 2000s, only about 66 are generally of a higher value and economically more important firms. An additional 92 transactions took place in transport, some of which might have been classified as infrastructure. Moreover, activity has been concentrated in very few countries. Of the USD nine billion raised from the African privatisation between 1991 and 2001, a full third was generated by a handful of privatisations in South Africa (South Africa was in the first place in the African Privatisation with USD3.1 billion). Another 33 per cent came from sales in a group of four actively privatising countries such as Ghana, Nigeria, Zambia and the Ivory Coast.

Ghana, launching privatisation in 1988, realised USD one billion through a sale of 212 PSUs as of 2001 (Nellis, 2003:8). Nigeria privatised substantial portion of its PSUs through the full or partial privatisation of 110 PSUs and the commercialisation of 35 others. At one point, the programme aimed at collecting about USD one billion a year (Business Africa, 2000). Zambia is one of the successful countries in privatisation. The Zambian Privatisation Agency privatised 253 out of the 254 firms privatised since 1991 which constituted 99.6 per cent share in the total PSUs slated for privatisation (Nellis, 2003:16). The total proceeds collected from these transactions between 1991 and 2001 amounted to USD 828 million. It is creditworthy to mention that the privatisation programme has made satisfactory progress with a substantial attraction of foreign investors, including previous owners of some of the firms.

To conclude, African privatisation albeit having its own success, is still deemed to be confusing, inconsistent, erratic and, above all, route-less. For instance, enterprises were sometimes reported as sold when they were merely up for sale. Sometimes, sales were recorded when the privatisation agency and a buyer reach a preliminary agreement (World Bank, 1994: 105). Such errors were among so many others traced by various studies.

Ideologically, in many, probably most African countries, the principal motivation of privatisation was to pacify the funding Agencies and major financial donors who forced those countries in the name of conditionalities (The Reporter, February 2003). Eventually, the issue for them was no longer whether to privatise, but when and how best to do so. Most of the empirical studies, although it proved a modest superiority of private over public ownership in the firms' efficiency, failed to give a clear picture and concrete finding of some macro issues such as reform measures, government's interference in privatised ones, pace of process, ownership distribution, labour-employment, and the society's access to price and product and management autonomy.

Finally, the African governments do increasingly recognise the PSUs problems. Many African countries emptied their exchequer by spending huge amounts for rehabilitating those weaker PSUs which was considered a mere wastage of a country's welfare budget. Nows, numerous African leaders and observers preach the gospel of financial discipline and market-oriented reform. Yet, commitment to privatisation as the best way to solve PSU problems has been neither widespread nor strong. It accounts for many reasons inherent in Africa, but to be frank, the prevalence of a unique political set-up and the attitudes of politicians are still posing a continuous threat to the on-going privatisation process.

NOTES

1. It is also referred as state owned enterprises, public enterprises, parastatal bodies and Government undertakings. It is difficult to define the term

since any attempt to define public sector involves financial, legal, and control aspects on one hand; and matters of flexibility, territory and allocation of power among various ministries and departments, on the other hand. However, it is consistently referred to as 'Public Sector Undertakings (PSUs)' in all chapters of this thesis. PSUs in Ethiopia are viewed as enterprises in which the Government holds almost all the equity, and include even small-scale enterprises such as retail shops and super markets.

2. Popular capitalism means widespread share ownership in privatised enterprises. In capitalistic countries, the concept was already mentioned in 1947 by Ludwig Erhard with the intention to promote capitalistic feeling in the population by establishing many small shareholders. It was Austria which first actually applied the concept in 1957, 40 per cent of the share of the two largest nationalised banks were privatised by selling the 'people's shares.

3. The conservative-liberal government in West Germany comprised of Christian Democrats of the CDU-CSU [its Bavarian Sister Party] and the liberals of the FDP, which was the first to include in its programme its intention of reducing state influence on the private economy and of strengthening market forces.

4. Voucher is a legal right evidenced on printed certificates, which could be used to purchase shares of stock in state owned business. The countries like Czech Republic used a voucher system to privatise over 2000 SOEs. Under this system, vouchers are issued to adult population, although in some cases children are allowed to participate, as a primary mean for transferring ownership rights in enterprises to be privatised. Usually vouchers are distributed free of charge, while in some other countries particularly in Czech, Russia and Romania, a small fee was collected to cover administration costs to weed out those not interested in the programme. See *more about voucher system in Radomir Sabela, Terézia Hrnèíové and Josef Vais(1995).*

REFERENCES

Abu Shair, J.A.R.O. (1997), *Privatisation and Development,* London: MacMillan Press Ltd., p. 86.

Ajayi, I. S. (2001), "What Africa Needs to do to Benefit from Globalisation", *Finance & Development,* A Quarterly Publication of the International Monetary Fund, Vol. 38, No. 4, pp. 6-7.

Bhatia, H.L. (1989), *History of Economic Thought,* New Delhi: Vikas Publishing House Pvt. Ltd., pp. 380-401.

Bierstelley, T.J. (1997), "The Triumph of Liberal Economic Ideas in the Developing World", in Shephany Griffith Jones and Barbara Stallings (eds) *New Global Financial Trends Implications for Development,* Cambridge: Cambridge University Press.

Bös, D. (1992), "Privatisation in Europe: A Comparison of Approaches", *Oxford Review of Economic Policy,* Vol. 9, No. 1, pp. 97-101.

Business Africa (2000), *"A Long Way to Go: Special Report-Nigeria",* Vol. 8, No. 9, pp. 35-6.

Cook, P. (1998), "Privatisation in the UK: Policy and Performance", in Parker, D. (ed) *Privatisation in the European Union: Theory and Policy Perspectives,* London: Routledge, pp. 219-41.

Dhameja, N. and Sastry, K.S. (1998), *Privatisation: Theory and Practice,* New Delhi: Wheeler Publishing & Co. Ltd.

Donaldson, D. and Wagle, D.M. (1995), *"Privatisation: Principles and Practices",* IFC Lessons of Experience Series No. 15007, September, Washington. D.C.: IFC, pp. 1-11.

Dornbusch, R. and Fischer, S. (1981), *Macro Economics,* New York: McGraw-Hill Book Company, pp. 544 -53.

Esser, J. (1998), *"Privatisation in Germany: Symbolism in the Social Market Economy?",* in Parker, D. (ed). p. 116-7.

George (2002), 'Aid Listen', *New African- IC Publication,* Vol. 2002, No. 411, p. 51.

Hill, C.W.L. (1998), *Global Business Today.* Washington: Irwin/McGraw-Hill, pp. 68-69.

Hoody, N. and Young, S. (1999), "The United Kingdom", in Dunning, E.J. (ed.) *Governments, Globalisation, and International Business,* Oxford: Oxford University Press.

Keefe, Joseph O'. (2003), "The Private Sector Drives Economic Growth", *Development Outreach,* March, p. 6.

László Neumann (1998), "Privatisation of Telecommunications in Hungary", in Rolph Van der Hoeven and Gyorgy Sziracközi (eds.) *Lessons from Privatisation: Labour Issues in Developing and Transitional Countries,* Geneva: ILO.

Megginson, L.M. (1998), 'The Impact of Privatisation', *Economic Reform Today* (Centre for International Private Enterprises (CIPE)), No. 1, p. 11.

Mutebile, E.T. (1999), "Better Public Sector Management: Capacity Building and Good Governance", in Wallace Laura (ed) *AFRICA: Adjusting to the Challenges of Globalisation* (Proceedings of a Seminar held in Paris, May 4-5, 1998), Washington, D.C.: IMF and Ministry of Finance of Japan, pp. 107-13.

Nellis, J. (2003), *"Privatisation in Africa: What happened? What is to be done?"*, Working Paper No. 25, Centre for Global Development.

Nicholas, H. (2001), *Public Administration and Public Affairs*, New Delhi: Prentice Hall of India Pvt. Ltd., pp. 318-25.

Pamela Ann Smith (1999), "Gulf Privatisation Gathers Momentum", *The Middle East*, November, pp. 33-6.

Parker, D. (1998), *"Privatisation in the European Union"*, in Parker, D. (ed.), pp. 8-12.

Posner, M.V. and Woolf, S.J. (1967), *Italian Public Enterprise*, London: Gerald Duckworth and Co.

Radomir Sabela, Terézia Hrnèíové and Josef Vais (1995), *"Process of Privatisation in Field of Industry and Trade in the Czech Republic"*, Study No. 5, June 1995, Institute of Economic Studies: Prague, pp. 12-24.

Ram Mohan, T.T. (2004), "Privatisation in China: Softly, Softly Does it", viewed on 02/10/2004 at *http://www.iimahd.ernet.in/publications/public/Fulltext.jsp?wp-no=2004-09-04*.

Rondinelli, D.A. (1999), "Privatisation and Economic Transformation: The Management Challenge", in Prokopenko, J. (ed) *Management for Privatisation: Lessons from Industry and Public Service*, Management Development Series No. 32. Geneva: ILO, pp. 3-41.

Sadar, F. (1995), *"Privatising Public Enterprises and Foreign Investment in Developing Countries, 1988-93"*, Occasional Paper 5, World Bank: Washington, D.C., pp. 1-45.

Sastry, K.S. (1988), "Privatisation of Public Enterprises", *Productivity*, Vol. 28, No. 2, pp. 45-9.

Savas, E.S. (1999), "Global Perspectives on Local Issues", in Yul Kwon, O. (ed) *International Privatisation: Global Trends, Policies, Processes and Experiences*, Saskatchewan: Institute of Saskatchewan Enterprises.

Sampson, C.I. (1999), *"Privatising Banking Services in Jamaica"*, in Prokopenko, J. (ed), pp. 207-28.

Shirley, M.M. (1995), "Getting Bureaucrats Out of Business: Obstacles to State Enterprise Reform", *Economic Reform Today*, No. 4, p. 2-3.

The Reporter (2003), *"IMF Urged to Understand Privatisation Concerns"*, Vol. 5, No. 219, 16 February, p.13.

World Bank (1995), "Congo-Privatisation and Capacity Building Project", Report No. T-6654-COB, July 25, p. 1-2.

Young, P. (1998), "The Lessons of Privatisation", *CIPE Economic Reform Today*, No. 1, p. 3-9.

CHAPTER - 2

Review of Literature and Conceptual Framework and Methodology

This chapter deals with the review of literature followed by the conceptual framework and methodology of the study. The review helps this research to know the research gap which exhibits the importance and uniqueness of this study, whereas the latter part provides the overall research design and methodology of this study.

Literature search is an important part of problem definition. The intent is to see whether the problem has surfaced previously, to examine the environment from which it was drawn, and to evaluate proposed solutions to the problem. The rationale is to avoid unnecessary repetition in research (Buckley, 1976).

The literature pertaining to this research is reviewed under different headings which contains the related literature—analytical, theoretical and empirical—on the particular issue. The literature that has been collected focuses more on various issues in privatising the PSUs to the private sector. The issues are nothing but the processing, political, economic, socio-labour, managerial, as indicated in the objectives of the study, have widely been tapped, through this chapter, for a comprehensive understanding of the research problem. As this part seeks normally, the literature from different sources conducted at the International level, Regional (Continental) and the National level which are either published or unpublished are furnished in the following headings:

- Literature related to Processing Issues
- Literature related to Political and Economic Issues

- Literature related to Social and Labour Issues, and
- Literature related to Managerial Issues.

LITERATURE RELATED TO PROCESSING ISSUES

Processing (transformation) issues are those issues which arise in transforming or converting PSUs to the private sector. Processing issues include privatisation policy issues, programming issues, methodological issues (methods and techniques), implementing and monitoring issues. Such issues are inherent in the processing of privatisation which determines the success or failure of a privatisation activity.

Preliminary Approach and Legal Framework

Donaldson and Wagle (1995) stress in their research conducted for the IFC Lessons of Experience series that a strong preliminary approach and legal framework on privatisation is a high priority work to make privatisation work well. It could be any approach but it must be transparent in the public domain. The appropriate institutional framework and approach depends largely on the government's strength and commitment.

Timmorthy (1996) has proposed in his empirical study that a strong groundwork should be done to make any privatisation work well. The groundwork is nothing but property rights and institutional support which must clearly be prescribed. He also suggests that the countries seeking a transition from command socialism to market capitalism must develop a legal system comparable to those who evolved in market capitalist countries.

Gibbon (1996) shares the experience that the governments at all levels in the United States own commercialisable enterprises—in fields of electricity, water and waste water services, parking facilities, insurance, hotels and convention centres and mail delivery. He also says that interest by public officials in privatising such enterprises is growing, fed in part by knowledge of the large volume of such transactions overseas. The actual sales of government enterprises in the United States have been very few, most public officials have little idea how to actually carry out such a sale.

According to Welch & Frémond (1998), privatisation law that guides the process is always important. Such laws define the rules of privatisation programme and empower the institutions charged with executing it. Privatisation law is so indispensable to those countries with the weaker institutions, that it may not be able to ensure the transparency of privatisation.

According to Gopal (2000), appointment of the committee or agency on privatisation would be the first step at streamlining the process of privatisation. This establishment should have its own legal framework even to advise the government on the extent, strategy, methodology, and timing of privatisation.

The empirical evidences of Parker and Kirkpatrick (2003) are consistent with the notion that privatisation works best in developing countries when it is integrated into a broader development framework. According to them, a framework includes articulation of objectives, institutional capacity needs assessment, evaluating administrative competence, ransparency and striking a balance between the pressure of external donors and legitimacy of process and long term social welfare. These findings are arrived at by their study after surveying the empirical literature on the impact of privatisation on economic performance in developing countries based on both the econometric and case study evidences. The basic regulatory work is, undoubtedly, essential to determine the efficiency of privatisation process of any country which is strongly authenticated and agreed upon with the authors' views.

Sridhar (2003) cites in his article 'Disinvestment: Air port for Sale', that a regulatory body and system were not formed well in time before the privatisation starts, it is natural that the government would give a lot of room for mal-practices to happen, which may enable the private players even to set the rules first that will govern their business; the regulator will have no choice but to accept these when constituted.

Pace of Privatisation, Methods and Techniques

Winter (1995) defines that privatisation is after all a process of converting a government owned enterprise into a private owned enterprise. He also points out that during the process, there are so many issues that are confronted and remain critical such as the transfer of know-how and ownership which have slowed down privatisation in many countries.

Radomir Sabela et al. (1995) are of the opinion that the methodology (methods and techniques) that be used is always a crucial factor determining the ownership and its relation and involvement to management. They affirm that in direct sales of part of privatised entities, the management is identical with owners. In bigger entities and in most of the task of privatisation is to find stimuli for both short-term and long term development of private companies. They also found out that the feasibility of the application of individual methods of privatisation was influenced by the position of individual branches of industry on the market. From this viewpoint, the methods, according to them, significantly differed e.g., in the branch of domestic trade. The decisive methods of privatisation were predominantly auctions of sales units and their acquirers were individual physical persons. The decisive method in the branch of engineering was transformation in the form of joint stock companies with the application of voucher privatisation.

The speed at which privatisation goes on matters a lot for its success. In the opinion of Miller (1998), the rapid move towards a market economy, though, not free of problems, has seemed to work better than the go-slow approach. He also warns that the slower the transition occurs, the more the former entrenched bureaucrats in the PSUs have been able to maintain their power over the use of resources, which ultimately ends in inefficiency.

Muegerwa-Kayizzi (2002), in the conclusion of their study, say that the pace of privatisation in African experience has greatly been determined by the political considerations. The findings indicate that the African politicians went ahead only when they were sure that the benefits to them exceeded the costs.

Auditing and Valuation of Assets

A study done by Mishra et al. (1993) cautioned about the practices prevailing in under valuation of assets in SOEs before disinvesting them. They quote in their empirical study that the Indian disinvestments, which initially brought down so many controversies, failed to bring the actual amount to be supposedly collected. The amount could have been realised, if the best value method was followed.

Any disinvestments must, ultimately, be made in the best interests of the public, Government of India's Disinvestment Commission

Report (1997) emphasised. It also stressed that to carry out the disinvestment properly, the audit of each disinvestment by the C & AG is conducted thoroughly, expeditiously and with the involvement of professionals familiar with the working of the industry and the capital markets.

Chandrasekhar (2003), in his investigative article, disclosed that the issues such as under valuation of assets, poor processing and other irregularities undermining the value of privatisation by taking the case of the Centaur Hotel, Mumbai, India.

LITERATURE RELATED TO POLITICAL AND ECONOMIC ISSUES

Political and Economic issues cover the change of political ideologies, distribution of ownership, technical assistance and aid from external agencies, terms and conditionalities of external agencies and foreign dominance which are often confronted as either villainous or heroic actors in privatising.

Economic Performance: Public Vs Private

In spite of many empirical and analytical evidences on the relationship between privatisation and economic performance, there are still many studies supporting the existence of state owned enterprises. Caves and Christensen (1980) and Bolnick (1987) draws a conclusion from the foregoing, stating that the poor performance is not an inherent characteristic of PSUs, unlike what is predicted in the property rights literature. With good management and sound policies, PSUs can justify their economic rationale, while contributing to social goals. These conclusions are contrary to the results obtained by Plane (1997) and Barnett (2000) which favour the privatisation as a catalyst for economic growth. Their studies firmly conclude that there is a positive correlation between privatisation and economic growth.

Against all the odds, Cook and Uchida (2003) assure through their study which resulted in a robust partial correlation between privatisation and economic growth. They also concluded that privatisation contributed negatively to economic growth. The study firmly assures this fact by using an Extreme Bound Analysis[1] and a larger sample of countries.

Mkandawire and Soludo (2003) criticise the structural adjustment programme (SAP) by referring to a number of acrimonious debates and tons of evaluation reports. They decline to accept that SAP has brought no betterment to the economy rather it has made the African states weaker. They even doubt the sustainability of macro economic stability which SAP reportedly brought to African states, would be attributed to volatile external finance. Padmanapan (2003) in his report defends the existence of SOEs, which can definitely succeed if they work with new ideas, and strong determination aiming only at market forces.

Structural Reforms, FDI and Political Considerations

The issues regarding reforms, FDI and politics often arouse people who deeply involve themselves in privatisation. Though these issues seem to be materialistic but bother a lot even sentimentally despite its own advantages. For instance, Itoh, & Kiyono (1988) in their study reveal that in order to avoid the FDI bringing negative implication, the countries adopt a pragmatic stance, pursue policies designed to maximise the national benefits and minimise the national costs. It favours the FDI, if its benefits outweigh the costs. In this line, many countries have adopted neither a radical policy nor a free market policy toward FDI, but instead a policy that can best be described as pragmatic nationalism.

Reich (1991) argues against pragmatic nationalism, which tightens the speedy reforms. He says that in a world where firms from all advanced nations are increasing investing in each other's markets, it is not possible for one country to hold another to economic ransom without hurting itself in the process.

Scholars like Befedkadu (1994) and Kibre (1996) support the state role that needs to remain in crucial economic activities. The scholars hold firm to the state intervention saying that no country ever industrialised relying solely on market principles without state intervention. According to them, a strong and visionary state can expedite the development of the economy and private sector. This is a major lesson that we learn from the economic history of the developed nations, including those that became developed in the recent past.

Yet, privatisation is very seriously pursued in most of the developing countries (Oxford, 1996) for political as well as economic reasons. The dictionary defines 'privatisation' giving justification to that point that a company will be more efficient as a result of competition, whereas politically, privatisation in the form of share offers to the general public are seen as a means of widening the share-owning public and thus increasing the commitment of working people to conservative values.

Sadar (1995) in his critical study proves a positive correlation between privatisation and FDI through regression analysis over a cross-section of thirty-six countries for the period of 1988-93, the co-efficient of which conforms to the result of the Edwards Model[2].

Larrain (1996) has assessed the potentiality of FDI in Africa which is not yet properly tapped, but he says that it could be possible through private players. The FDI potential, according to him, can be calculated with FDI/GDP ratio. The countries with a low FDI/GDP ratio relative to the average have unexploited FDI potential. The slow privatisation rate is seen as one reason for the large number of African countries with significant FDI potential.

Miller (1997) questions the credibility of legislators and officers, who obviously impede the privatisation activity as they themselves feel too comfortable to stick to state run enterprises. He has also found that the pressure coming from their side has mal-proceeded some of the privatisation activities across the world.

Stiglitz (1997), a Nobel laureate on economics and former chief economist of the World Bank, out rightly rejects the doubt on the invalidity of 'social well-being' and government losing control at the advent of privatising PSUs. As the government is always in the driver's seat, it is so easy for the government to mandate the desired action. A mandate is simply a requirement back-up by the threat of legal punishment. He illustrates for instance that the government may mandate private firms and provide health insurance to their employees. In all such mandates, the government requirement does not show up as a cost on the government budget. He, however, does not want to hide the fact that these mandates do have costs which can be very high and are borne indirectly by workers, firms and consumers.

Winter (1999) acknowledges the PSUs' poor performance, which emptied many economies, particularly Nigeria, a leading member of the OPEC. According to him, the findings were not in favour of PSUs in Nigeria as they picture out that the PSUs were abusing monopoly power; creating bureaucratic bottlenecks; were badly managed and were infected by corruption and nepotism; their capital structures were defective, hence they were overly dependent on the treasury for funding.

New African (1999) in its special report has depicted the Tunisia's economic development which is on a high. The analysis shows that a number of measures by the government are in place to help the private sector cut production costs, improve quality, delivery and marketing and generally become much more competitive. Results, officials say, have been positive—turnover improvement is around 10 per cent this year and exports have increased.

Sheel (1999) and New African (1999) admonish that if entry barriers and other obstacles to free competition are not removed, the gains from privatisation will be limited. So, the state reformers should structural reform of the economy and privatisation to go in hand in hand. Moreover openness in reforms and efficiency in its execution, which has already proved in the quickening of economic tempo of some countries, can't ever be discouraged. The structural reform has been given much importance these days as it widens a chance for attracting more FDI. Griffith (1998) says that FDI represents an alternative aid and has been increasing in some developing countries. He also discloses a fact that the bulk of this investment, however goes to those countries that are already growing. Since the poorest countries are less attractive investors, they are falling further behind.

Fosu (2000) says that political instability acts always against any economic reforms, which may be either on export or structural adjustments like privatisation. His empirical results confirm a hypothesis that political instability reduced the overall GDP growth of many Sub-Saharan African countries. He also stressed that a solution to political instability problem in SSA may be crucial for sustainable development of the region.

Anderson (2000) has a critical note about government policies of poor countries toward privatisation. He strongly criticises the government's policies, programmes or intervention that failed to create a favourable condition, rather it impedes the process and development. This is, due to the poor quality of government institutions, the high level corruption, and the influence of special interest groups including the private sector that manipulates the government for its own profit.

Chakravarthi (2001), in his article, emphasised about waiving of trader barriers and easing inter-state trade for attracting private entrepreneurs. He discloses that there are some countries like India, where there are no restrictions or barriers or inter-state commerce, and once goods and services are imported, they can be spread or sold across the country in all its streets. None of the states can control or restrict it; rather they can only provide incentives for foreign investors with clearance for establishment in the country within the federal jurisdiction.

The state should always see that there is adequate information disseminated among community as to what privatisation yields actually. Most of the time, privatisation receives antagonism from the people, which may threat the political sustainability. Tagema (2002), in New African, reports that in spite of it a large number of PSUs have been privatised, public opinion is, all of a sudden, turned against the programme claiming that the government is selling the country to foreigners.

Nellis (2003) argues in his study that structural reforms should always precede a successful privatisation. He concluded in his study that the sound investment climate is one of the components to be reformed for a successful execution of privatisation. According to him, the sound investment climate includes macro-economic stability, freedom to entry and exist, reasonably well functioning markets, adequate physical infrastructure, sound property rights and effective legal and judicial system.

Political factors play a giant role in policies and decisions pertaining to privatisation. As politicians are the powerful actors, their attitude and perception contribute to the performance of the privatisation. Geeta and Syed Mohmood, (2003) reveals that inaction to PSUs reforms sometimes reflects not simply the lack of expertise, resources on institutional capacity, but rather intent, spurred by political hostility to privatisation. They also pinpoint that African intellectuals and officials have long been educated to view the public sector as the promoter and defender of indigenous interest, and believe that it will improve and enrich foreigners.

Nature of Ownership and its Distribution

Taylor (1995) confirms controversial issues such as ownership issue of PSUs before privatising them as happened in Polish privatisation.

The workers and managers at these firms argued that they, rather than the government, owned the enterprise. If the government sold or gave away shares, the workers and managers wanted compensation, where as in Russia the local governments also claimed ownership.

The distribution of ownership matters a lot to see whether or not the expected results have been brought out as a result of change in ownership composition. It was, thoroughly, examined in the study done by Radomir Sabela et al. (1995), who confirm that the process of privatisation and transformation of economy represented mainly a significant change of ownership relations, resulting in a different approach to the management of business entities from the level of state administration. One of the decisive tasks of the Government during the transition was to develop a regulatory and institutional framework and incentives supporting economic growth. The change of ownership relations brought a new quality of responsibilities on owners with regard to the acquired property and the relation of owners to the executive management.

Voszka (1999) gives another picture about the extent of ownership changes. He emphasises that the ownership change is not something, which moves from the state to the private sector but also to the length, to which it is extended. Even after the privatisation, if the ownership remains in a few hands, it may not serve the purpose for which, the privatisation on ownership is intended.

Oumar (1999), in his study on Zambian privatisation, reveals that in some cases, shares remained under the government ownership with the intention to open to public floatation once the capital market develops. For such a purpose, the authority specially designated for the purpose held shares in some enterprises. He, however, acknowledges that ownership changes are usually a good indicator of the extent to which the government is willing to relinquish its involvement in a particular sector.

Preper and Taylor (2000) criticise about the cosmetic ownership changes which seldom bring technology, skill, managerial know-how and capital for restructuring. An ownership change, unless brings all these components, the effectiveness of privatisation may be at a great stake. He proves this statement underscoring the Czech voucher scheme that was turned down in 1997.

Chandrasekhar (2003) questions the necessity of changing the ownership from the public to the private. He argues that the only instance where privatisation of potentially or actually profitable assets can be defended is when it is presumed that the government is incapable of running a unit as well as the private sector and, therefore incapable of earning the higher potential return. But that argument is also irrational, since there are many areas, from national security to poverty alleviation, where the government must perform since they cannot be privatised. If the government is seen as capable of delivering on those fronts, there is no reason why it cannot be reformed to deliver in spheres of production, which for a variety of reasons were seen as areas in which public presence was a must.

Cook and Uchida (2003) argues, in their theoretical literature, that the change in ownership alone at the micro economic level is not sufficient to guarantee greater enterprise efficiency, then other reforms, more directly related to enterprise development, may indeed play a crucial role.

External Conditionalities and Constraints

The World Bank, the IMF and other funding nations and donors take always their own role in the host economies. While they fund, they do it along with a lot of restrictions but not deficiently, with justifications. Massod et al. (2001) confirm the IMF Conditionalities which some observers criticise as 'beyond the limit' and allowing the scope of its conditionality to become excessive, and a big talk among the politic-economic observers. They cite that whatever the extremity of the problem, when the IMF comes forward to financing, it always asks the member country to commit to necessary policy changes and reforms, and keep those policies and reforms on track, adjusting them if circumstances warrant. These conditionalities are nothing but, according to them, a warrantee that the money it has lent is being used for the purpose—to facilitate the adjustment process—and that the member country will be able to repay what it has borrowed from the IMF's pool of funds.

A comprehensive review of IMF conditionality has started since 2000. The decision making power at the IMF rests with the creditors' group—mostly affluent countries—due to the lopsided distribution of the quotas and hence, the voting power, reveal Sitikantha and

Sangita (2003). According to them, many empirical estimates show a negative correlation between number of conditional measures and programme success (both in terms of completion of the programme and attainment of objectives).

Ahluwalia (2003), Director, Independent Evaluation Office of IMF pinpoints that member country guaranteed to undertake those IMF Conditionalities should advisably go in that path if the IMF desires so. If the Conditionalities are not met, and as a result of if any damage happened, it might close its eyes if any immediate assistance is sought from the member country. Moreover, these countries cannot escape from the severe criticism.

LITERATURE RELATED TO SOCIAL AND LABOUR ISSUES

There are so many social and labour issues, some of which are difficult to identify with either political or social features like ownership, distribution and employment. These issues are nothing but in between political and social which could interchangeably be used. Nevertheless, changes in employment, labour productivity, labour relations, prices, society's access to produce and community reactions are considered as strong social and labour issues.

Schiller (1991) argues that privatisation, if properly regulated, can cause no damage to the social and other environmental issues, According to him, even in the strategy of protecting environment, privatisation can be used as a regulatory option. Private owners are always so quick in responding to any damage or pollution control in his environment for which, he is responsible.

Fundanga and Mwaba (1997) present an interesting fact in favour of privatisation on employment. They disagree with the criticism that privatisation affect the employment pool as it restricts a number of people, thereby aiming at cost reduction. In their assessment, in many of the companies that have been sold so far, the existing jobs have been preserved, while in a number of others, new jobs have been created. But at the same time, their study accepts the fact to a limit that privatisation has led to loss of jobs, therefore it can be mainly attributed to those companies that have been liquidated.

Baumol and Blinder (1997) examine the privatisation and pricing practices. They appeal to the states to circumvent those inappropriate pricing practices, when the privatisation is in process. Those that had previously been held at ludicrously low levels would be freed from control, though, in varying degrees. They also agree that such measures may bring forth inflation as a result, reducing the standard of living of most people. In a competitive market, Ekelund and Tollison (1997) say that, producers are so numerous that they are unable to affect prices. It normally ends in the well-being of the buyers, who can get all that he/she desires in the market.

Miller (1997) has agreed to the labour issues, which often have come up as a bottleneck in privatising PSUs. It is because of this reason that managers of PSUs typically have had life-time job-security, better working conditions than they could obtain elsewhere, and little threat of competition. Not only are managers, even the workers in state run firms also believe often rightly that, their life will not be quite as good if the PSUs are sold to private sectors.

Hymen (1997) describes that the transition to free markets will not be painless. As old and inefficient public undertakings are privatised or shut down, many workers will lose their jobs and have to seek new ones, while the prices of many of the products they need will be rising. Higher prices will eliminate shortages but will also reduce the purchasing power among low incomes. The unemployment, reduced living standards and soaring prices are the unfortunate consequences of the painful transition to free markets. He has not, however, denied that albeit these consequences, the privatisation has improved resource usage and income status, which he authenticates with the former communist countries.

Miller (1998) cautions that whatever the efficiency in the usage of resources, the privatisation in the process may worse the fate of some workers and managers. It is also proved by Kühl (1998), who says that the economic performance of privatised firms in term of sales, investment, productivity and wage was far better than that of THA firms, a public holding in Eastern Germany. Nevertheless, it had brought an adverse effect on employment and the position gets worse as the rate of employment was expected to decline with an overall loss of more than 200,000 jobs.

Bothelho and Addis (1998) assesses about the privatisation and employment in a study conducted on the Mexican Telecommunication (Telmex), which states that the operators, who constituted 20 per cent in Telmex, are the group of union workers most threatened by new technologies but, despite the changes, the expected lay-offs have not materalised.

Eardledy (1999) and Ernest and Helen (2000) are very clear that both liberalisation and privatisation may result in improved environmental performance, provided the government succeeds in channelling these developments in the desired course. If a government, for any political reason, gives pressure to private enterprises, it may not be conducive for those organisations to take the real advantage of privatisation. For instance, a competitive private enterprise, as due to the government's pressure, cannot carry redundant workers and overstaffing.

LITERATURE RELATED TO MANAGERIAL ISSUES

Changing management philosophy, work culture, preparedness to take challenges, management efficiency and effectiveness are deemed managerial issues, and are ideally to be discussed at micro level, i.e., at the companies of transition.

Many studies have already proved that private owned enterprises are doing much better in productivity, cost effectiveness and, efficiency, which is authentically proved in an empirical study conducted by Bennet and Johnson (1979). Boardman and Vining (1989) also say that there is a strong evidential record of private ownership that can improve efficiency.

Navak (1991) and Pack (1992) go one step further by preferring the private sector to the public sector in respect to the market, which both agree that the market in private sector economy serves as an efficient disseminator of information, skills, methods and new possibilities (innovation). Novak confirms authentically that the former USSR was not scientifically backward and also lacking a vital market place; it succeeded poorly in bringing its research to the service of the common people.

Voszka (1999) assesses the relationship between the economic reform and management autonomy which resulted in a positive outcome. The findings of Hinds (1999) show that the net profit margin before tax and interest of Guyana Telecom Ltd. effected three fold increase within three years from the date of privatisation.

Many case studies like (Shirley, 1995; Leon, 1999; Rahn, 1999) have clearly stated that privatisation brings a radical performance change, which makes the managerial efficiency of organizations to a zenith. Earle (1999) agrees with positive impact of privatisation by rejecting the null hypothesis of ownership-performance relationship. Case study of Fundanga and Mwaba, (1997) agrees with the positive effect of privatisation on the performance of enterprises. They found that private over public ownership is superior in efficiency and productivity. One of the three case studies (Vácha, 1999) on the Slovakian Steel Works (SSW) also showed that privatisation resulted in an increase of efficiency and so was entrepreneurial potential, which was suppressed under Command economy.

Sheel (1999) and Ernest and Helen (2000) give another finding which is some what different in conception comparing to aforementioned findings, and have agreed upon one point that monopolies are sloppy in nature, whether public or private. If monopolist nature continues in companies even after privatisation, it is doubtful to extract the expected advantages from the process. Ernest and Helen add more, by putting forth their points that a private monopoly can afford to be just as lazy as a public monopoly. In private monopolies, only those innovations, which increase profit, can count on an enthusiastic response, and external pressure groups may find it difficult to push the company to adopt other types of innovations. Innovation, after all, is not something that can be enforced.

As a surprising reply to all aforementioned authors and analysts, scholars like Ahmed (2000) gives a warning so as to not get into a stereotype assumption that privatisation always brings out benefits. His analysis on performance of privatised organisation declines to accept that privatisation has generally improved enterprise performance. He asserts the statement with the review of various theoretical literature and empirical studies, which failed to find a definite correlation between privatisation and enterprise efficiency.

PROS AND CONS OF PRIVATISATION–A SPECIAL REVIEW

It is a tough job to come to a concrete idea about the cost and benefits of privatisation. First of all, many studies and analytical conclusions differ in their views, which are rather confusing than untying knots on pros and cons of privatisation.

Many affirm that privatisation brings forth a lot of advantages to enterprises and economy as well. As a first evidence, Ethiopia is no exception. According to Girma (1993), SAP led the Ethiopian economy stabilisation which attained; an overall economic growth; declined in exports had been reversed and agricultural production and exports had increased. The scholar attributed these positive changes to nothing, but specially to the removal of major distortions from the economy, and a warm welcome to private sector into the economy.

Another case done by Kidane (1996) on the Eritrean privatisation shows that the pre-privatisation rehabilitation measures of public enterprises resulted in some improvement at the efficiency of the enterprise. Two out of three sample studies showed a positive result on the performance of the enterprises. That performance-improvement was attributed to the measures taken to rehabilitate those enterprises, which were on the verge of privatising.

Hill (1998) puts his statement that many host countries worry that the economic reforms and privatisation brings a substantial amount of FDI accompanied by some loss of economic independence. The concern is that of a foreign parent that has no real commitment, makes key decisions that can affect the host country's economy.

ILO (1999) report acknowledges that even a basic issue whether or not private enterprises outperform public enterprises in efficiency is not uniformly answered. Many evidences and studies around the world noted that private enterprises usually do well but due to their inclination towards adopting new technology, operating in a competitive environment and executing performance based incentive systems.

In general, most of the findings at the International level (Parker and Kirkpatrick, 2003; Megginson and Neller, 2001) certify positively about privatisation, which was at the beginning of 1990s as a structural reform led a number of developing countries gained competitive strengths in response to the changing economic environment (Rangarajan, 2002).

Ramakrishna et al. (2003) examine the impacts of globalisation in India as well as in Ethiopia. Using neo-classical growth model, the study indicates that there was a positive effect on economic growth and poverty on account of introducing globalisation and privatisation in these respective countries. However, the study disapproves the same impact on other aspects, particularly the income inequalities existing among the people.

Irrespective of these findings, the so-called advantages that are supposed to be brought by privatisation in developing countries remain controversial. Bamenjo (2002) condemns privatisation in his paper presentation on the Second International Conference on Energy for Sustainable Societies. He strongly quoted in his paper that foreign multinational companies winning electricity markets through privatisation scheme marginalise rural areas. There is, therefore, the need for public investments to be consecrated to rural electrification.

Stifanos and Henk von Eije (2003) finds by using a top-down triangular approach in their case study that the process of privatisation itself can endanger profitability, if privatisation is assumed wrongly that it relieves government budget deficits by an account of the direct cash revenues of selling companies.

RESEARCH GAP—FOR THIS STUDY TO FILL UP

From the foregoing review of literature, it is found that there are a lot of studies conducted on different issues of privatisation. However, these studies have concentrated largely on: economic and financial measures of performance; narrow and specific issues; and finally, these studies have amply been done in the industralised countries and higher income developing countries which leave the world a dearth of study on privatisation in the least developed African countries. Moreover, it is from the researcher's point of view, there is no study so far conducted empirically on the transitional issues and approaches of privatisation in Sub Saharan Africa, particularly in Ethiopia. Hence, this study is done to fill up this gap.

STATEMENT OF THE PROBLEM

Privatisation has been promoted in the developing countries since 1980. Although recent reviews of international effects of privatisation have been generally favourable to privatisation, the consequences of privatisation within the developing countries remain controversial.

Privatisation process, in fact, has given a rise to contentious issues and conflicting interests such as privatisation vs. processing effectiveness, privatisation vs. economic growth, privatisation vs. investment, privatisation vs. national sovereignty, privatisation vs.

public(society) concern, privatisation vs. labour concern and employment, and privatisation vs. efficiency and productivity. With theses issues, privatisation at this moment is no more a rhetoric statement because it has become a big debate among intelligentsia pertaining its merits and demerits. As a matter of fact, privatisation is believed to have brought conflicting interest and confusing state as post-privatisation effects.

Yet, there is a strong belief on market system that privatisation can bring into an economy, resulting in growth and stabilisation and reduction in budget deficit and national debt. Moreover, a shift towards a market system involves competition and incentives which are seen as driving forces towards efficiency in resource allocation and use, as well as accelerated economic growth. But experience shows that most of the developing countries have not achieved the expected outcomes and overall growth which goes against market-driven policies, and the World Bank, the IMF and other donor countries. The severity of the case is so high in poor countries which are with little resources, and spare frequently its national policy to food security and poverty reduction. Ethiopia, which is a typical case of this kind, nevertheless, adopted privatisation as a structural adjustment programme since 1994.

Privatisation in Ethiopia is nothing but is considered an outcome popped up as a result of the new economic policy of the Federal Democratic Republic of Ethiopia which was announced in 1992. The policy clearly envisaged a quickest development of its economy through the process of planning and implementation of multi-sector programme, especially to establish an efficient private sector and a market economy.

Ever since the introduction of the new market-oriented economic policy was announced, a number of policy measures and reforms have been undertaken to attract private investment either domestically or internationally. These measures include short-term economic stabilization, and structural adjustment measures, such as deregulation of domestic prices, abolition of export taxes and subsidies, liberalisation of foreign trade, privatisation of public enterprises and the promulgation of liberalised investment law for the promotion and encouragement of domestic and foreign private investment.

Privatisation as an economic process needs to be handled systematically with a careful plan and policy especially in the third world countries since their resources and capacity to meet any repercussion in mishandling privatisation are very much limited to bearing the after shock. If the process and their issues were well handled, it would yield expected outcomes which have already been experienced in many developing countries.

The privatisation entails enormous number of issues to be contemplated and analysed in such a way that the impact of privatisation can easily be judged. Four specific issues underscore the urgency of the breakthrough: first, processing issues that the application of legal framework, valuation of assets, use of methods and techniques, buyers' response and pace of privatisation in general which all determine the success of privatisation. Processing issues are business environment, regulatory and executing issues that are very much interrelated to other succeeding issues of privatisation. If the processing issues were not properly approached, it would increase chances of failure muddling up political, economic and other social issues which could turn out to be anti-elements to economy and community as a whole.

Second, economic and political issues include economic growth, budget deficit and external debt reduction, openness (export orientation) and investment which are main targets of privatisation. These issues are direct causes to why privatisation is imposed on the least developed countries (LDCs).

Third, the socio-labour issues, such as standard of living, education, health, road construction and social welfare, poverty reduction, unemployment and labour conditions after privatisation should carefully be seen during the privatisation process. Many studies reveal that privatisation has brought a negative impact on social and labour issues, albeit its better performance in political and economic issues; fourth and final, the performance and managerial issues of privatised ones are the most visible issues contributing a lot to judge whether privatisation works well at the bottom level of economy.

Ethiopia is no exception to all these issues, queries and complication in handling privatisation which have been raised above. It has, therefore, become a strong reason, and necessitated this research to be undertaken in Ethiopia, a poverty-stricken nation. The research design for this study is basically built up to accomplish its objectives on empirical and analytical basis in order to give a full proof about some of the hidden issues and impacts of privatisation, which are not yet properly diagnosed in Ethiopia, a Sub- Saharan African country.

RESEARCH QUESTIONS

This research is mostly empirical that attempts to address the following questions:

- How much worth are economic reforms in Ethiopia? What has necessitated Ethiopia to adopt privatisation?
- What are the issues and impacts of processing issues that decide the over all performance of privatisation process in Ethiopia?
- What are the economic and political issues of privatisation, and their impacts, particularly on the issues of economic growth, reduction of budget deficit and national debt, export orientation, investment, ownership creation and foreign dominance?
- What are the socio-labour and managerial issues of privatisation and impacts that privatisation brings to Ethiopia?

OBJECTIVES OF THE STUDY

The objectives of the study are as follows:

- To study about the Ethiopian economic reform, a corollary to privatisation, and its impact on the Ethiopian economy in general.
- To analyse the initiative symptoms that necessitated Ethiopia to practise privatisation as one of the structural adjustment programmes.
- To study thoroughly the processing issues and approaches during the transformation of PSUs into private sector.
- To ascertain and investigate economic and political issues of privatisation, and its impact on the economy.
- To study socio-labour, and managerial issues and its impact on the working class and community as a whole.

HYPOTHESES

The following hypotheses are formed to verify at the end of the research:

- Privatisation in Ethiopia is slow and absurd.
- Privatisation in Ethiopia as an economic reform has failed to bring a desired change in the economic issues.
- Privatisation in Ethiopia has failed to show any positive outcome in the social and labours' conditions, and
- The privatisation in Ethiopia has not effected any betterment in productivity, profitability and management working environment in the privatised enterprises.

DEFINITION OF THE CONCEPTS

Privatisation: It refers to the transfer of ownership or control of PSUs from public to private individuals and entities. It also includes the transfer of ownership of land or housing to private individuals and entities. However, this study limits privatisation to PSUs only.

Transitional Issues: The emergence of those issues in the sphere of economy, polity, society, labour and management while transferring PSUs to private hands. It also includes processing issues concerning with the conversion of legal form from public entity to private entity.

Transitional Approaches: It refers to approaches of those issues by the country in terms of the objectives set forth for privatisation.

CONCEPTUAL FRAMEWORK FOR ANALYSIS OF THE STUDY

Figure 1 shows the conceptual framework for analysis of this study. The conceptual framework gives the basic research theme or the research base on which the collection of data and structure of analysis are made. Moreover, it serves as a guide as to the kind of data to be collected and the method of analysis to be made.

Moreover, the framework used here to explore and explain how the transitional issues—categorized as processing, economic and political, socio-labour and managerial issues which, as per small arrows indicated, are interrelated and interdependent, deciding success of one another, and eventually determining overall performance of Ethiopian privatisation, resulted in success or failure. The big arrows indicate various actors coming across through out the privatisation process, influencing the transitional issues.

Processing Issues: Processing issues are the basic and fundamental issues. These issues consist of assessment of business

Figure 1
Conceptual Framework for Analysis of this Study

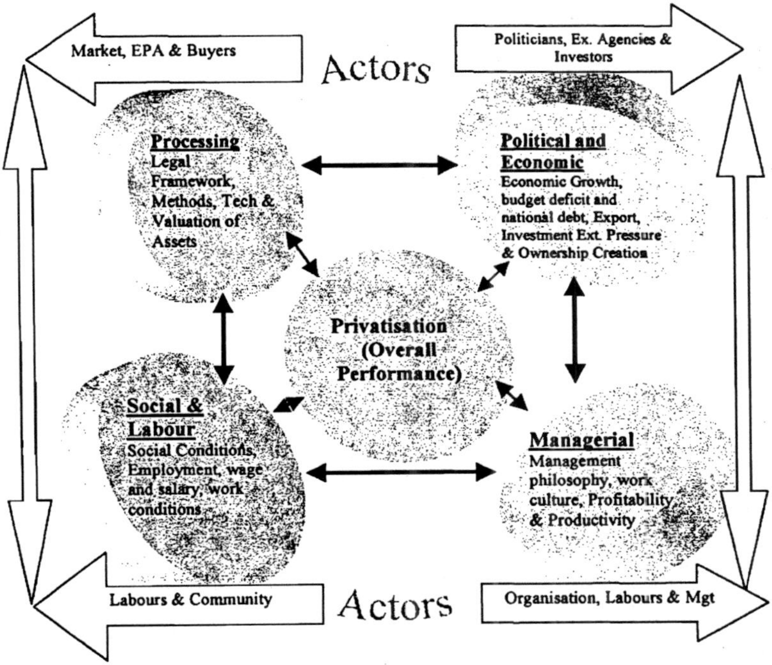

environment including market, legal and commercial framework, conducting the formalities such as asset valuation, deciding the methods and techniques, selection of buyers and monitoring the post-privatisation impacts. Furthermore, these issues include buyers' response to privatisation and tender convertibility. The main actors in the privatisation process are Ethiopian Privatisation Agency (the regulatory body) and buyers. Quality lies on how best the Agency plans and executes the privatisation, particularly in the way that the national policy directs, whereas the buyers oblige and execute the business in the way that the expected advantages of privatisation, such as professionalism and efficiency are achieved. It is, therefore, the responsibility of the Agency to act very carefully in processing the privatisation activities and to choose the best buyers not only based on their higher purchasing capacity but also their attitude, experience and character.

Economic and Political Issues: Political and economic issues are the major issues which determine success of the privatisations process. These issues are nothing, but the ultimate targets, such as economic growth, budget deficit and external debt reduction, export orientation and investment attraction, and politically external pressures and foreign dominance and ownership creation which determine the overall performance of privatisation. Economic growth and a substantial investment including FDI need to be well accomplished as an outcome of the privatisation process; otherwise the government will be held responsible for further retrograding economic condition. It is a well known fact that if privatisation is not properly surged, the side effects of it will become worse.

Political and economic issues are the initiators, organisers, and sometimes, destructor of the process. Either success or failure of privatisation can easily be attributed to these issues. Political ad economic issues are much considered well before the privatisation, and will become remain as vital ones through out the programme. The actors in this context indicated in the framework—importantly, politicians, legislators, investors and public—are the deciding factors as they give shape to the programme. Their attitudes and aptitudes are not only indispensable for the fate of the programme, but also for upholding efficiency and overall performance of the programme.

Socio-Labour Issues: Investigation about the social variables such as improvement of the standard of living, education, health, road construction, social welfare and poverty reduction is stressed at this point of the research framework. After all, privatisation as an economic reform is also aimed at improving the living standard of Ethiopians, who have been suffering for long without the basic necessity for their livelihood. Moreover, labour issues such as employment creation and work conditions are the haunting issues in privatisation. It is, therefore, a felt need in this study to bring about the facts whether the privatisation in Ethiopia has improved the socio-economic conditions of labourers and the community as a whole.

Managerial Issues: Managerial issues consist of management philosophy, work culture, employee and employer relationship, efficiency and productivity of the enterprises. The focus is whether privatisation has turned out a positive effect on these issues of the enterprise, which is, in fact, going to be the spokesperson for privatisation. Managerial issues as well as some of the labour issues are studied in terms of comparing domestic privatised enterprises with foreign ones in order to know their success in the light of privatisation.

METHODOLOGY

This study is both descriptive and empirical. The overall data set up for analysis in this study includes national economic indicators, statistical data from the concerned ministries, manuals, and financial statements. For the analyses of most of the labour and managerial issues, survey method was conducted.

Selection of Samples

The labour, who were chosen as samples based on the purposive random sampling for this study, were ensured to have worked during the pre and post privatisation process of the enterprises. As a result, 1200 were identified out of 11,500 labourer population. Out of which 120 labourers—10 per cent of the identified lot—were drawn as samples. These samples were distributed based on the size of the business they acquired from the state which was, in turn, found in much proportionate to the number of labours. For much closer look, these samples were distributed after a stratification of privatised enterprises as the domestic and foreign which help this study to investigate thoroughly as to how these issues are handled by these enterprises. To analyse about other issues such as retrenchment and employment generation, fifty five enterprises were taken as samples out of 220 privatised enterprises, i.e. 25 per cent of the total enterprise population.

To analyse the financial performance of those privatised enterprises, a purposive random sampling was applied. Forty five potential enterprises were identified. Out of which, six enterprises, i.e., 13 per cent were chosen as samples on the justification: the enterprises were relatively bigger in operation, and moderately with a wider area of network; the enterprises employed a relatively large number of workers and the enterprises that were with adequate accounting data and approved statements and they should, moreover, be suitable for in-depth studies.

Data Collection

Primary and secondary data were collected. Pertaining to primary data, a questionnaire was prepared to collect relevant data and so were interview schedules. Primary data for this research aims at collecting first hand information from important actors such as EPA (Ethiopian Privatisation Agency), the labour, and donors. Interviews were conducted, particularly with officers working in pre-privatisation and post privatisation departments of EPA and an expert in the World Bank.

Secondary data was collected from different stakeholders of Ethiopian privatisation like Ministry of Finance & Economic Development (MoFED), Ministry of Economic Development & Cooperation (MEDaC), Ministry of Industry & Trade, Ethiopian Investment Authority, EPA, World Bank, IMF, and importantly, from those privatised companies.

Quantitative Data

Accounting data is the mirror that reflects where exactly an organisation stands. Financial data was collected in such a way that the basic requirement of the study is not, at any phase of study, undermined. Reports and statistical data were collected from the concerned ministries and the Agency, and a detailed schedule was prepared to collect the relevant financial conditions of the selected enterprises for analysing changes in their conditions. Financial statements—though limited—such as income statements, balance sheets and annexes for accounting justification for the required period were carefully examined in spite of a lot difficulties confronted in seeking them. Governmental accounts and statistical data relating to economic performance were also deeply pursued for studying the relationship between different variables under study.

Quality of the Financial Data and Economic Indicators

The data either of financial data or economic indicators were ensured to be reliable and dependable. As it is already quoted in the cases selected, the way the enterprises were sampled to show that they had their accounts properly audited by the certified or chartered auditors. Statistics at the National level was collected from the National Accounting Department of the MoFED, which is duly audited by

FAG. In addition to these sources, the World Bank data was highly useful, as the World Bank computes its statistics as per the 1993 United Nations System of National Accounts (1993SNA).

Qualitative Data

Most of the actors studied in this research were interacted with or interviewed (structured or unstructured or both) or given a questionnaire. A comprehensive questionnaire (Appendix II) was prepared to target the labour (employees) of the privatised enterprises for the study of the labour and managerial issues. A two set of Structured Interview Schedule (SIS) with closed and open ended questions were prepared and administered respectively for the officials in the Agency (Appendix III), and for the external agency official (Appendix IV).

Managers and Administrators of the selected enterprises were focused and discussed for labour and managerial issues. The details of issues taken up for the discussion are given in Appendix V. A high degree of attention and vigilance was taken in preparing and administering the questionnaires, interviews and discussions as not to prevent the study from missing any needed result. Each interview took approximately forty five to fifty minutes. Questionnaires, SIS and discussions were administered in 2003/04.

Tables 1 and 2 show respectively for history of response to interviews and nature of people interviewed, and average time taken by each respondent.

Table 1
History of Response to Interviews

Organisation	*Position*	*Interviews*	
		Conducted	*Not Conducted*
EPA	Post Privatisation Manager (He was then acting General Manager)	X	
	Senior Privatisation Impact Analyst	X	
	Senior Economist	X	
	Senior Engineer (who involves in valuation)	X	
External Agency (World Bank)	Private Sector Specialist	X	

Table 2
Average Time Taken for Interviews and Discussions

The nature of Interviewees	*Average Time Duration*
EPA and WB Officials	50 Minutes each
Managers of the Privatised Enterprises	45 Minutes each

Period of the Study

Data concerning this study covers a period of ten years which ranged between 1994/95 and 2003/04, Ethiopian Fiscal Years (EFY). However, for investigating the pre-impact reforms and causal analysis of privatisation, period ranging from 1986/87 EFY to 1991/92 EFY was used only in Chapter III.

Data Analysis

Data collected from the different sources was analysed through SPSS Version 12 (Statistical Package for Social Sciences). Financial statements of the selected enterprises were interpreted through financial analysis. As financial analyses are helpful to understand the strengths and weakness of the organisation, the analysis has carefully been done, and the most widely used method in this study is ratio analysis. The ratio analysis was used to know the proportion between two variables: productivity, profitability, liquidity and return on investment.

To know the growth rate of each and every economical and social variable of the study period, the compound growth rate was applied. To calculate the compound growth rate, the following formula is used:

$$y = Ax^b$$

$$\text{Log } y = \log A + b \log x$$

$$Y = a + b\,x$$

Here, y = Dependent variable, x = Time period (1, 2, 3...), b = (1+r); r = compound growth rate, and Compound growth rate = (Antilog b–1) 100

The significance of b value is tested by 't' value:

$$t = \frac{b}{S.E}$$

At the macro level, especially the economic performance of Ethiopia during privatisation was analysed through simple measures of central tendency and regression analysis. Pertaining hypotheses testing, t-tests were performed. Multiple linear regression analysis based on heterodox model was widely used in this research, and the formula for multiple linear regression model is:

$$y = b_0 + b_1 x_1 + b_2 x_2 + b_3 x_3 + \ldots\ldots\ldots\ldots\ldots\ldots\ldots b_n x_n$$

Where y is the dependent variable and $x_1, x_2, x_3, \ldots\ldots\ldots x_n$ are the set of independent variables, $b_1, b_2, b_3, \ldots\ldots\ldots\ldots\ldots\ldots b_n$ are called the regression coefficients and b_0 is called the intercept term. Most of the time series data was linearised through logarithms, in particular ones that are growing at a constant rate having no significant negative signs.

To find out the relationship or association between two variables, correlation analyses were applied. It is computed by using the formula:

$$r = \frac{N\Sigma XY - (\Sigma X)(\Sigma Y)}{\sqrt{N\Sigma X^2 - (\Sigma X)^2}\ \sqrt{N\Sigma Y^2 - (\Sigma Y)^2}}$$

Here, the significance of 'r' is tested by the formula:

$$t = \frac{r\sqrt{n-2}}{\sqrt{1-r^2}}$$

During the analysis labour and managerial issues, an attempt was made to distinguish through Chi-square distribution (χ^2) whether there is any significant difference in results between domestic and foreign privatised enterprises after privatisation. The formula for χ^2 is

$$\chi^2 = \Sigma \left[\frac{(fo - fe)^2}{fe}\right]$$ with degree of freedom (df)=(r–1) (c - 1),

where

r = number of rows; c = number of columns

f_0 is the observed frequency

f_e is an expected frequency

In addition to these statistical tools, scatter diagram and simple graph methods were widely applied. Furthermore, data was tabulated in order to show the ups and downs of different economic indicators and other important privatisation proceedings. To show more accuracy, geometric mean was used to calculate the annual growth rate if data was found either in percentage or in ratio.

LIMITATIONS OF THE STUDY

This study may not represent the whole effect of privatisation because it deals only with the privatisation of PSUs. In Ethiopia, as a process of political change, the land and housing once nationalised have also been in the process of privatisation which is not included in this study.

Owing to a lack of time series data on poverty, the study lacks an in-depth insight into its relationship with privatisation. Other limitation of this study is the availability of data which the researcher found them inconsistent between different organisations, owing to the lack of proper coordination on the relevant data and statistics bank which is supposed to be archived between concerned and inter-dependent organisations.

Some of the enterprises, which were randomly selected, had either denied to receive or failed to send back the questionnaires while primary data was sought. Particularly, the questionnaires supplied to the labour in small scale enterprises were in a partial failure since the owners of those small scale enterprises refrained the working class to fill the questionnaire.

This research may lack an in-depth analysis of the financial aspect of the privatised enterprises, owing to the rigidity of the management in disclosing their financial statements.

There are a few analytical gaps in the empirical study, but within a permissible error limit which may also be a limitation if a high degree of comprehensiveness and accuracy is expected. The research place, Ethiopia, which is not the home country of the researcher, posed for sometime a cultural shock during his initial stay for data collection.

NOTES

1. The EBA was developed by Leamer and Herman and has been applied since 1978. This analysis is used widely when a cross country growth needs to be found. The EBA can be conducted by applying the following linear ordinary least squares(OLS) regression:

$$Y = \beta_1 I + \beta_2 M + \beta_3 Z + u$$

Where Y is the GDP per capita growth rate, I is a set of variables that are commonly included in the regression, M is the policy variable of particular interest, and Z is a set of up to three variables chosen from a pool of policy variables. In accordance with the EBA procedure, the combinations of a set of the Z variables are changed to examine whether or not the co-efficient of M is statistically significant and maintains the same sign through out the process. To conduct the EBA, all possible combinations of regressions are estimated to obtain β_2 and the corresponding standard deviation, σ, for each regression. Then, the upper or maximum extreme bound is defined as the minimum value of β_2 plus σ_2. The lower or minimum extreme bound is defined as the minimum value of β_2 minus σ_2. If theses maximum and minimum extreme bounds keep the same sign, the result is interpreted as robust than fragile.

2. A model, which was originally used by Edwards, applied to estimate the importance of privatisation as a determinant of FDI in developing countries. On the basis of empirical and theoretical literature on FDI, Edwards selected a set of structural variables he deemed relevant to the decision making process of a foreign investor. He used these variables to estimate the average level of FDI relative to GDP, as well as the percentage share of total FDI, for a cross section of fifty-eight developing countries during 1971-81.

REFERENCES

Ahluwalia, M. (2003), "Some of the Criticism Directed at the IMF is not valid", an Exclusive Interview, *D+C [Development & Cooperation]*, September, Vol. 30, pp. 436-7.

Ahmed, M.U. (2000), "Privatisation in Bangladesh" in Gopal Joshi (ed.) *Privatisation in South Asia: Minimising Negative Social Effects through Restructuring.* New Delhi: ILO. pp.24-39.

Anderson, R. (2000), "How Government Can Help Business in Poor Countries", *Journal of Economic Integration'*, Vol. 15, No. 1, pp. 145-61.

Fosu, A.K. (2003), "Political Instability and Export Performance in Sub-Saharan Africa", *Journal of African Economies,* Vol. 39, No. 4, pp. 68-82.

Barnett, S. (2000), *"Evidence on the Fiscal and Macro Economic Impact of Privatisation"*, IMF Working Paper, July, Washington, D.C.: IMF.

Baumol, W.J. and Blinder, A.S. (1997) *Macro Economics: Principles and Policy.* Florida: Dryden Press, p. 484.

Befekadu Degefe (1994), "Strategies and Macroeconomic Policies for the Development of the Private Sector in Ethiopia" (ed) *The Ethiopian Economy: Problems and Prospects of Private Sector Development-Proceedings of the Third Annual Conference of the Ethiopian Economy.* Addis Ababa: AAU Press.

Bennet, T. and Johnson, M.H. (1979), "Public Vs Private Provision of Collective Goods and Services: Garbage Collection Revitalised", *Public Choice,* No. 34, pp. 55-64.

Boardman and Vining (1989), "Ownership in Competitive Environments: A Comparison of the Performance of Mixed, Private and SOEs", *Journal of Law and Economics,* April, No. 32, pp. 1-36.

Bolnick, B.R. (1987), *Economics of Development: Study Guide and Work Book.* New York: W.W. Norton & Co., pp. 122-8.

Botelho, A. and Addis, C. (1988), "Privatisation of Telecommunications in Mexico" in Rolph Vander Hoeven and Gyorgy Sziraczki (eds) *Lessons from Privatisation: Labour Issues in Developing and Transitional Countries.* Geneva: ILO, pp. 71-90.

Buckley, J.W. (1976) *Research Methodology and Business Decisions.* New York: National Association of Accounts. p. 37.

Caves, D.W. and Christensen, L. (1980), "The Relative Efficiency of Public and Private Firms in a Competitive Environment: The Case of Canadian Railroads", *Journal of Public Economy,* No. 88, pp. 95-6.

Chakravarthi, R. (2001), "The World Bank, Globalisation and Poverty", *Third World Economics: Trend and Analysis,* 1-15 December, No. 270, p. 3.

Chandrasekhar, C.P. (2003), "Economic Perspectives: Privatisation on Hold", *Frontline,* October, Vol. 20, No. 20, pp.102-3.

Cook, P. and Uchida, Y. (2003), "Privatisation and Economic Growth in Developing Countries", *The Journal of Development Studies,* Vol. 39, No. 9, pp.121-54.

Government of India (1997) "Disinvestment Commission Report V", November, New Delhi, p. 16.

Donaldson, D. and Wagle, D.M. (1995), *"Privatisation Principles and Practices: IFC Lessons of Experience Series* No. 15007", September, Washington: IFC, pp. 3-22.

Eardley, R.F. (1999), "Privatising Bus Transport in Sri Lanka" in Prokopenko, J. (ed) *Management for Privatisation.* Geneva: ILO, pp. 233-51.

Earle, J.S. (1999), "Privatisation in Russia Offers Lessons for Others", *Economic Reform Today*-CIPE (Privatisation in the Digital Age), No. 2, pp.12-9.

Ekelund and Tollison (1997), *Micro Economics: Private Markets and Public Choices.* New York: Addison-Wesley Publishing Company, Inc., p. 118.

Ernest ten Heuvelhof and Helen Stout (2000), "Sustainable Utilities: New Opportunities for Sustainability through Liberalization and Privatisation", *UNEP Industry and Environment,* Vol. 23, No. 1-2, p. 60.

Fundanga, C.M. and Mwaba, A. (1997), *"Privatisation of Public Enterprises in Zambia: An Evaluation of the Policies, Procedures and Experiences",* Economic Research Papers No. 35, African Development Bank, pp. 15-7.

Geeta, B. and Syed Mahmood (2003), *"Direct Support to Private Firms: Evidence on Effectiveness",* World Bank Policy Research Working Paper 3170, November, IMF, pp. 5-6.

Girma, S. (1993), *"Ethiopia's Private Sector under Structural Adjustment Response to Foreign Trade Liberalisation and Exchange Rate Policy Reforms",* A Paper Submitted for the Third Annual Conference on the Ethiopian Economy, The Department of Economics, AAU and EEA, December 3-6, 1993, Nazereth, Ethiopia.

Gopal Joshi (2000), "Privatisation in India" in Gopal Joshi (ed) *Privatisation in South Asia: Minimising Negative Social Effects through Restructuring.* New Delhi: ILO, p. 57.

Griffith, R.J. (1998) *"Developing World 1998/99: Political Economy and the Developing World",* Guildford (CT): Dushkin/McGraw-Hill, pp. 38-9.

Gibbon, H. (1996) *"A Guide for Divesting Government Owned Enterprises",* How to Guide, No. 15. July, p. 1.

Hill, C.W.L. (1998), *Global Business Today.* Washington: Irwin/McGraw-Hill.

Hinds, B. (1999), "Opportunities and Constraints of Privatisation" in Gormley, W.T. (ed.) *Privatisation and its Alternatives.* Oxford: Oxford University Press, pp. 281-306.

Hyman, D.N. (1997), *Macro Economics.* Boston: The Mc Graw-Hill Company, Inc. p. 98.

ILO (1999), *"Report of the Sub-Regional Workshop on Privatisation in South Asia",* 24–26 November, Kathmandu, ILO, pp. 211-18.

Itoh, M. & Kiyono, K. (1988), "Foreign Trade and Direct Investment" in Kamiya, M. Okuno, M. & Suzumuru, K. (eds) *Industrial Policy of Japan.* Tokyo: Academic Press.

Kühl, Jürgen (1998), *"Privatisation and its Labour Market effect in Eastern Germany"* in Rolph Vander Hoeven and Gyorgy Sziraczki (eds), pp. 119-42.

Kibre Moges (1994), "The Role of the State and Private Sector under Economic Liberalisation–Theoretical Perspectives", in Getachew, Y. and Abdulhami, B. (eds) *The Ethiopian Economy: Problems and Prospects of Private Sector Development*-Proceedings of the Third Annual Conference of the Ethiopian Economy. AAU Press: Addis Ababa.

Kidane, T. (1996), *"Challenges and Prospects of the Privatisation Process of the Public Enterprises in Eritrea"*, A Paper Submitted for the Partial Fulfilment of the Degree, March, University of Asmara, Asmara, p. 58.

Leon Louw (1999), "What Would Make Privatisation Work in South Africa", *Economic Reform Today*-CIPE [Privatisation in the Digital Age], No. 2, p. 17-21.

Lorrain Eden (1996), "Whither WIR?", *Transnational Corporation*, Vol. 5, No. 2, pp. 145-55.

Masood Ahmed, Timothy Lane, and Marianne Schulze-Ghattas (2001) "Refocusing IMF Conditionality", *Finance & Development*, December, Vol. 38, No. 4, pp. 40-1.

Megginson, W.L. and Neller, J.M. (2001), "From State to Market: A Survey of Empirical Studies on Privatisation", *Journal of Economic Literature*, November, Vol. 39, pp. 321-389.

Miller, R. Le Roy (1997), *Economic Today: A Micro View*. Boston: Addison-Wesley Educational Publisher, pp. 122-3.

Miller, R. Le Roy (1998), *Economic Today*. New York: Addison-Wesley Educational Publisher, pp. 124-5.

Mishra, R.K., Nandagopal and Lateef Syed, A. (1993), "Sale of Public Enterprise Shares: Frittering Away Nation's Wealth", *Economic and Political Weekly*, Vol. 28, No. 48, pp. 163-8.

Mkandawire, T. and Soludo, C.C. (2003), "Towards the Broadening of Development Policy Dialogue for Africa" in Mkeandawire and Soludo (eds) *African Voices on Structural Adjustment*. New Jersey: African World Press, pp. 2-5.

Nellis, J. (2003), *"Privatisation in Africa: What happened? What is to be done?"*, Working Paper No. 25, Centre for Global Development, pp. 3-19.

New African (1999), *"A Giant Step Forward"*, Special Report: Tunisia, October, No. 378, p. 11.

Novak, M. (1991), "Transforming the Democratic Capitalistic Revolution", *International Journal of Value Based Management,* Vol. 4, No. 2, p. 22.

Oxford (1996), *Dictionary of Business.* Oxford: Oxford Printing Press, p. 395.

Oumar Makalou (1999), *"Privatisation in Africa: A Critical Analysis",* A paper presented on the 9th International Anti-Corruption Conference [IACC], 10-15 October 1999, Durban, South Africa, p. 10.

Padmanapan, B.S. (2003), "Towards Total Solutions" in Focus: MTNL-DELHI, *Frontline,* July, Vol. 20, No. 14, pp. 89-94.

Parker, D. and Kirkpatrick, C. (2003), *"Privatisation in Developing Countries: A Review of the Evidence and the Policy Lessons"* Working Paper Series 55, Manchester: Institute for Development Policy and Management, pp. 20-32.

Preper, U. and Taylor, L. (2000), "The Revival of the Liberal Creed: the IMF, the WB, and the Inequality in a globalised economy" in Dean Baker, Gerald Epstein and Robert Pollin (eds) *Globalisation and Progressive Economic Policy.* Cambridge: Cambridge University Press, pp. 53-4.

Plain, P. (1997), "Privatisation and Economic Growth: An Empirical Investigation from a Sample of Developing Market Economies", *Applied Economics,* Vol. 29, No. 2, pp. 161-78.

Radomir Sabela, Terézia Hrnèíové and Josef Vais (1995), *"Process of Privatisation in Field of Industry and Trade in the Czech Republic",* Study No. 5, June 1995, Institute of Economic Studies: Prague.

Rahn, R.W. (1999), "Money: The Ultimate Privatisation", *Economic Reform Today,* Privatisation in the Digital Age, No. 2, p. 7.

Ramakrisha, G., Sivarama Krishanan, V., & Abdul Hamid Sukar (2003), "Impact of Globalisation on Growth, Poverty and Income Inequality: A Study of Ethiopia and India", *Asian Economic Review,* August, Vol. 45, No. 2, pp. 326-39.

Rangarajan, C. (2002), "Economic Reforms: An Assessment", *The Indian Economic Journal,* July-September, Vol. 49, No. 1, pp. 1-3.

Reich, R.B. (1991), *The Work of Nations: Preparing Ourselves for the 21st Century.* New York: Alfred A. Knopf.

Sadar, F. (1995) *"Privatising Public Enterprises and Foreign Direct Investment in Developing Countries, 1988-93",* Occasional Paper 5, Foreign Investment Advisory Service, Washington: IFC, pp. 1-44.

Schiller, B.R. (1991), *The Economy Today.* New York: McGraw-Hill, Inc. p. 693.

Sheel, A. (1999), "The Privatisation Wheel", *The Economic Times,* 4 September, Vol. 39, No. 177, p. 2.

Shirley, M.M. (1995), "Getting Bureaucrats Out of Business: Obstacles to State Enterprise Reform", *Economic Reform Today,* No. 4, p. 2-9.

Sitikantha, P. and Sangita, M. (2003), "The Spectre of IMF Conditionality: Some Streamlining Option", *The Indian Economic Journal,* Vol. 50, No. 1, pp. 17-8.

Sridhar, V. (2003), "Disinvestment: Airport for Sale", *Frontline,* October 24, Vol. 20, No. 21, p. 127.

Mugerwa-Kayizzi, S. (2002), *"Privatisation in Sub-Saharan Africa: On Factors Affecting Implementation",* Discussion Paper No. 2002/12, Helsinki: UNU/WIDER, pp.1-19.

Stifanos, H. and Henk von Eije (2003), *"The Impacts of Slow Privatisation in the Beverage and Textile Industry in Eritrea",* Viewed on 12th January, 2005, http://som.rug.nl/

Stiglitz, J. (1997), *Economics.* London: W.M. Norton & Company Inc. pp.162-3.

Taylor, J.B. (1995), *Principles of Macro Economics.* Boston: Houghton Mifflin Co. p. 661.

Tagama, H. (2002), *"Who's for Privatisation",* New African, July/August, No. 409, p. 17.

Timmorthy, T. (1996), *Macro Economics.* New York: Worth Publishers. pp. 492-500.

Vácha, S. (1999), "Privatisation in Three Large Manufacturing Companies in the Czech Republic and Slovakia" in Prokopenko, J. (ed), pp. 51-84.

Voszka, E. (1999), "Privatisation in Hungary: Results and Open Issues", *Economic Reform Today*-CIPE [Privatisation in the Digital Age], No. 2, p. 9.

Welch, D. & Frémond, O. (1998), *"The Case-by-Case Approach to privatisation: Techniques and Examples",* World Bank Technical Paper no. 43, Washington D.C.: World Bank, pp. 1-12.

Winter, J. (1999), "Taking Stock: Is Nigeria Prepared to Privatise?", *Africa Economic Digest,* 31 May, pp. 5-6.

CHAPTER - 3

Economic Reforms and Privatisation in Ethiopia

This chapter begins the empirical part of the study describing Ethiopia, the research location, in context of its economic position over the past four decades, particularly from the Imperial government to the present government. This chapter also serves—preceding the economic background—to the extent that it describes the history, topography and cultural and societal characteristics of the country. The main purpose in analysing these backgrounds is to know why and how this country moved into neoliberalism[1], particularly into economic reforms and privatisation despite its cultural and trade conservatism.

The phase-to-phase analyses of economic conditions and reforms made in this chapter reveal the necessities which urged the country to go in for privatisation. Hence, highly emphasized in this chapter are the economic reforms and its drive to privatisation in Ethiopia.

ETHIOPIA: A PROFILE

Ethiopia is one of the poorest countries in the world, with an estimate per capita income of about USD100 (World Bank, 2004). As of 2003/04, 44 per cent of the people live below the basic needs poverty line. Non-monetary indicators of poverty are equally severe amidst its richest historical background, natural advantages and beautiful topography, which are described below as an attempt to introduce the country to this study.

The Country

Ethiopia is a country of thirteen months of sunshine with a weather property of lowland, highland and temperate climate. Located in the Horn of Africa, with an area of 1.1 million square kilometres and with a population of 69.13 million (CSA, 2004). It is the third most populous country in Africa, and ninth in terms of geographical area in the whole of Africa (MoFED, 2002a).

Ethiopia lies in the northeast of Africa. It borders Sudan in the west, Somalia and Djibouti in the east, Eritrea in the north and Kenya in the south (Map 1). The land surface of Ethiopia shows great variation. Some of the highest mountains in Africa, such as the Semien Mountains, and some of the great depressions, such as the Dallol, are found in Ethiopia. High plateaus, deep river canyons, rolling plains and lowlands, crisscross its land surface. Ethiopia, with its 14 rivers, 18 artificial and natural lakes have only developed 15 per cent for cultivation. According to MEDaC (1999), 69 per cent of the entire size of Ethiopia is arable land and also has a large size of farmland that is yet to be tapped in spite of its conducive room for agro-investment.

With regard to its animal wealth, Ethiopia has about 30 million cattle, 40.5 million of sheep, goats, horses and donkeys, 19 thousand pigs, one million camels, and 56.5 million chickens. This makes it first in Africa and 16th in the entire world. What is more, Ethiopia is a home to 103 animal and bird species. Of these, seven are mammals and 23 of the bird species are endemic to Ethiopia.

Ethiopia is located from 3°-15° north of the equator. One would expect the country to have a tropical climate. However, in the highland areas, the average temperature is 20° (68° F). It is here that the majority of the people live. Naturally, the lowlands do have a tropical climate. As the 'water tower' of Northeast Africa (Abraham, 2001), it has a country wide average rainfall during the summer season (June to September). There is a lesser amount of annual rainfall during the Belg season (February to April). The capital city of Ethiopia is Addis Ababa.

The People

The population has been growing annually at the average rate of 2.2 per cent with a life expectancy of 42.1 years (World Bank, 2003).

Map 1
Political Map of the People's Democratic Republic of Ethiopia

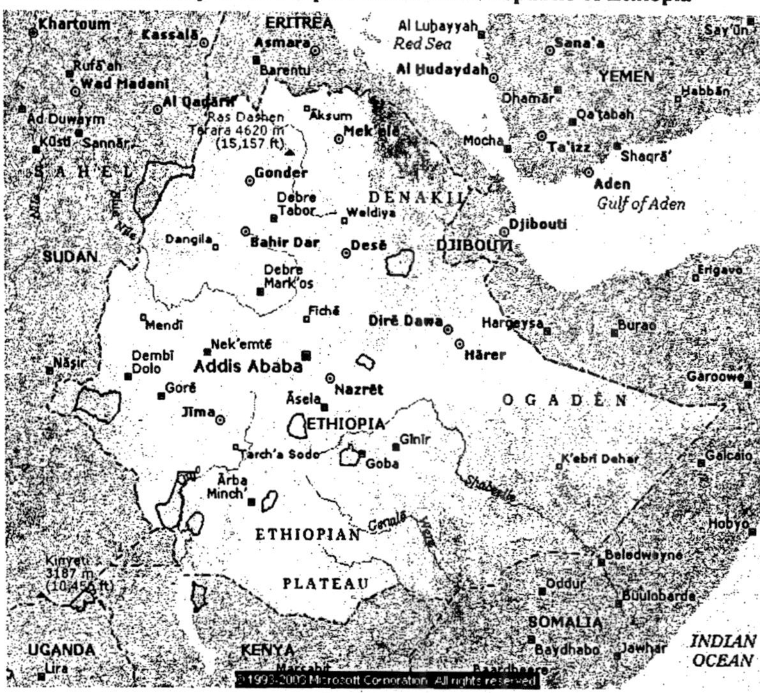

Source: Microsoft (2004)

The country is a melting pot of various ethnic groups who speak numerous languages. There are Semitic, Cushitic, Omotic and Nilotic people. Rural dwellers account for 84 per cent of the population. They are mostly smallholder peasant agriculturists. The illiteracy of the population accounts for 58 per cent of the population age 15 and above.

The Government

Ethiopia has come a long way from the centralised rule of the Haile Selassie, the emperor during the Imperial government and Derg regimes. It now has a federal government structure. After a brief administration by the Transitional government of Ethiopia, following the fall of the military regime, the Federal Democratic Republic of Ethiopia was established in 1995 under a new constitution.

Table 1
Profile of Ethiopia

ABOUT LAND	
Total Land Area	1.1 Million Square Kilometres
Total Arable Land	759,000 Square Kilometres
Total Area Under Cultivation	165,000 Square Kilometres
POPULATION	
Total Population	69.13 Million
Population (Average annual growth in percentage)	2.4
Labour Force (Average annual growth in percentage)	2.2
Urban Population (percentage of total population)	16
Life Expectancy at birth (years)	42
Infant Mortality (per 1,000 live births)	116
Child Malnutrition (percentage of children under 5)	47
Illiteracy (percentage of population age 15+)	58
Gross Primary enrolment (percentage of school-age population) Male	76
Female	52
GOVERNMENT	
Official Name	Federal Democratic Republic of Ethiopia
Form of State	Federal Republic
National Legislature	The 548-member House of Peoples' Representatives is the federal assembly. Nine regional state councils have limited powers, including that of appointing the supervisory Federal Council.
Head of State	President, has a largely an officiating role and is appointed by the House of Peoples' Representatives.
Head of Government	The Prime minister and his cabinet
Regional States	Oroma, Amhara, SNNPR, Somali, Tigray, Afar, Benishangul-Gumuz, Gambella, Harari, Addis Ababa, Dire Dawa

Source: Various World Bank and CSA Reports.

The federal government is responsible for national defence, foreign relations and general policies of common interest to all states. The Federal Government recognises that Ethiopia is composed of numerous states. It accepts their right to self-determination, giving them regional autonomy in the areas they inhabit. Hence, there are nine autonomous states in Ethiopia with the power of self-determination. The Federal Government has a bicameral parliament, the members of which are democratically elected by universal suffrage for a term of five years. Regarding other details, a glance of Ethiopia is given in Table 1.

ECONOMIC BACKGROUND AND POLICY CHANGES IN ETHIOPIA

At this point of research, Ethiopia is examined in relation to its economic policies and performance from the period of Haile Selassie to the present. There are so many factors that can be taken to review and evaluate the economic performance of a country. Among all factors, gross domestic product (GDP) and its growth are the crucial indicators. According to the World Bank's Development Report of 2000/01 (World Bank, 2002a), Ethiopia remains the poorest country on the earth, if ranked in dollar denominated per capita income terms as it has been with USD100. It is so tragic that the cursed status has continued for so long, whereas Sub Saharan Africa records its per capita income of USD450. In a nutshell, it is better to review Ethiopian's economic performance during different regimes especially from the mid 1960s.

Imperial Government and its Economic Policies

In the Imperial era, Ethiopia was a kingdom ruled by the Emperor, Haile Selassie. During his period, the Ethiopian economy was a type of mixed economy, where the private and the public sectors coexisted. The economic structure of that time was characterised by a predominant subsistence sector with extremely low levels of output, productivity, saving and investment.

Although the planning for economic development was started in 1937 (IEG, 1968: 23-4), it is very difficult to analyse the economic status of Ethiopia, as there was not enough data pertaining to the economy before 1950. However, this study enables to give a glance over the three five-year plans for discussion: the First Five Year Plan as already mentioned, but owing to delay in its implementation, it started to work from 1958; the Second Five Year Plan (1963-1967) and the Third Five year Plan (1969-1974).

The first document of macro economic and social policy known as 'The First Five Year Development Plan 1957-61' enables experts to have a meaningful review of the macroeconomic objective of the Ethiopian economy. Ethiopia was, perhaps the first African country to prepare comprehensive planning for socio-economic development. During the fist five-year plan, the actual GDP growth slightly fell short of the target standing at 3.2 per cent. The first five-year plan was completed with a trial and error process of reforms, but gave ample lesson for the second five-year plan.

In the second five-year plan, the economy registered an average annual growth rate of 4.6 per cent of GDP against the 4.3 per cent target. It was an achievement partly thanks to those reform measures targeted at the foreign private investment. To activate reform measures, several proclamations including investment and legal notices were passed, the essences of which were summarised in the 1967 Investment proclamation. Reforms on FDI, tax concessions, tariff and remittance of profit were observed. In essence, these incentives were similar to those commonly employed as reforms in many advanced countries (Bulti, 1992).

In the third five-year plan, it was initially planned to attain GDP average growth rate of six per cent. Later, in the mid plan review, the average annual GDP growth rate was revised down to five per cent because the target set at six per cent was found to be infeasible. The average growth rate of GDP in real terms for the period 1967-68 to 1971-72 (Figure 1) was four per cent per annum. In per capita terms, the average growth rate was about 1.7 per cent. However, in 1972/73[2], the GDP growth rate began to decrease amounting to 2.5 per cent, which means that per capita GDP was stagnating that year. The lower performance of 1973/74 was mainly due to the revolutionary confusion which created economic disruptions and uncertainties. The major underlying cause for the deceleration of the growth of aggregate output during 1973/74 was the poor performance of the agricultural sector—generated then around 57 per cent of GDP—which in turn had a serious impact on the dynamics of the industrial sector.

Figure 1
Growth Rate of GDP and Per Capita Income During the Imperial Government (In Percentage

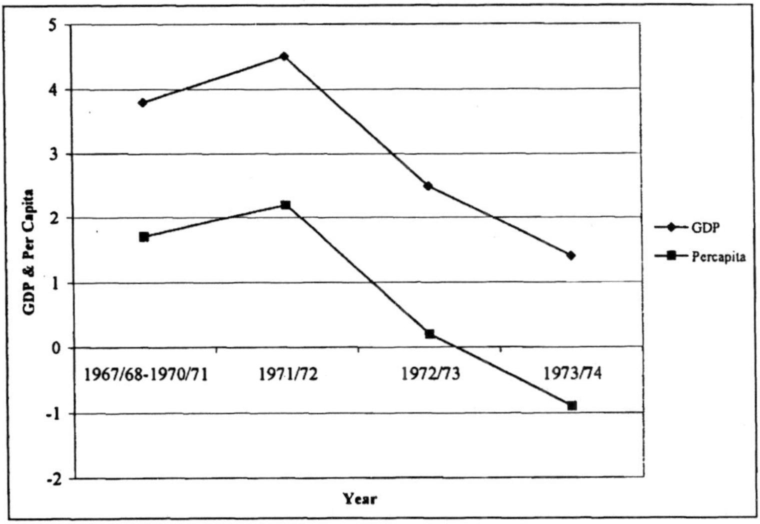

Derg Regime and its Economic Policies

During this period, the pattern of economy was moved from more or less outward looking to a rigid inward looking socialist regime, otherwise called as the Derg Regime[3]. Economic performance during this period showed the poorest record which the country has ever had for a century (MEDaC, 1999).

During that period, the rate of growth of GDP averaged 1.9 per cent. It fell considerably short of the population growth assumed to have been 2.7 per cent. This represents a decline in per capita income of about 0.8 per cent, revealing that the standard of living of the average Ethiopian, already one of the lowest in the world, suffered further deterioration during the era of military rule.

Figure 2 represents the overall picture showing the uneven performance over the years. During the 1974-78; a period of intensive internal conflicts and the war with Somalia, GDP grew by a mere 0.4 per cent. This was followed by a period of recovery (1979-83) when GDP registered a respectable growth rate of 4.2 per cent. There were the so-called zemecha (community cooperative) years, when an all-

Figure 2
Growth Rates of GDP & Its Components During Derg Regime

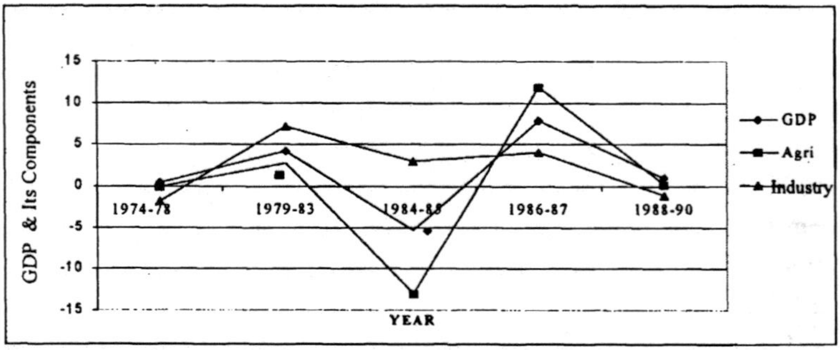

out effort was made to boost production on the basis of annual development campaign. Then followed the lean year of 1984-85, the period of catastrophic draught and famine, in which GDP declining to negative 5.3 per cent caused disastrous consequences for the economy and society. This drastic decline was due to the poor performance of agricultural sector which recorded its growth rate at negative 13.1per cent.

Surprisingly, the year 1986-87 was a period of recovery in which GDP grew by 7.9 per cent, largely as a result of improved rains. However, the recovery was bound to be short-lived and it gave way to the years of deepening crisis (1988-90) in which a rapidly accelerating war situation combined with other factors generated a GDP growth rate of a mere one per cent. This was to be the beginning of the end.

It should also be realised that this record apart from being poor in absolute terms, also stands in stark contrast to the overall goal the military government had set itself in the Ten Year Perspective Plan as 6.5 per cent annual growth rate of GDP and 3.6 per cent growth in per capita GDP. In total, Derg regime brought a devastating state which necessitated the successor to adopt economic reforms.

Transitional Government and its Policy towards Economic Reforms

The crisis carried forward by the Derg regime to the Transitional Government of Ethiopia (TGE), which was formed in 1991, turned down the Ethiopian economy more badly. The government was then suffering from other problems: weak economy with loss of productive capacity and competitiveness; increased food insecurity; severe macro economic imbalance and instability; and social crisis involving millions of displaced persons, refugees, demobilised soldiers, homeless and unemployed people.

It was against this background that the then TGE initiated a broad spectrum of reform measures to address both the immediate need of economic recovery and reconstruction to restart its economy to free it from the long term structural problems of underdevelopment. The primary notable achievement in Ethiopia in the early 1990s was the end of internal conflict followed by successful transition made towards peace and democracy. Since then, a federal system of Government has been put in place with the 1994 Constitution guaranteeing democratic and human rights as well as laying the basis for decentralisation of decision making power and responsibilities to regional states, thus creating the foundation for participating development and empowerment.

Ethiopia actually began the 1990s with a clear vision of reversing the socio economic crisis of the 1980s and rapidly transforming the economy. The clear vision was nothing but the economic reforms, facilitated by the Transitional Economic Policy (TEP) which was then announced by the EPRDF (Ethiopian People's Revolutionary Democratic Front) government in November 1991. Following that policy, a three year Policy Framework Paper was also developed and agreed with the IMF and the World Bank in October 1992. The Policy Framework Paper, which forms the basis for the economic reform programme, sought to revitalise the economy and create a more market oriented economic system, giving room for privatisation and thereby, replacing the rigidly centralised command economy (GoE, 1992: 3-12). In 1992/93, the government began its first series of economic reform programmes. The reform programmes were at re-orienting the economy from command to market economy, rationalising the role of the state and creating legal, institutional and policy environment to enhance private sector investment. The adoption of Agricultural Development led Industrialisation Strategy (ADLI) provided long-term development framework for economic transformation.

The macroeconomic policy then gave, in fact, room for the first time in Ethiopia, the removal of cost-price distortions, improvement in market related incentives, promotion of private enterprises and exports and progressive liberalisation of the economy, with a corresponding reduction in the size and role of the public sector. Ever since these reforms were initiated by that policy, the Ethiopian economy has successfully recovered from the consistently deteriorating trends of the late 1980s and the two transition years preceding the reforms (MoFED, 2002a). In order to have a comprehensive understanding about economic reforms and its impacts, it is better to discuss them in different phases:

First Phase of Economic Reforms and its Impacts, 1992/93-1994/95

The first phase of the structural and economic reform programme, can accurately be named the Comprehensive Macro-economic and Structural Reforms, was undertaken during 1992/93-1994/95 including the devaluation of ETB by 58.6 per cent in USD terms, reforms on exports and imports and interest rate and tax system. It is worth mentioning in this period that the first PSU was sold and the new investment, labour and PSU laws were enacted (GoE, 1998: viii). During this period, Ethiopia achieved a commendable record as GDP growth registered 13.4 per cent. Moreover, a real average annual growth rate of 7.6 per cent was observed during 1992/93-1994/95 and inflation averaged 8.2 per cent accounted over the period.

Second Phase of Economic Reforms and its Impacts, 1994/95-1996/97

The second phase of economic policy reform was implemented during the period 1994/95–1996/97. This phase showed a way for the promotion of private sector activity and investment which led to the establishment of the Ethiopian Privatisation in February 1994.

During this phase, real economic growth slowed down from 6.2 per cent in 1994/95 to 5.6 per cent in 1996/97, with an exceptionally high growth rate of 10.6 per cent in 1995/96. The inflation rate dropped from 13.4 per cent in 1994/95 to negative 6.4 per cent in 1996/97 and the value of exports rose by about 33 per cent while imports grew by about 32 per cent.

Third Phase of Economic Reforms and its Impacts, 1996/97-1998/99

In October 1996, Ethiopia entered a three-year ESAF ((Enhanced Structural Adjustment Facility) arrangement with the IMF and began the third phase of the reform programme which covered the period 1996/97–1998/99. Under this programme, the government committed itself to reducing poverty by achieving broad based economic growth in a stable macro-economic environment. Hence, its policies were to be geared towards maintaining financial sustained economic growth through increased savings and investment.

This phase also focused on fiscal consolidation, further liberalization of the exchange and trade system, undertaking rapid pace of structural reforms, strengthening of human resource base of the economy, rebuilding the environment and physical structure. And other reforms such as civil service reforms, reduction of import tariff by 10 per cent, elimination of retail price control on fertilizer, entry of Forex Bureaus in the commercial banks, and notably foreign exchange retention and inward remittance provisions for exporters.

Furthermore, the government introduced financial service tax and unified the hitherto diversified taxes on coffee. It began institutional reform of the revenue and customs authority to boost revenue collection and enhance tax administration. On the expenditure side, it revised allocation formula of federal transfers to regions and continued to implement civil service reforms. Regarding, financial sector and trade reforms, the government accelerated the liberalisation of interest rates by decontrolling commercial bank lending rates and setting only a minimum deposit rate while maintaining positive real interest rates. In the trade sector, import tariff system was further rationalised as the average import tariff rate was reduced from 24.5 per cent to 21.5 per cent while maximum tariff rate remained at 50 per cent.

On structural reforms, the investment code was revised to allow foreign participation in the telecommunication and power sectors, and a foreclosure law was enacted. The economy achieved a negative 1.2 per cent growth in 1997/98 (against 5.2 per cent in the preceding year), owing mainly to the adverse weather effects. Average inflation was kept at 2.33 per cent in 1997/98. The government deficit (excluding grants) registered 7.2 per cent of GDP compared in the same period.

In early 1998, the government reached agreement with the IMF to resume the programme under the ESAF arrangement including an economic programme for 1998/99 to be supported by a second annual ESAF arrangement. The second annual arrangement under the Enhanced Structural Adjustment Facility for 1998/99 was approved by the IMF Board on 23rd October, 1998. Ethiopia envisages forging ahead with its new structural and reform programme and to further stabilize its economy and to reduce poverty (GoE, 1998: xii-xiii).

Reform that started in 1992 continued with a strong vision to decentralise the economy and stimulate the engine of development through wider private entrepreneur participation. In order to facilitate such vision, the Government of Ethiopia (GoE) took many facilitating-reform measures including the protection of intellectual property rights, patents and/or copyrights, easy access to credit, speedier customs clearance and very importantly anti-corruption measures.

Impact of Economic Reforms: An Empirical Analysis

Here an attempt is made to analyse the impact of economic reforms to conceptually prove a hypothesis that whether the economic reforms have made imprints on the economic development comparing to the pre-reform period. The impact analysis of economic reforms includes privatisation because the Ethiopian economic reforms undoubtedly include privatisation as a reform measure. The important logic behind this impact analysis is to measure in advance the scale of effect on the different, but selective economic and social variables before measuring the impact of privatisation on those variables.

This analysis helps the result of research in two ways: First, what degree of difference the Ethiopian economy has observed on the socio-economic variables during the post reform period, compared to the pre-reform period. Second, it may help to know if there were any difference between the impact of economic reforms and that of privatisation. Supposing a result of positive impact on GDP between the pre-reform and the post reform period may not be true in case of privatisation if privatisation variable is applied as a predictor. Such difference is always common.

Probe on reasons for this difference may be owing to the impact or effect, varying over the period for many factors which are either difficult to be quantified or they change their intensity according to the nature of policies. It is nothing but a certain factor works in different degrees for the economic reforms in general, and for privatisation in particular. Another reason, much relevant for this study, is the difference over their time of implementation. Economic reforms actually started in the fiscal year of 1992/93, where as the real privatisation came into effect in the fiscal year of 1994/95 that received the first privatisation proceeds.

Table 2
Ethiopia's Economic Performance between Pre-Reform and Post Reform Period (Annual Average in Percentage)

Economic Variables	*1986/87-1991/92*	*1992/93-2003/04*
Real GDP Growth	1.7	5.7
Agricultural Output Growth	0.2	2.78
Industrial Output Growth	0.4	7.3
Per Capital GNI Growth	-8.28	0.67
External Debt/GDP	110.55	97.19
Budget Deficit/GDP (excl. grants)	-10.96	-15.3
Trade Balance/GDP	-16.37	-25.54
Current A/C Balance/GDP	-10.2	-13.0
Export /GDP	7.55	13.71
Gross Private Investment/GDP	2.33	9.14
FDI*/GDP	0.08	0.27
Inflation	-1.26	3.94

Note: *FDI doesn't include foreign privatisation proceeds
Sources: World Bank (1997), MoFED (2003a), MoFED (2003b) and World Bank (2004)

The summary in Table 2 shows that the economic growth during the post reform period was satisfactory as compared to the pre-reform period, the fact of which is also supported by Meenakshi et al. (2005) and Ramakrishna et al. (2003) in their studies respectively on economic reforms and globalisation impact in Ethiopia. Agriculture and industrial output grew at the rate of 2.78 per cent and 7.3 per cent respectively over the post reform period which, in fact, pushed up the GDP to 5.7 per cent as compared to 1.7 per cent in the pre-reform period. But the growth rate of GDP and their components in the post reform period appears to be fluctuating with a higher degree of variations than that of pre-reform period. Leave alone the beginning year of economic reforms after the fall of the Derg Regime and the war-prone period of 1997-98, other periods also showed an unsteady pattern of growth, as shown in Figure 3, which was not expected to occur if reforms were carried out in a right way.

Figure 3
Economic Trends during the Post Reform Period
1992/93–2003/04

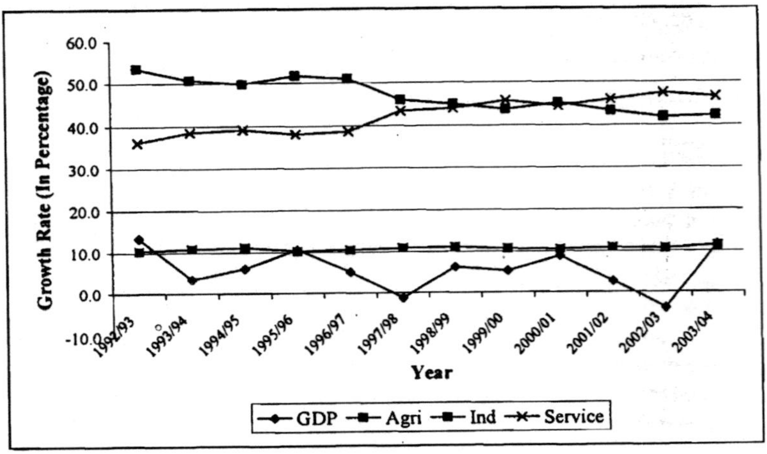

Reforms and Growth Pattern

When the growth pattern is analysed, the importance of agriculture in the national economy cannot be underestimated. A simple fluctuation in agriculture affects the total production of the country. It is evident in 1996/97, 2001/02 and 2002/03 fiscal years where agricultural production was not up to the mark, recording negative 1.4, 3.1 and 3.9 per cents respectively (MoFED, 2004a). This poor performance was attributed not only to the war broken out with Eritrea, but also to the drought conditions.

But question comes to its economic development because economic development is different from economic growth. Economic development means not only more real output but different kinds of output than were produced in the past. This study finds little evidence on economic development as three things are found unsupportive: first, the industrialization in Ethiopia is absolutely slow in progress despite the fact that there is an increase in the total volume of output they produced; second, Ethiopia is still a major importer even for the basic and necessary raw material for its industrial sector and finally, the technological advancement in Ethiopia is still poorer than any other Sub-Saharan African (SSA) countries.

Reforms and Living Standards

From the analysis, Inflation and Consumer Price Index (CPI) were found normal, but they were inflated too high in some of the fiscal years of the post reform period. It is well known that the rising inflation needs to be brought under control because even a moderate increase in inflation particularly affects the poor in Ethiopia very severely. Meenakshi (2003) in his study reveals that reform process affects the poor people adversely by inflation which reduces purchasing power, and the relatively better performance of an economy and its exports can be overshadowed by the fall in living standards of large numbers.

Ethiopia stands the lowest in GNI per capita. Economic reforms made no change in GNI Per capita which was rather declined from USD158 in the pre-reform period to USD103 in the post reform period. It is found that the post reform failed to bring the GNI per capita to a normal platform, attributing notably to weather related shocks and Ethio-Eritrean border conflict. Otherwise, it is believed to have well attained. However, many Ethiopians particularly in the rural areas were not affected of this lowest GNI per capita and rising inflation because the availability of food to them is found self-sufficient. Nevertheless, the danger is imminent as this rural mass moves to urban areas for economic purposes (MoFED, 2002b).

Reforms and External Debt and Trade Balances

The analysis also reveals that the economic impact on the external debt, trade and current account balance were far from satisfactory. The main objective of any reform is to rid these developing countries from the clutches of external debt which has been increasing at an alarming rate in the post reform period. But, it is ironical that the external debt to GDP recorded only 78.07 in the fiscal year of 2001/

02, thanks to the waiving-off the substantial portion of debt by the donors. This fact rules out any contribution of economic reforms in the debt reduction. External debt to GDP was, however, increased to 97.19 per cent in 2003/04, owing to an increase in external borrowing (World Bank, 2004).

The study affirms the failure of economic reforms in reducing trade balance and current account balance deficit. Trade and current deficit in percentage of GDP were increased in the post reform period by 56.02 and 27.45 per cent respectively despite the export to import increased from 49.11 per cent in the pre-reform period to 50.40 per cent in the post reform period along with a supplementary finding of an increase of export to GDP from 7.55 to 13.71 per cent over the period. The capital account, which improved from the deficit balance of USD90.6 million in 1994/95 to USD363 million, also failed to curb the increasing trend of deficit in these balances. Capital account to GDP grew at an annual average of 4.9 per cent over the reform period (MoFED, 2004b).

Other impressive finding of this study is that the budget deficit to GDP over the post-reform period was reduced to 9.36 per cent, compared to 10.96 per cent in the pre-reform period. As far as investment receipts are concerned, the post reform period was impressive as there was an increase in private investment by 292 per cent, and FDI moved from 0.08 per cent but insignificantly to 0.27 per cent over the period. The above discussions on the impact of different economic variables in the light of economics can be statistically proved.

Table 3 presents the result empirically on the selected variables which are tested at 5 per cent significance level. Any result obtained from this regression that exhibits a significant level of multi-collinearity (that is, a regression showing that a variance inflation factor (VIF) is greater than 10) is discarded from these results..

The empirical findings underscore the fact that the economic reforms played an insignificant role in the economic growth of the country. It reveals that the adoption of economic reforms in the country is too incomplete and slow to capture the expected objective of economic growth.

Agricultural and industrial growths are significant, and have positive signs. The growth observed in agriculture influenced and sustained the economy to the extent that the country could survive with a reasonable growth rate. Industrial development is a new phenomenon contributed significantly to the economic growth. However, investment during the post-reform period, which is the first priority of any economic reform, is insignificant despite its positive sign. It is due to the fact that the economic reforms failed to create a conducive monetary environment for the local as well as foreigners to come forward for investment. The major problem with the locals is that their savings pattern is too weak to contribute enough to capital accumulation of the country. Furthermore, the foreigners' response to the country's economic reforms is so poor that it could attract only little from them.

Table 3
OLS Model: Impact of Economic Reforms in Ethiopia

Dependent Variable: GDP Growth $[y]_t$
Method: OLS (Ordinary Least Squares)

Variable	*Co-efficient*	*T-statistic*	*Significance*
Constant	2.287	1.589	0.138
Agriculture Output $[A]_t$	0.698	12.390	0.000
Industrial Output $[R]_t$	0.547	7.214	0.000
Capital $[K]_t$	0.103	1.040	0.319
Economic Reforms $[O/Y]_t$	-0.162	-1.644	0.126
D_i	0.084	0.835	0.420
R^2	0.982		
Adjusted R^2	0.950		
F-statistic	65.869		
Significance (F. Statistic)	0.000		
D/W Statistic	2.041		

Note: Economic reforms (O/Y)—an explanatory variable calculated as an average of exports and imports to GDP

Impact of Economic Reforms on Inequality and Poverty

In the case of Ethiopia, studies on inequality and poverty are limited. Lack of consistent and long period data is a big problem. Countrywide studies are yet to be done. As far as inequality and poverty are concerned, Ethiopia is still a poorer performer even after the reforms.

According to UNDP (2003), there has been 82 per cent of the total population living below one-USD a day, standing 169th rank in the World with the human resource index of 0.359 as compared to 0.305 in the pre-reform period. There has been a little reduction in the depth, and severity of poverty that symbolises a decrease of 0.0285 within four years of time. In absolute term, it slipped from 45.5 per cent in 1995/96 to 44.2 per cent in 1999/00. Although it is insignificant, it is so interesting to note that the decrease in the incidence of poverty was observed in rural areas than in urban areas (MoFED, 2002a). Christiaensen et al. (2002) also confirm this finding through their international cross-sectional growth regression model applied over fifteen countries including Ethiopia.

The percentage of population access to sanitation facilities in the post reform period went up to 12, compared to 8 per cent in the pre-reform period. Illiteracy rate also reduced from 71 per cent to 58 per cent with the primary school gross enrollment ratio has gone up to 57 per cent of eligible adult population, compared to 38 per cent in the pre-reform period. But no improvement is found on the inequality because the percentage of the population below two-third of national mean per capita income was 50 per cent in the rural areas, whereas it was only 21 per cent in the urban areas (World Bank, 2004).

The result of economic reforms on the human development was far from satisfactory on the expected poverty alleviation, income distribution and some of indices of human resource development. For instance, the population access to safe water decreased from 25 per cent to 24 per cent, worsening the rural where access to safe water reduced substantially from 17 per cent to 12 per cent (World Bank, 2004). But it is assumed that had there not been any abnormal condition such as war and drought, Ethiopia would have achieved a substantial reduction in consumption poverty and other human development impediments by 1999/00 (MoFED, 2002: p. 22).

The analysis and discussion over the economic reforms over the study period shows a mixed result. The analysis also discloses that the economy after the reforms started walking on a tight rope of economic development. A moderate success in economic indicators such as GDP and private investment are not overruled as a positive statement of the post reform period, but may be overshadowed by the dangers of increasing inflation, external debt and trade and current balances in the post reform period. Moreover, the achievement on economic stability and poverty reduction was found either negative or little in the post reform period. Hence, it can be questioned that can the minimum economic achievement without steady development and poverty reduction be called a success? If the country's progress were defined in this way, it may be said that the attainment of economic reforms in the country is far from satisfactory.

This study reveals some reasons and flaws behind the mixed result of economic reforms: first, the programme started just after the formation of Transitional Government which rushed with the reform policy without any feasibility study. So that the first phase of the reforms went in vain through trial and error process; second, the lack of clear, predictable and transparent rules and regulations (regulatory reforms), third, Ethiopia was then to create for private entrepreneurs a strong and conducive financial climate; fourth, no stock market was found as is being witnessed in other countries that have taken financial reform measures; and fifth, no reforms in the area of banking such as restricting foreign firm participation in the domestic banking or insurance services.

Finally, a large amount of state intervention in different reform bodies and institutions was considered a major flaw, for instance, the five permanent board members in the Ethiopian Privatisation Agency (EPA) were designated by the government and it was accountable to the Prime Minister in all matters. Along with these flaws, other sentiments such as the coercive nationalisation policy of previous government and the ongoing Ethio-Eritrian border conflict also served as impediments for the execution of Ethiopian reforms.

PRIVATISATION: AN OUTCOME OF THE ETHIOPIAN ECONOMIC REFORMS

Economic reforms are the ones which urged the country to review the conditions of their PSUs and their impact on the total economic conditions of the country. Structural Adjustment programme in PSUs normally brings out a clear picture of what PSUs are meant for the economy of the country. Not compulsory that if these PSUs performs poorly, they have to be privatised. Nonetheless, privatisation as policy matter comes out as a deliberation of the government with political justifications, coupled with economic reasons. Under this circumstance, the poor state of PSUs cannot be underestimated to stimulate the government to go for privatisation option.

Here, an attempt is made to examine what exactly urged the country to go for privatisation. In this regard, the causal analysis helps this study to ascertain through some of the selected indicators as to what factors were behind privatisation of the country. As a prelude to it, the forthcoming discussion deals with: first, the background of the Ethiopian PSUs, and second, causal analysis of privatisation.

March of Public Sector Undertakings from 1974 to 1991

The institutional framework under which economic enterprises operated prior to 1974 was a free enterprise system with an open policy in the sense that no minimum requirement was imposed on the establishment and operation of enterprises. The role of government was mainly to encourage potential investors both from within and outside the country to commit resources in industrial investment. The economic enterprises especially the PSUs of that time had shown fast growth and expansion, but did not continue after 1974, leaving a lesson (though it is not new) that the state is an uninspired entrepreneur and a bad manager.

After the emergence of Marxist Military government in 1974, the political philosophy changed and ownership moved toward the state. On 7th February 1975, the government released a document outlining socialist Ethiopia's economic policy. The policy identified three manufacturing areas slated for state involvement; basic industries that produced goods serving other industries and that had the capacity to create linkages in the economy; industries that produced essential goods for the general population; and industries that made drugs, medicine, tobacco and beverages. The policy also grouped areas of the public and private sectors into activities reserved for the state, activities where state and private capital could operate jointly, and activities left to the private sector.

As a result, the industrial enterprises was more affected than any other sector as the necessity of public ownership was forced especially on almost all medium and large-scale industries. In the line with socialising the national properties, 87 manufacturing enterprises were nationalised in 1975. In the following few years, their number grew to 134, and by 1983 as many as 159 enterprises were nationalised. However, many of the nationalised enterprises were very old, and more than 50 per cent of which were operating beyond their technically expected life, and were financially weak.

It is distressing to note that even then operating medium and large-sized enterprises were declined from 479 in 1970 to 399 in 1984, owing to closure caused by their inherent structural, managerial and financial weaknesses. Altogether the experiment of Derg regime on expanding public ownership proved to be failure, owing to mismanagement and overstaffing, inappropriate investments, poor coverage and quality of services, high debt and fiscal losses and increased corruption. It was the Transitional Government that came into power in 1991 which initiated privatisation aimed at stopping this hemorrhage. In 1992, there were 211 large and medium sized manufacturing plants under state control, of which 164 were under the management of the Ministry of Industry, while the remaining 47 firms were under other ministries.

As of 2002/03, there are only 141 enterprises (Large and medium industries) under public ownership, employing around 56,588 employees out of 98,136 in this sector, where as the private sector with 769 establishments has employed 41,551 (CSA, 2003: 45). Privatisation was, however, carried out for the past ten years, the public sector seemed to be dominating in terms of the value added and number of people employed.

INITIATIVES AND CAUSES FOR PRIVATISATION

Almost in all cases of privatisation in the Least Developed Countries (LDC), the reasons (causes) are crystal clear: (a) higher fiscal pressure on governments (high budgetary deficit, large domestic public debt, and large external debt), (b) higher dependency on loans from international organizations (WB and IMF), (c) a large share of PSUs in total investment, (d) inferior and poor performance of PSUs in production and profitability, and (e) lower long term growth. These causes are the main syndromes for privatisation of PSUs in LDCs. Many studies have proved that privatisation occurs in countries with higher financial problems, such as large budgetary deficit and external debt in per cent of GDP.

In the Ethiopian context, privatisation is conceived as an important ingredient of the transformation from a command to a market oriented economy, reduction of alarming budget deficit and external debt, injection of openness into economy and development of private sector at macro level, and alleviation of problems such as managerial inefficiency and poor performance of PSUs at the micro level. It is also said that the Ethiopian government keeping these objectives in mind adopted privatisation as an immediate reform measure to redress the economy being affected from ill-syndromes. The forthcoming analysis of the study deals with the privatisation causal analysis to measure the extent of causes and their validity to justify the privatisation in the country.

Performance of PSUs

Privatisation has been implemented for many reasons. The first and foremost reason that expedited the privatisation programme in Ethiopia was the poor performance of PSUs particularly in production and utilization of plant capacity. A rise in the number of weak PSUs and their disappointing performance in production became major syndromes for privatisation.

According to the financial reports of the Ministry of Industry at the end of 1990/91 fiscal year, the liquidity balance of 53 enterprises was less than one, indicating that most firms could not cover their working capital requirements. It is a known fact in many countries that post-privatisation has brought positive changes in finance and operation in the enterprise (Megginson et al. 1994). It is so natural that Ethiopia was also bound by this fact to change the fate of the enterprises which had been making a loss, and consequently troubling the economy.

Table 4 indicates that as of 1991/92, 33 per cent of a total number of PSUs including small sized enterprises were under the category of loss-making enterprises, in which industries accounted 55 per cent and whereas, agriculture constituted 27 per cent (MoI, 1992) resulted in widening the deficit in federal budgets. Obviously, this reason may justify for the government privatising its PSUs. Gupta et al. (2001) support such justification to privatise if the government cares about efficiency. But Guo and Yao (2005) argues that efficiency is not a concern in the government's decision on privatisation which is because of the reason that an unprofitable firm may still be able to deliver taxes to the government and maintain sizable employment.

Moreover, the GDP by industrial sector (at constant factor cost) over the period of 1986/87-1991/92 was reduced from USD714.29 million to USD326.93 million (MoFED, 2003). A high slash in the

Gross Value of Output (GVO) made the average growth rate to negative 3.8 per cent in 1987/88 that was raised to the same negative growth but of highest standing at 19.1 in 1991/92. Such bad show cannot be justified with the political uncertainties and restless, which went to a high drama only in 1990/91. It is a strong witness to prove that poor performance in the overall industrial GVO was mainly due to the structural and managerial incapability of PSUs which is authenticated in Table 3, showing the constant decline started well early from 1988/89. Hence, it is found that the rise in the number of weak PSUs and their dismal performance in GVO may be one of the strong reasons for privatising PSUs in the country.

Table 4
Classification of PSUs by Profitability, 1991/92

Sector	*Profit Making*	*Loss Making*	*IIA•*	*Total*
Industry	63	40	10	113
Agriculture	8	20	9	37
Mining and Energy	2	2	1	5
Construction	6	5	7	18
Transport and Commodity	10	2	1	13
Housing	1	0	4	5
Trade	10	1	3	4
Hotels and Tourism	5	2	1	8
Health	3	0	0	3
Finance	4	1	0	5
Others	2	0	1	3
Total*	114 (50.9)	73 (32.6)	37 (16.5)	224 (100)

Note: *Figure given in the parentheses indicate the percentage in the column total
• Information Inadequate.

Source: MoI (1992).

Capacity Utilisation of PSUs

Capacity utilisation is one of the factors, determining the viability of PSUs in a country. Capacity utilisation in this regard is analysed to justify the need for privatisation.

Table 5 analyses the capacity utilisation in PSUs over the period, 1987/88-1991/92 showed a poor performance on the utilisation of business capacity. Except printing and wood industry, others showed a dismaying performance over the period. Food and beverage industries, which constitute a major portion in the economy, were no exception to this trend.

Table 5
Capacity Utilisation of PSUs

Sub Sector	1987-88	1988-89	1989-90	1990-91	1991-92
Food	83.9	93	97.2	69.3	41.8
Beverage	100.2	94.8	83.5	60	53.5
Tobacco	81.4	74.8	68.3	72.8	51.2
Textile	87.3	72.9	82.8	52.2	36.2
Leather	99.0	105.7	95.0	67.2	59.1
Wood	106.2	102.7	99.6	78.0	87.9
Non-Metal	99.7	104.9	83.7	80.3	66.5
Printing	100	98.0	92.8	94.2	93.6
Chemical	96.2	85.7	87.4	41.8	39.6
Metal	37.6	28.1	19.8	11.6	7.1
Average (In Percentage)	82.2	78.8	76.5	54	40.9

Source: MoPED (1994).

The capacity utilisation of food industries which stood at 83.9 per cent in 1987/88, declined to 41.8 per cent in 1991/92, whereas the beverage section had a decrease of 50 per cent over the period and the same case was approximately found in other sub-sectors of industry such as tobacco, textile, leather, wood, non-metal and chemical. The overall capacity utilisation of the Ethiopian industries was, in fact, decreased by 50 per cent, i.e. it was cut down from 82.2 per cent in 1987/88 to 40.9 per cent in 1991/92. Most of the industries with a high share in manufacturing production operated below 50 per cent of their respective attainable capacity (MoPED, 1994). The down-trend of capacity utilisation of industries is shown in Figure 4.

What is more to initiate privatisation programme is that those PSUs were running under the heavy loss which continued the same speed over the study period. At the end of 1999/00, the major loss making PSUs registered over USD 23.44 million losses, out of which 54.8 per cent was in state farms while 25 per cent was in industry. In a market- oriented economy, the motive force behind production is profit. To the contrary, the profit motive was choked off from the PSUs in the past and present eventually leaving them at the point of collapse.

Figure 4
Capacity Utilisation in the Major PSUs
1987/88–1991/92

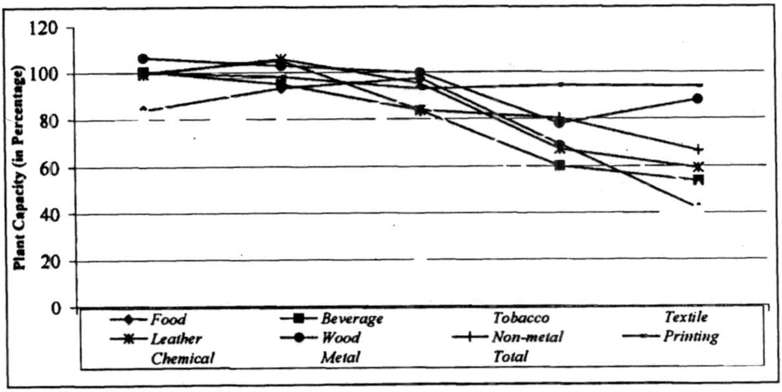

The above discussion proves that the poor performance, under capacity utilisation and financial loss of PSUs created skepticism about the ability of the government to manage and operate enterprises efficiently. This study reveals that mismanagement, shortage of raw materials and spare- parts, inadequate allocation of foreign exchange, non-overhauled and outdated machineries were found as the major reasons for this disappointing performance which is same as a result found in Tefera (1993). Out of these reasons, the shortage of raw materials and inadequate allocation of foreign exchange may not be the inherent problems of PSUs. Unless and otherwise, the government liberalises its financial and trade protection, a higher performance would not have been possible even for the private sector. Other mounting reasons to privatise were said to be the wider budget deficit (Fekru, 1993) and severe heavy debt burden which is discussed hereunder.

Budgetary Deficit and External Debt

As all economic studies confirm that the main reason for budget deficit is that the money the government spends aimlessly in the name of renovation and rehabilitation of PSUs, resulting in no returns. Assume that had the government neither borrowed the money from the external funding agencies nor spent for such weaken PSUs, it would have rather narrowed the budget deficit that, in fact, benefited the society.

Spending any more on the PSUs is of an economic waste; rather they can be privatised.

Figure 5 shows a constant increase of budget deficit-GDP ratio, which stood at 0.069 in 1986/87, had jumped to 0.097 in 1991/92 (MoPED, 2003). Deficit to GDP ratio shows how much the GDP should contribute to compensate the gap between the federal revenues and expenditure, that is, in the GDP of 1986/87, 6.9 cents of every USD was additionally required to balance the budget, that is, the revenue equals expenditure, whereas in 1991/92, it was 9.7 cents extra needed from every single USD of GDP to arrive at a zero-deficit budget. Over this period, the deficit/GDP grew at the average rate of 0.112 per cent with standard deviation of 0.0237 which was not underestimated by then the newly formed government to go for an alternative that was nothing but the reforms and privatisation programme.

Figure 5
Budget Deficit to GDP Ratio

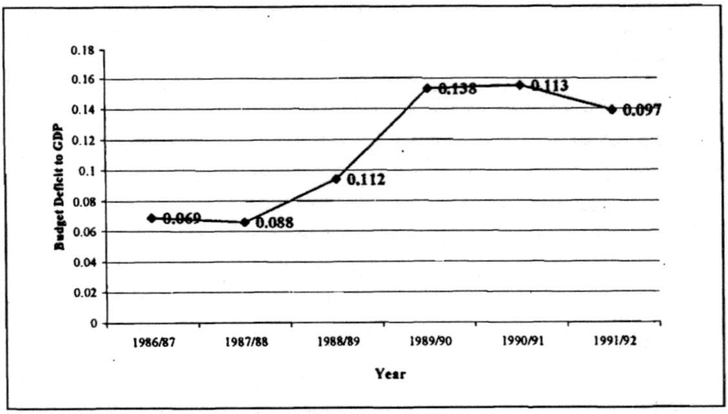

Note: Budget Deficit excluding grants.

The national debt is perennially at the centre of economic policy debates. In recent years, the government's expenditures have abundantly overtaken the revenues which make the budgetary position so pathetic that the government is forced to borrow from external sources. As for Ethiopia, budget deficit and poverty have become the most critical challenges, the effect of which negatively turns out the country to highly indebted. The pattern of Ethiopian external debt had changed into a bad fashion after the Imperial government was overthrown by the Derg regime.

During its 17 year tenure, the Derg government increased the country's total debt by 30 fold owing not only to its extravagant spending on defence and also to the high expenditure on PSUs due to an increase of government intervention. It is also found that as of 1991/92, defence expenditure accounted for 31 per cent in the total expenditure, whereas the government's expenditure on PSUs took a share of 4 per cent in the total expenditure shown in the budget (MoFED, 2003a). Eventually, the annual average of external debt for the period 1974/1975-1983/84 stood at USD1,656 million which became USD9,341million in 1991/92. .

The syndrome analysis clearly exhibits a burden of external debt in relation to GDP of the country. The debt/GDP ratio stood at an alarming rate of 0.98 and 1.30 in the fiscal years 1987/88 and 1991/92 respectively. Over the period, the debt/GDP ratio grew at the average rate of 1.04 with standard deviation 0.12367. The analysis shows that no significant debt reduction was made over the period.

Figure 6
Debt/GDP Ratio

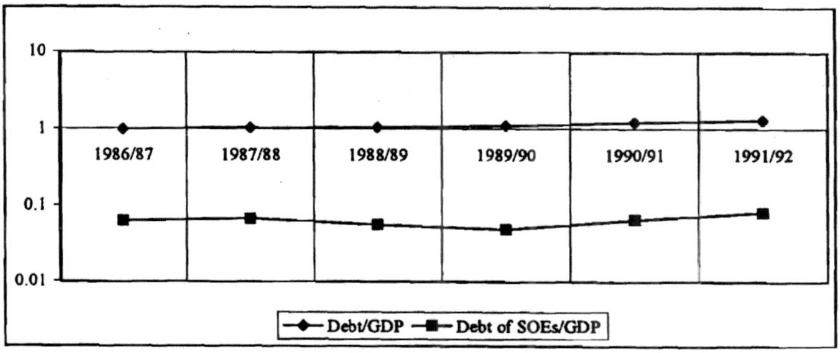

Figure 6 discloses the magnitude of external debt and its share to PSUs. The external debt of PSUs/GDP ratio which stood at 0.062 in the fiscal year 1986/87, increased to the ratio 0.08 with an annual average increase of 6.6 per cent. This type of burden is too heavy for a government which is heavily indebted. This empirical finding shows that these PSUs are not only inefficient themselves, but also do encroach upon the fund that is meant for other developmental activities.

Table 6
Summary of Privatisation Causal Analysis, 1986/87-1991/92

Major Syndromes	*Year*						
	1986-87	*1987-88*	*1988-89*	*1989-90*	*1990-91*	*1991-92*	*Annual Average*
Industry's GVO (Growth Rate)	8	-3.8	-6.7	-4.7	-19.1	-7.1	-5.57
Capacity Utilisation	Na*	82.2	78.8	76.5	54	40.9	55.4
Profitability**	114	128	119	65	17	-24	69.83
Budget Deficit/GDP Ratio***	0.069	0.088	0.112	0.138	0.113	0.097	0.088
Debt/GDP Ratio****	0.98	1.03	1.04	1.1	1.22	1.3	1.3
Debt of PSUs/GDP Ratio	0.062	0.066	0.055	0.048	0.064	0.08	0.064

Note: *Not available **As a percentage of Net Sales.
***Budget Deficit excluding grants ****Debt indicates the external debt.
Source: MoI (1992), MoPED (1994), World Bank (1997) & MoFED (2003b)

Table 6 shows a summary of the major causes which activated privatisation as one of the major macroeconomic and structural adjustment policies in Ethiopia. Among all causes analysed, the declining trend of industrial output and capacity utilization of PSUs in the pre-privatisation period may be the major causes at micro level behind the privatisation of PSUs in the country. The growth rate of industrial output stood at 5.57 per cent below zero level and capacity utilisation recorded only 55.4 per cent. Profitability was reduced from 114 per cent in 1986/87 to a negative 24 per cent in 1991/92 which reduced the annual average growth rate to 69.83 over the period. The steady growth in the debt of PSUs/GDP may also be another haunting cause why privatisation was necessitated.

Moreover, the macroeconomic structural objectives such as reduction of budget deficit and external debt were found to be strong obstacles in the pre-privatisation period, were aimed to be brought down in due course of privatising PSUs. The ratio of budget deficit and external debt to GDP that recorded 0.088 and 1.3 respectively over the period may be the other strong macro reasons for causing the country to adopt privatisation. Having analysed the major macro and micro indicators, it was found that neither visible comparative advantages of retaining PSUs nor strategic significance of continuing public ownership may be justified.

Furthermore, the pressure of the WB and IMF as external factors may not be ruled out for implementing privatisation programme because the country's dependence on these externalities was found to be very high. Many empirical evidences as in Abu Shair (1997) and Debebe (1993) indicate that a high degree of dependency of the economy on external debt, particularly provided by the WB and the IMF, indicating a positive correlation between the implementation of privatisation and dependency on loans from international organizations. But Ethiopia may not fall completely in this category as there was a strong justification found behind the privatisation programme in this study.

To conclude over the overall analysis, economic reforms were found to have given an impetus to privatisation owing to the failure of PSUs not only in preventing their own financial and managerial constraints, but also in reducing the national burdens such as budget deficit and external debt. Economic reforms analysed over the study period shows a mixed result in which the total output of the country, no doubt, increased, but the findings on the other economic and social variables were far from satisfactory. Privatisation, which was introduced after a two years of reforms with a strong justification, may not be expected to fetch the same result because of its strong dominance in the whole process of economic reforms. It is, therefore, indispensable to investigate and analyse how privatisation was carried out and what impact the privatisation programme brought on various issues as articulated in the objectives of this study.

NOTES

1. Neo-liberalism refers to a political-economic philosophy that had major implications for government policies beginning in the 1970s—increasingly prominent since 1980—that de-emphasis or rejects positive government intervention in the economy, focusing instead on achieving progress and even social justice by encouraging free-market methods and less restricted operations of business and "development". Its supporters argue that the net gains for all under free trade and capitalism will outweigh the costs in all, or almost all cases. It can be contrasted with economic nationalism, fair trade and anti-capitalism. Critics of neo-liberalism associate with globalisation, and with the rise of

multinational corporations, as well as monetary and fiscal austerity at the expense of social programmes (Wikipedia, 2005).

2. The oblique stroke ('/') between two years e.g. 1972/73 signifies a Gregorian fiscal year covering 12 months period from July 7 to July 6 of the following year. The 1965 E.F.Y (Ethiopian Fiscal Year) covers the period Hamele 1, 1964 to Sene 30, 1965, which is equivalent to the 1972/73 G.F.Y. Use of hyphen (-) between dates representing year, e.g. 1972/73-2001/02 signifies the full period involved, including the initial and final year. The Ethiopian Calendar is approximately seven years behind the Standard Western Calendar. In all data of this research, Ethiopian fiscal year is converted into Western Calendar.

3. After the 1974 ouster of Haile Selassie, the last emperor of a dynasty claiming descent from the Biblical Solomon, Ethiopia had a Marxist Military government, which was headed by Colonel Mengistu Haile Mariam, ruled the country between 1974 and 19991.

REFERENCES

Abraham, K. (2001), *Ethiopia: The Dynamics of Economic Reforms (Economic Liberalisation and Political Transformation)*, Addis Ababa: EIIPD (Ethiopian International Instt. for Peace and Development), pp. 1-2.

Abu Shair, J.A.R.O. (1997), *Privatisation and Development.* London: MacMillan Press Ltd., pp. 86-7.

Bulti, T. (1992), "Recent Trends in the Development of Manufactured Industries in Ethiopia" in Mekonen Taddesse (ed) *The Ethiopian Economy: Structure, Problems and Policy Issues,* (The Proceedings of the First Annual Conference on the Ethiopian Economy), Addis Ababa, pp. 139-156.

Christiaensen L., Lionel, Demery and Paterson, S. (2002), *"Growth, Distribution and Poverty in Africa: Messages from the 1990s"*, Washington, D.C.: World Bank/IBRD, pp. 21-7.

Cook, P. (1998), "Privatisation in the UK: Policy and Performance", in Parker, D. (ed.) *Privatisation in the European Union: Theory and Policy Perspectives.* London: Routledge, pp. 219-41.

CSA (2003), "Report on Large and Medium Scale Manufacturing and Electricity Industries Survey", Statistical Bulletin 281, October, (Central Statistical Authority), Addis Ababa: CSA.

CSA (2004) Ethiopia: Statistical Abstract, 2003, January, Addis Ababa: CSA.

Debebe, F. (1993), *"Privatisation in Sub-Saharan Africa: Origins, Trends, and Influences on Development Strategies"*, New Jersy: Centre for Economic Research on Africa, pp. 1-18.

Fekru, D. (1993), *"Privatisation in Sub-Saharan Africa: Origins, Trends, and Influences on Development Strategies"*, New Jersey: Centre for Economic Research on Africa (CERAF), p. 3.

GoE (1998), "Ethiopia: Economic Reforms for 1998/99-2000/01, The Policy Framework Paper", Prepared in Collaboration with the IMF and the WB), September 28, Addis Ababa: FGDRE, pp. v-xv & 1-69.

Guo, K. and Yao, Y. (2005), "Causes of Privatisation in China: Testing Several Hypothesies", *The Economics of Transition"*, Vol. 13, No. 2, pp. 211-38.

Gupta, N., Ham, J. and Svejnar, J. (2001), *"Priorities and Sequencing in Privatisation: Theory and Evidence from the Czech Republic"*, Working Paper No. 323-1, University of Michigan Business School, William Davidson Institute, pp. 1-32.

IEG (1968), "Third Five Year Development Plan-1968/73", Berhane Selam Hailai Selassie Imperial Printing Press: Addis Ababa, pp. 23-4.

Meenakshi S. Rajan, A. (2003), "Globalisation and its Impacts on Social and Human Development in India- an Analysis" in Mukhopadhyay et al. (eds) *Globalisation and Challenges of Education: Focus on Equity and Equality*, New Delhi, Shipra Publications, pp. 419-20.

Meenakshi S. Rajan, A., T. Iyappan and Selvam, J. (2005), "Impact of Economic Reforms on Economic Issues: A Study of Ethiopia", *African Development Review*, Vol. 17, No. 1, pp. 138-150.

Megginson, W.L., Nash, R.C. & van Randenborgh, M. (1994), "The Financial and Operating Performance of Newly Privatised Firms: An International Empirical Analysis", *Journal of Finance*, Vol. 49, No. 2, pp. 403-52.

MEDaC (1999) "Survey of the Ethiopian Economy: Review of Post Reform Developments (1992/93-1997-98)", June, Addis Ababa: MEDaC, pp. 1-35.

Microsoft (2004), *"Microsoft Encarta Encyclopedia Standard 2004: Ethiopia"*, USA, Microsoft Corp.

MoFED (2002a), "Development and Poverty Profile of Ethiopia (Analysis Based on the 1999/00 Household Income, Consumption and Expenditure and Welfare Monitoring Surveys)", March, Addis Ababa: MoFED, pp. 1-3 & 22.

MoFED (2002b), "Ethiopia: Sustainable Development and Poverty Reduction Program", July, Addis Ababa: MoFED, p. 1.

MoFED (2003a), Economic Indicators, Department of Policy Analysis, Addis Ababa: MoFED.

MoFED (2003b), Economic Indicators, Department of National Accounts, Addis Ababa: MoFED.

MoFED (2004a), Economic Indicators, Department of National Accounts, Addis Ababa: MoFED.

MoFED (2004b), "Annual Report on Macroeconomic Development in Ethiopia (2003/04), September, Addis Ababa: MoFED.

MoI (1992), "Industrial Restructuring in Ethiopia", Vol. I, August, Addis Ababa: MoI, pp. 21-4.

MoPED (1994), "Survey of Current Economic Conditions in Ethiopia", Vol. II, No. 1, February, Addis Ababa: MoPED, p. 2-9.

MoPED (2003), Economic Indicators, Department of Policy Analysis Computation, MoPED: Addis Ababa.

Ramakrishan, G., Krishnan, V.S., & Sukar, A (2003), "Impact of Globalisation on Growth, Poverty and Income Equality: A Study of Ethiopia and India", Asian Economic Review, Vol. 45, No. 2, pp. 326-40.

Tefera, A.H. (1993) *"Privatisation Initiative in Ethiopia"*, September 1993, Addis Ababa: Ministry of Industry, p. 26.

GoE (1992), "Ethiopia: Transitional Government's Policy Framework Paper, 1992, 1992/3-1994/95", Addis Ababa: TGE.

Wikipedia (2004), "Privatisation", Viewed on 18/02/05, *http://en.wikipedia.org/wiki/Privatisation*

World Bank (1997), African Development Indicators, Washington, D.C.: World Bank.

World Bank (2002a), Development Report 2000/01, Washington, D.C.: World Bank.

World Bank (2002b) African Development Indicators (Drawn from the World Bank Africa Data Base), Washington, D.C.: World Bank.

World Bank (2003), World Development Indicators Database, August, Washington, D.C.: World Bank, *(http://www.devdata.worldbank.org/external/cppprofile).*

World Bank (2004) African Development Indicators, Washington, D.C.: World Bank.

CHAPTER - 4

Processing and Mechanism Issues in Privatisation

The discussions in the earlier chapter indicate that there have been many reforms measures including privatisation geared towards socio-economic development and growth. The findings show that the economic reforms in the country brought a insignificant result—not necessarily reflecting the impacts of privatisation in the country.

The earlier discussions and analyses also reveal that the privatisation was introduced in the country with many visible reasons which were found as strong justifications for the privatisation in the country. The causal analysis of privatisation in the previous chapter serves a high degree proof for the necessity of privatising PSUs. Hence, it can be said that the privatisation programme in the country was really a strongly felt need or drive which was to bring a positive change not only in the enterprise level, but also in the country's level.

As the experimentation all over the world has revealed, privatisation is a complex process (Kebede, 1993) which needs prior preparation and a comprehensive plan for the correct processing and implementation. In the Ethiopian context, this transformation is not only a simple transformation of PSUs into private, but also a transformation from a socialistic command economy to a market oriented economy. Hence, the study of these processing issues is considered as the vital ones since they play a significant role in determining the success of privatisation. The forthcoming discussions include issues on the business environment and legal and regulatory framework issues—the pre-condition issues for privatisation, followed by the legal framework issues of the implementing agency, transformation issues and magnitude(size) and speed of privatisation in the country.

BUSINESS ENVIRONMENT AND LEGAL AND REGULATORY FRAMEWORK ISSUES

A State's effectiveness in preparing and managing a privatisation programme and private investors' perception and response to this programme is to a large extent to determine the success of privatisation. This has a number of implications for the establishment of a stable political and economic climate, a conducive business environment and a transparent, non-discretionary legal and regulatory framework. First, the economic and political stability must be ensured; second, a conducive business environment needs to be established; and third, the legal and regulatory framework must be devised to guarantee a smooth operation of business. These three conditions, which can be achieved through a well-tailored economic reforms, are inter-related, affecting the process of privatisation programme.

The findings in the previous chapter already authenticate that the reasons for mixed results owe to the unstable political and economic environment, attributing the reasons to the unpredictable climatic conditions, and the war with Eritrea. The instability in the political and economic environment affects any reform measures, the fact of which is, in this regard, applicable to privatisation. Many investors perceived the pre-conditions of political and economic instability as potential hindrance for purchasing or investing in PSUs. Out of twenty factors studied (World Bank, 2001: 16) to determine the country as a potential destination for investment, the least score was given to these two conditions by investors, thus, hampering privatisation.

Business environment and legal and regulatory framework include market conditions, commercial framework and tax systems, property rights, judiciary system and agency implementing privatisation programme. Market conditions in the country improved significantly compared to the pre-reforms period. The open and market oriented economy set up in the early 1990s contributed a lot through its reforms and liberalisation—though not fully but—to the development of market. The measures taken over the period were found directly connected to improving the market conditions. Among all, the relaxation of price control, particularly for petroleum and pharmaceutical products is worth-mentioning but not on all products.

Liberalisation of financial sector, permitting private financial intermediaries and policy and administrative measures to support export development played an important but a limited role in converting the market conditions somewhat conducive. It is also agreed that a country, having the advantage of large population, enhances the potentiality for growth of local market (World Bank, 2001: 15) which was out rightly objected by the officials in the EPA, rating it an obstacle. Moreover, connecting the local market to the rest of the world was found lagging amidst the initiatives through Common Market for Eastern and Southern Africa (COMESA), African Growth and Opportunity Act (AGOA) and recently, New Partnership for Africa's Development (NAPED). A fair and healthy competition also ensures for an ample private participation in general (Gómez-Ibáñez and Meyer, 1993) and privatisation in particular (Kebede, 1993), but the country has, unfortunately, got the weak domestic competition and market contestability in many sectors (MoFED, 2004), coupled with a highly monopolistic structure of the economy with state run or controlled enterprise in many sectors. Large sized enterprises were with the state control. Eventually, no competition existed to force for reducing costs and improving the quality. Moreover, the economic isolation (Sach, 2005) is the special phenomenon in the African continent which hampers the country to capitalise the increasing internationalisation of production and globalisation.

Commercial framework and tax system play a vital role in determining the fate of privatisation of any country. They consist of anti-competitive or informal practices, access to electricity and telecommunications, customs and trade regulations, access to financing, business licensing, labour regulations, availability of skilled labours and tax administration. Excepting elements such as business licensing, labour regulations and availability of labour, other said elements in the country were diagnosed as chronic worry to foreign and domestic buyers of PSUs.

Of all, the most hatred element was the tax administration, followed by access to financing and electricity, customs and trade regulations (World Bank, 2002). Tax and custom rates were reduced to some extent for the industries which are export oriented and so was on importing heavy equipments and infrastructure. Whatever be the case, it was eventually considered an unfavourable condition to the privatisation programme in the country. Availability of labour was not a major problem, but meeting the demand for highly skilled or trained human capital in the advent of increasing technology was a big question.

Most land in Ethiopia belongs to the Government, and the current policy is that no land can be obtained or transferred other than on a leasehold basis. The land issue is the most dissuading factor in the country since the investors can only buy the factory infra-structures and business, but not the land. Many existing as well as potential buyers of PSUs were not at ease on land issue which was found to have adversely affected their move to buy or further investment on modernisation and expansion. One of the investors who purchased a PSUs uttered that "*much to disgust is the land of the enterprise; my balance sheet looks so deserted without any value of land*". There have been many cases of Ethiopian investors losing the value of their investment, owing to the wrong allotment of land due for the farmers or the Rental Commission of Ethiopia.

The study finds that there are limited means of protecting intellectual property rights, patents and copyrights in the country. Firms generally place notices in local newspapers to effect registration of their trademarks with the Ministry of Trade and Industry. Many foreign investors are found to be unhappy to sell their products or franchise use of technology due to the lack of proper protection of property rights. Furthermore, many investors see the country a poorly judiciary one, where several cases of expropriation remain unsettled or never to be settled. Although concrete efforts are taken, the judiciary system still operates in a rudimentary manner that many judges lack the commercial knowledge. Fear among the foreign investors exists despite the country signing the World Bank treaty the "International Convention on Settlement of Investment Disputes between States and Nationals of other States" (ICSID).

The foregoing discussion reveals that the business environment improved related to the pre-reform period. However, the required elitism and conduciveness in making privatisation were found discouraging, particularly the local market conditions and competitive environment. Competition in the market was absent despite some sort of growth found in the local market. Even if competition were created, the favourability and effectiveness of which would be a big question in the absence of a large sized privatisation programme (Bhardhan, 1998).

It is always certain that small economies experience the problems of limited extent of market owing to the existence of a few customers to make up a mass market and many potential customers without the economic means to buy the product (Gareth and Smith, 1998). But, the small developed economies may be an exception to this theory as many are potential and capable to buy the product. Ethiopia in this regard is rated poorly, leaving it as an impediment to the privatisation process.

Not only is this, the country's high dependability on raw materials may hamper privatisation. The existence of PSUs' monopoly, incomplete reforms on tax rates and its administration, poor commercial framework, absence of land ownership, and weak judiciary and legal system may need to be either reviewed or revamped. Otherwise, a simple act of ownership transfer may not serve to achieve the efficiency in the economic and social motives for which privatisation strives.

ISSUES ON THE PRIVATISATION LEGAL FRAMEWORK

Formalising the privatisation process is an important task of any government which adopts privatisation programme. The main aim behind formalizing or legalizing the privatisation activities is to guarantee the public that the programme is constitutional. Hence, it can be said that a separate legal framework is required for privatisation programme. Issues on the privatisation legal framework include the legalities and frame work not only for the implementing agency, but also for privatisation programme. Setting up a new agency to manage privatisation will similarly have to be done with knowledge of general legal framework discussed in the previous paragraphs of this study.

The country established an agency called, "Ethiopian Privatisation Agency" (EPA)–hereafter called "Agency" through out the study— which was established in February 1994 by proclamation No. 87/ 1994 made in accordance with Article 9 (d) of the Transitional Period

Charter. Since then EPA is the lead-agency in carrying out the process of privatisation of PSUs. A Board of Management, consisting of five permanent members, who are designated by the government and a General Manager, administers the agency. The Agency was directly accountable to the Prime Minister's Office in all matters. In addition, the chairman of the board of the enterprises under privatisation and one of the representatives of workers participate as a non-voting member in the Board (GoE, 1994).

Privatisation laws can be helpful, but are not always essential. But the countries with weaker institutions and law enforcement may not be able to ensure the transparency of privatisation. Such countries should draft a privatisation law that clearly defines privatisation procedures (Welch and Frémond, 1998: 11). The study finds that it was after four years, the Privatisation proclamation No. 146/98, a pure privatisation law, was enacted which provided guidelines for implementing privatisation, particularly on the objectives of the programme, pre-privatisation activities, valuation and modalities. With this effect, the programme's objectives became wider to attaining objectives such as: to generate revenue required for financing development activities undertaken by the government; to change the role and participation of the government in the economy to enable it exert more effort on activities requiring its attention; and to promote the country's economic development through encouraging the expansion of the private sector (GoE, 1998).

As per the latter proclamation, the Agency was re-established with the clearly defined powers and duties to: implement the privatisation programme in accordance with the provisions of the proclamation; determine privatisation sequence plan for all enterprises included in the privatisation programme; cause the undertaking of all necessary preparatory works for the privatisation of enterprises; determine bid evaluation criteria for the selection of investors participating in privatisation; prepare necessary documents to be used in the privatisation process; design ways and means of encouraging domestic investors to participate in the privatisation of enterprises; take necessary measures to publicise the privatisation programme and its implementation; through post privatisation monitoring, ensure compliance of investors' obligations, and undertake impact assessment of the privatisation in general; own property, enter into contracts, sue and be sued in its own name; and carry out other activities necessary for the fulfillment of its objectives (GoE, 1998).

In addition to the powers and duties vested in it under proclamation No. 146/98, the Agency has also, under Proclamation No.110/1995 and its amendment proclamation No. 193/2000, the power to investigate and decide on claims of ownership in respect of properties confiscated in extra-legal manner through directives as well as through written or oral orders.

It is also found in the study that clear provisions regarding privatisation came late when the second proclamation was enacted in 1998. Till then, it was completely on a trial and error process which caused a lot of inconvenience to the buyers. Furthermore, the study finds that the framework of the Agency pertaining to autonomy was also at stake since the members of the board were designated by the government. This is a common scenario in Africa giving autonomy to agencies only for name sake, while the composition of their boards was steered to a large extent by the government themselves (Mugerwa-Kayizzi, 2002). Ethiopia was no exception to this. The study also finds that the lack of experience and training among personnel working in the Agency may also be an impediment in carrying out the programme. Belema (2003) also confirms the result in his country in a study called "Economic Development".

It can be concluded from the above discussion that although the country has got its own legal framework including the Agency for executing privatisation, the Agency lacks the required expertise and trained manpower. Moreover, the government intervention –though opined supportive for the Agency–may hamper its independence in taking decision, causing a lot of delay in processing. Hence, this study, to sum up, rules out a possibility of a more conducive privatisation legal framework encouraging privatisation in the country.

TRANSFORMATION ISSUES

Transformation issues are nothing but the issues concerning with steps identified for transferring the PSUs into the private ones. Transformation issues normally include issues in privatisation processing such as identifying and sequencing PSUs (candidates) for sale, finding out its readiness for sale (re-structuring and valuation), fixing the modality, bidding and tendering, performing the sale and monitoring the sold enterprises. Phasing may be different from one country to another country, but these steps are unavoidable in privatisation which is otherwise called a case-by-case approach to privatisation (Welch & Frémond, 1998). Countries often privatise PSUs using a case-by-case approach in which they plan each divestiture and carry out individually (Sadar, 1995).

Figure 1 shows a pictorial description of the privatisation process in the country. The steps involved in the whole processing are categorized into the three major steps, having their own sub steps. The forthcoming section discusses various processing issues based on these steps illustrated in the figure.

Pre-Privatisation Phasing

Pre-privatising comprises identification and sequencing of PSUs candidates and preparation of PSUs through restructuring and

Figure 1
Privatisation Process

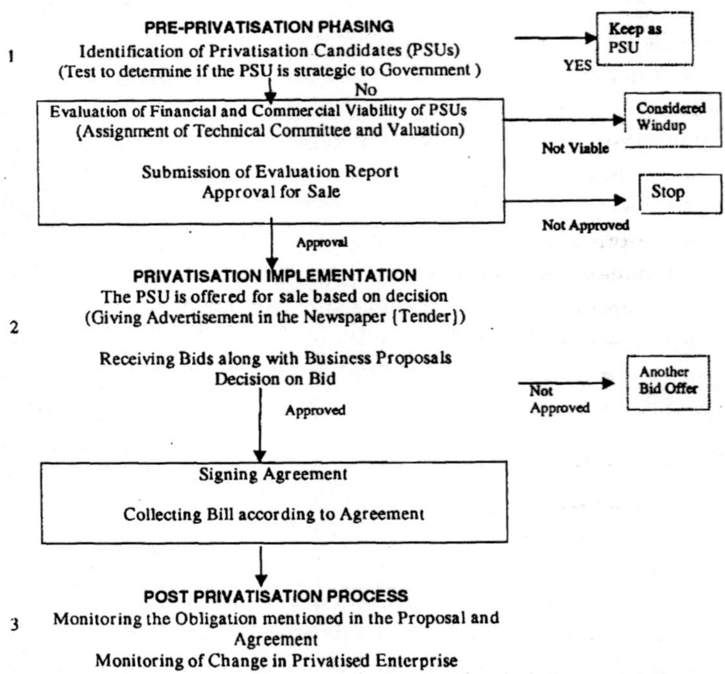

valuation for reading the sale. The forthcoming discussion analyses these two steps:

Identification and Sequencing of PSU candidates

The privatisation process in the country begins with the identifying the candidates for privatising, and performing a feasibility study which in turn comprises of identifying policy issues, valuing and providing options on timing and method of sale. While identifying the candidates, the strategically important ones have been filtered out and set apart for not privatising, i.e., those enterprises, which remain non-strategic as of that time, have been selected as the prospective candidates for sale.

The perception on "strategically important ones" may change from one time to another depending upon the views of the deciding authority and importance of the candidate at that particular time. There are many empirical evidences from other countries proving that public enterprises that were once deemed strategic—oil and gas companies, telecommunications firms, other utilities—were afterwards privatised (Welch, & Frémond, 1998: 11).

The diagnosis of candidates as to decide whether it is strategic or non-strategic is a crucial role in the pre-privatisation processing. While diagnosing, there are two parameters used: the first, from the political point of view or government's perception on the importance of the candidate and second, from the economic point of view. The government tends to classify enterprises as "strategic" or "essential" and "non-strategic" or "unessential". Economic analysis on the other hand, usually attempts to divide the enterprises into "viable", "potentially viable" and "non-viable" (Shirley and Nellis, 1991: 16-8). It is found from the study that the government of Ethiopia categorised the candidates by applying economic and political parameters as above explained. The most strategic and viable candidates were retained with the state control and the rest, which included a few potentially viable, have been slated and sold to buyers. The same pattern of identifying the candidates has been used in the countries such as Somalia and Madagascar (Shirley and Nellis, 1991: 19-20).

After categorising, it is common that a country may apply either Top-down approach or Bottom-top approach. Top-down approach refers to commencing the privatisation programme with large sized and strategically important enterprises. On the other hand, bottom-top approach deals with small-sized and non-strategic ones. Douglas and Wagle (1995) say that following either of this approach depends on their strength and commitment to reform. If the country were so committed, the route to privatisation can be top-down or vice versa. It is found that Ethiopia followed bottom-top approach by privatising the small ones initially. Out of 124 enterprises privatised during the initial period of privatisation, 102 were small and petty enterprises. Hence, it can be said that the Agency sequenced these enterprises in such a way that all small and micro enterprises (retailing and small petty businesses) appeared first, followed by medium scale enterprises, large industrial and commercial firms including agro based industries and at last, the financial institutions.

The sequencing was made not only based on the size of enterprise, but also to some extent based on their profitability. Although there was no proper record on the pre-privatisation performance of small and petty enterprises, the medium and large sized enterprises were found performing well during their pre-privatisation period. Douglas and Wagle (1995) affirm that for a privatisation programme to gain momentum, early sales have to be succeeded. This suggests privatising easy candidates first. This can be interpreted that they should preferably be small ones or as found in the case of Jamaica, the most profitable and attractive PSUs should be privatised at first (UNDP, 1989). Pirie (1988: 69) concludes this point of discussion that money making operations are always easy to sell.

It can, therefore, be concluded that Agency sequenced the PSUs from bottom to top approach through sequencing small enterprises at first helped the country not to make the privatisation an end in itself. It is evidenced during the initial study period of 1994/95 and 1995/96, out of 130 PSUs privatised, 102 enterprises, which accounted for 78.46 per cent of the enterprises over the period, were retailing businesses as a result of sequencing them first for privatising. In the first three fiscal years, over 121 out of 156 retailing enterprises—77.56 per cent of the total privatisation over the period—were privatised.

However, there were a few transactions in the initial period of privatisation gone on demand side (Kebede, 1993). A few food and beverage enterprises along with hotels sold out in this line. Hence, the absorptive capacity of private sector cannot be overruled owing to the costliness of two transactions. In 1994/95, Coca Cola and Pepsi Cola enterprises were sold out for USD10.76 and USD17.71 millions respectively in the fiscal year 1994/95 which were one among the largest transactions over the study period. Agro based industries, which started later as per the sequencing, performed its first disposal in 1997/98 and continued till the end of the study period. The study discloses that no financial institutions were then sequenced and privatised because they were considered strategic and important in the perception of the government.

Re-structuring and Valuation

Once the identification and sequencing of candidates was over, the Public Enterprises Supervising Authority (PESA) informed the concerned enterprises to get prepared for privatising and subsequently, the list of the candidates was dispatched to the Agency. In addition, the heads of the enterprises were briefed about the process of privatisation and the commencement of re-structuring and valuation regarding the enterprises in order to enable them to make necessary arrangements.

The re-structuring measures included debt-rescheduling or write offs, debtors write offs, stock write offs and creditors write offs to ensure the viability of each proposed share company. This financial re-structuring was immediately followed by the business valuation. In large number of cases, an enterprise needs to be carefully re-structured or readied to make the sale or offering feasible. Such re-structuring is not an obstacle where the enterprise has a good earnings potential (Vuylsteke, 1988:14). But in the Ethiopian cases, the re-structuring was found indispensable since the performance of the PSUs in general was visibly poor as discussed in the previous chapter.

Feasibility study began soon after the Agency received the list of candidates. The Agency assigned professionals to perform a preliminary review (due diligence) with the well-tailored guidelines (Appendix VI). Explanation along with a checklist (Appendix VII) was given to every enterprise that the gathering of information must be based on the cut-off date indicated. To fill up the checklist duly, the Agency guided and helped the technical committee constituted by the enterprise. The checklist can only be filled up after a thorough financial restructuring and valuation of assets and liabilities.

The study finds that the Agency carried out two types of valuation: Asset Valuation and Business Valuation. Although other valuation systems were also introduced by foreign consultants, the two methods only have been strictly used. It is also found that the asset valuation works according to the directive for the type of asset in which the valuations mainly exercised are Depreciated Replacement Cost and Open Market Value. The Business Valuation works based on the capacity of the enterprise's five or ten years of generating money and expense and is shown in different interest rates discounted in three or more alternatives.

During the valuation process, the fixed assets of enterprise were valued for coming up with financial statements that reflect market-based and going concern values. The fixed assets included buildings, process plant and machinery, non-specialist equipment, vehicles, and office furniture and equipment. Once the asset valuation was over, auditing of financial statements was done with a view to judging their state of true and fair view. This process was done according to the international accounting standards. Based on the results of financial audit, all problems in the audited financial statements were separated from the other items. Valuation of business was undertaken to get information which would serve as a bench mark that tells the Agency what an enterprise is worth. The value takes into account not only assets and liabilities, but also the performance of the enterprise overtime, market conditions, product popularity and financial strength of the enterprise (EPA, 2003). It is understood that the valuation as such performed was to assist in the negotiation of a final sales of an enterprise to be privatised.

It is also found from the study that completing verification and valuation enabled the enterprise to provide as much information as possible through the checklist distributed. The Agency through the apportioned professionals cross-checks all information furnished by frequent visits to the enterprise, and fed the information into the computer in order to prepare a feasibility report. The report was presented to the Deputy Manager of the privatisation section after a possible panel discussion is held. The report after the correction if need be by the Deputy Manager was handed over to the General

Manager who in turn after his comments handovers it to the Board of Management for deciding on the valuation and price of the enterprise.

The study finds that after approval of the report, the specification of Asset Valuation was sent to the concerned enterprise by the agency for further comments and suggestions. Nonetheless, the business valuation was not disclosed to the enterprise because of the reason that the confidentiality of the business price should be maintained in such a way that the sale action could be taken without any impartiality or price fixing in advance.

It is also found that after re-structuring and valuation, the enterprises were transformed into a new share company—otherwise called as corporatisation—using internationally accepted methodologies. The share capital was derived based on the value of net assets in the opening restructured balance sheet. It may be the last step in the pre-privatising process along with fixing modalities of privatisation. Welch & Frémond (1998: 16) articulate the reason for corporatisation: Corporatised public enterprises are treated as private businesses; they pay taxes, receive no subsidies, and must operate at a profit. Moreover, once it is corporatised, the government will not guarantee their debt.

From the foregoing discussion, it is understood that the privatisation programme, no doubt, followed the procedures and formalities in valuation of assets and business which was more or less in parallel with that of privatisation programme in other countries. However, the accuracy and dependability of valuation may be questioned owing to the following reasons: first, weak and lower performing PSUs present naturally valuation difficulties. No doubt, that some of the highly performing PSUs were privatised first, but the process followed by many of the rest found poorly performing; second, poorly performing PSUs poses weak financial management, accounting and control systems. So that, the reliable and up to date information may not be available; third, assessing future prospects of PSUs as a going concern may be difficult in the context of a new business and regulatory environment. The findings on the business environment and regulatory environment in the beginning of this chapter proves that the newly created economic environment and regulatory framework in the country were only a few years old and raw which was then yet to undergo a lot modifications suiting the present economic reforms.

As proved in the discussions of the previous chapter, the macro economic and political conditions, though their results improved relatively during the post-reform period, were unstable and difficult to predict. It may be argued from this hint that in the prevalence of instability in the economic and political conditions, expecting the full degree of integrity in the valuation of an enterprise as an on-going concern will be a great question mark. Moreover, it is found that the valuation did not take into account the impact of inflation and exchange movements in preparing the projections, doubting the in-depth review of PSUs before privatising. Nankani (1988) in her case studies on the selected countries stresses that a well-tailored and an in-depth review of the enterprise is necessary after an initial review with a view to examining all the issues associated with the privatisation of each enterprise. The loops holes in the review resulted in many flaws in valuation. As a result, many complained about the valuation of business, showing it either overvalued or undervalued, particularly from the investors towards overvaluation of the business.

Privatisation Implementation Issues

Privatisation implementation issues include bidding and tendering, assessment and selection of bidder and modalities used in the privatisation programme of the country. Each and every phasing is discussed under separate headings. However, an in-depth investigation is made on the buyers response in terms of the number of bidding attempts and bidders to the slated PSUs, and modalities applied in the privatisation transactions.

Bidding and Tendering

Implementation phasing starts after fixing the price of enterprise. The bid notice for sale was found to be announced in the appropriate media as well as in the notice board of the Agency. The interested bidders were given information memorandum and bid document. The information memorandum explains the historical profile and performance of the company, principal activities, markets, customers, competitors, sales outlets, suppliers, production processes, assets and human resources, where as the bid document contains the information such as paid up capital, par value and indicative price of shares and other major instructions to comply with the sale process. The study finds that the bidders were allowed to exercise their due diligence, i.e., they visited the company with a proper permission from the Agency. Unauthorised contacts were not allowed to, and said to have become a cause for disqualification. However, no such disqualification in this regard was found during the study period.

Once the bidder was satisfied with all required details and visit, the bid (Appendix VIII) along with bid bond and proposal were asked to be submitted. The bid bond was nothing, but a two per cent of the indicative price per share times the total number of shares for which the bid was to be submitted. The bid in wax-sealed envelopes, was delivered by hand, or by register mail, but it was ensured to reach the Agency before the closing date of the tender.

Table 1
Tender Floatation and its Convertibility

No. of Tender Attempts	*No. of Slated PSUs**	*Tender Convertibility (In Percentage)*
First Attempt	165	79.71
Second Attempt	29	14.01
Third Attempt	11	5.31
Fourth Attempt	2	0.97
Fifth Attempt and Above	nil	0.00

Note: No. of slated PSUs excludes restitution.
Source: EPA (2004).

The privatisation programme in the country was found moderately successful on the tender convertibility. Tender convertibility refers to a number of tender attempts at which the sale offer is converted into sale action. Table 1 shows the tender floatation and its convertibility to sale during the study period. The statistics given in the table excludes the restitution because tendering process is not applicable to restitution. It is found that 79.71 per cent of the total PSUs were sold out at the first tender attempt, showing the country's high degree of tender convertibility rate. Those PSUs, which were not sold out at the first tender, were gone for the second attempt to tender, constituting 14.01 per cent.

The result also reveals that over 94 per cent of the total enterprises were sold out within two attempts. About 90 per cent of the small scale enterprises were sold within the first attempt of sale. The remaining was extended to third and even to the fourth attempt for its convertibility. The expensiveness of these PSUs was the reason to stretch for the third and fourth attempts. The average indicative price of many of these enterprises came over USD500,000. Hence, it can be said that there is a relationship between the size and tender convertibility, i.e., the smaller the size of PSUs, faster the convertibility is.

Assessment and Selection of Bidders

Assessment and scrutiny plays a vital role in making the privatisation process successful. Experiences from many countries show that they do follow different criteria based on their objectives of the privatisation programme and their intuition. The total amount offered by the prospective buyer is an important factor in the sale. However, the government frequently develops a number of selection criteria in addition to the offered price which includes financial strength and credentials of bidders and their commitment to employees and customers. It is because of the reason that the government wants not only to simply sell an enterprise, but also it needs a strategic partner in the development of the country (Gibbon, 1996).

Table 2
Criteria for Evaluation of Bidders

Criteria	*Weight (in Percentage)*
Price offered	70
Business Plan	20
Technical and Managerial Expertise	10
Total	100

Source: EPA (2004)

The privatisation programme in the country has followed its own criteria which almost resemble the internationally accepted ones. Three major criteria were examined to select the right bidder: price offered, business plan and technical and managerial expertise. The criteria given in Table 2 are considered a typical model which has been followed in many countries.

Table 2 shows that price offered by the bidder constitutes the major weight to win the bid. It was given 70 per cent in the overall weight in selecting the buyer. It is natural that the price offered determines the capital and capacity of the bidder. Moreover, the sale is after all for generating revenues for the government. Business plan was weighed for 20 per cent, followed by the technical and managerial expertise of the bidder, accounting for 10 per cent. Business plan shows the bidders vision to run the business successfully, particularly the benefits açcrued to the government in terms of export development and foreign reserves. In selecting the buyer, the technical and managerial expertise was assessed as to how capable the bidder is in managing the business, and as a result, the firm becomes profitable to fetch enough tax to the government. The criteria as discussed could only be applied extensively provided there were overwhelming responses to the tenders.

Response to Privatisation

Bidders' response decides the fate of privatisation programme of any country. Bidders or the prospective buyers, if they are rationale, before applying, they could choose the best enterprise for their venturing. Not only is it, they are also the first-hand evaluators of the position of enterprise in particular and the conditions of economy in general. If they are satisfied with these conditions, their response can be expected to be high and vice versa.

Table 3 shows the bidders response to the sale over the study period which examines the extent of choice available to the agency to choose the buyers. It is a known fact that more the bidders respond, the greater will be the choice. But the result was disappointingly small. The result reveals that the average number of the bidders to the slated enterprises was 1.79, that is, less than two bidders responded to each sale offer. In 1993/94, the bidders to the slated ratio recorded about two. Since then it never exceeded beyond it in any fiscal year of the study period except in the fiscal year of 2001/02. But one thing noted in this point is that there was only one transaction in this particular year. In 2003/04, the ratio was observed to be better, accounting for 4.0. In total, the result reflects the dismaying as well as the poor response of bidders to the slated enterprises for privatisation.

Table 3
Bidders Response to the Slated PSUs

Year	*No. of Bidders Responded*	*No. of the Slated PSUs*	*Bidders to the Slated Ratio*
1994/95	27	14	1.93
1995/96	121	116	1.04
1996/97	41	26	1.58
1997/98	21	9	2.33
1998/99	24	16	1.50
1999/00	16	12	1.33
2000/01	10	7	1.43
2001/02	3	1	3.00
2002/03	4	3	1.33
2003/04	12	3	4.00
Total	279 (27.9)	207* (20.7)	(1.79)

Note: *Total number of Slated PSUs excludes restitution.
Figures in parentheses are mean values of total column.
Source: EPA (2004).

Table 4
Bidders Response to the Sectors

Sector	*No. of Bidders Responded*	*No. of Slated PSUs**	*Bidders to Slated Sectors*
Hotel & Tourism	27	18	1.50
Food & Beverage	29	19	1.53
Retailing	135	126	1.07
Cement & Chemicals	10	4	2.50
Wood & Furniture	6	4	1.50
Leathers	5	3	1.67
Farm & Agriculture	48	25	2.18
Textiles	3	2	1.50
Mining	5	1	5.00
Pharmacy	11	5	2.20

Source: EPA (2004).

Table 4 reveals that no sector attracted more than three bidders for offering for each sale except a sale for mining. Cement and Chemicals, farm and agro industries and pharmacy convinced more than two bidders for every sale action. The mining sector was the only one of its kind during the study period which attracted five bidders, whereas the food and beverage, hotel and tourism, wood and furniture and textiles, recorded for each only 1.50 bidders to the slated ratio. The least one was retailing which could make the ratio only for 1.07. It can, therefore, be concluded that the choice to select the reasonable buyer was very much limited due to the lower response of the buyers. It questions the credibility of evaluation criteria which were said to have been strictly followed.

Modalities of Privatisation

After having selected a buyer, the privatisation process in the country proceeded in such a way that a legal transfer of the enterprise from the government to the buyer took place depending upon the modality of privatisation. The modalities differ from one country to another country depending upon their objectives, strategies and existence of capital markets.

Vuylsteke (1988: 8) classifies the basic methods of privatisation into seven: public offering of shares, private sale of shares, new private investment in an PSU, sale of government or PSU assets, reorganization (or break up) into component parts, management/employee buyout (MEBO), lease and management contract. However, for all practical purposes, privatisation methods can be grouped into two broad categories: sale and contracting out services. The main difference between these two categories is that, while in the former, the ownership is transferred from public to private, whereas the ownership is still retained by the public in the latter and management is privatised (Dhameja and Sastry, 1998: 76).

Transferring ownership takes different forms. It can be total or partial or specific to bidders or to the management or to the workers of the enterprise and so on. The study finds that there were four major methods adopted: largely asset sale, followed by the management and employees buy-out (MEBO), lease and restitutions. Asset sale, for this study, includes full or partial sale, and restricted and negotiated sale.

Under the modality of asset sale, the state sells the assets directly by which the PSUs dispose their major assets. This kind of sale is suitable only when distinct sections or divisions are identified which can be sold separately and independently. It is evidenced in Table 5 that the most of sale was performed in the country through the asset sale, particularly on open competitive bidding. Out of 161 asset sale transactions, six transactions were concluded after direction negotiation and restricted tender, and one was made under joint venture.

Table 5
Privatisation Modalities

Year	*Asset Sale*	*MEBO*	*Lease*	*Restitution*
1994/95	13	1	nil	nil
1995/96	73	43	nil	nil
1996/97	25	1	nil	nil
1997/98	8	nil	1	nil
1998/99	16	nil	nil	5
1999/00	12	nil	nil	4
2000/01	7	nil	nil	4
2001/02	1	nil	nil	nil
2002/03	3	nil	nil	nil
2003/04	3	nil	nil	nil
Total	161 (73.18)	45 (20.45)	1 (0.45)	13 (5.91)

Note: Figures in the parentheses indicate the per cent share of modalities in the total transactions

Source: EPA (2004).

Table 5 also indicates that the asset sale as a modality in the privatisation programme accounted for the majority of 73.18 per cent in the total number of sale transactions. Next to asset sale, MEBO was widely used, where 44 PSUs were sold out directly to either the existing management or employees of the enterprises, whereas one transaction was totally different as it is found that only the marketing activities of the enterprise was given to the employees. The analysis shows that MEBO was extensively followed among the small enterprises which recorded 45 transactions, accounting for 20.45 per cent in the total number of sale transactions. The main purpose of applying this modality was to promote employee-share ownership.

Furthermore, as the public in general is not involved in this type of modality, the process of privatisation can be smooth and does not attract any criticism (Dhameja and Sastry, 1998:80). This method is found politically the easiest way for a country to privatise an enterprise. Sach (1992) claims that MEBO is the simpler method of privatisation in transferring the ownership of the enterprise because the ownership goes to insiders of the enterprise. However, unlike asset sale, the bidding process is absent in this modality of sale since outside investors are not allowed to take part, causing a lack of competition, resulting in under pricing of asset.

In addition to the modalities discussed above, lease is another modality which has been seldom experimented in the privatisation of other developing countries. Under lease, government sells or enters into long-term leases out assets such as airports, utilities or real estate and mines to private buyers, thus turning physical capital into financial capital. This transaction was very unique in the country's privatisation programme in the way it applied as it was mixed with the other sub-modality of concession. It is also found that it was a single transaction in which the buyer was specially called up to takeover the enterprise since the offered price was found much higher than that of other buyers. Lease as a modality is normally preferable when the government decides against the complete transfer of ownership. In many instances, particularly those involving natural resources, a complete sale may be politically difficult (Sadar, 1995: 20). It is true in the case of this single transaction occurred in 1997/98, in which the business was leased for 98 years. While ownership remains with the state, the buyer is responsible for management and carries out desired improvements.

As the country transforms from socialism to market led economy, it is found that the privatisation programme attempted to restitute the then nationalised properties during the Derg regime. There were 13 transactions of this type by which the enterprises were given back to their previous owners. Restitutions in this regard accounted for 5.91 per cent, followed by the lease—a single transaction of this modality—falling below one per cent in the total number of transactions.

Table 6 shows the extent of modalities used in terms of the privatisation proceeds received during the study period. The analysis reveals that asset sale dominated not only in the number of transactions, but also in the total privatisation proceeds received during the study period. The reason is clear that this was the only major option availed to the privatisation programme since the choice of public offerings of shares cannot be exercised in the context of having a weak capital and zero stock market. Moreover, the asset sale is more preferable when some parts of assets either by deliberation or constitution cannot be transferred to the private buyers and the slated PSUs are small in size.

Table 6
Extent of Privatisation Modalities

Type of Modalities	*Modalities in the Total PP (In USD Million)*	*Share in Per cent of PP*
Asset Sale	250.99	57.87
Ordinary	231.22	53.31
Joint Venture	18.45	4.25
Negotiated and Restricted Sale	1.32	0.30
MEBO	8.48	1.96
Lease	172.00	39.66
Restitution	2.23	0.51

Note: The figures that are not highlighted shows sub-totals.
Source: EPA (2004).

Table 7
Asset Sale: Full and Partial

Year	*Full**	*Partial***	*Total*
1994/95	08	5	13
1995/96	69	04	73
1996/97	11	12	23
1997/98	5	3	08
1998/99	12	4	16
1999/00	10	0	10
2000/01	4	3	7
2001/02	nil	1	1
2002/03	2	1	3
2003/04	3	0	3
Total	124	33	157***

Note: *It refers to sale of building and business, **refers to sale of business only ***It excludes the sale under MEBO.
Source: EPA (2004).

Under asset sale modality, as shown in Table 7, 124 transactions were made on full sale, where as 33 transactions were done on partial sale. Full sale refers to a sale of building, business assets(excluding land) and management. Partial sale includes all these, but excluding the building. The reason for the emergence of such partial sale is that the buyers' reluctance to buy building without land.

The study also discloses that the major assets of PSUs in the country have got their own identity in their ownership: Land belongs to the government, i.e. it is not subject to sale or to other means of exchange (GoE, 1997); buildings in some cases belong to the Rental Commission of Ethiopia and finally the business belongs to the enterprise. A few earlier buyers of PSUs were victims of this type of assets segregation. To avoid these complications, PSUs were valued on the basis of business which includes all properties and machineries (excluding land), and building. Hence, the asset sale was considered the only option in this scenario. The analysis indicates that there were a few sub-modalities applied in addition to the ordinary sale. The ordinary sale is nothing but a sale of assets without any special arrangement with the buyer either in the processing or contract of sale. The ordinary sale accounted for USD231.22 million, representing 53.31 per cent in the total privatisation proceeds.

It is also found that there was only one transaction carried out on joint venture—otherwise called as public and private partnership—yielded 4.25 per cent in the total privatisation proceeds. The buyer on this transaction held only 21.1 per cent of shares. Negotiated and Restricted Sale is another possibility, which is as shown, accounted for 0.3 per cent from the six transactions. Out of six of this type, two transactions—restricted sale—were made purely on the government decisions. Moreover, such type of sale normally occurs when an offer from one particular bidder or set of bidders is unlikely to be equaled in open competition through more than one attempt. Alternatively, it may be opted in order to reduce the expense and time involved in the sale process (Gibbon, 1996:8). It came true in our study that these six sales attempted more than one bid owing to their costliness in nature.

On MEBO, the analysis discloses that there were 45 transactions sold on MEBO basis, but surprisingly 43 of them transferred to the existing employees of a single enterprise, narrowing the distribution of ownership. MEBO yielded USD8.48 million, but contributed insignificantly to the total privatisation proceeds, showing only 1.96 per cent in the total privatisation proceeds. It is instructive to mention that one of the MEBOs was made on Employee Stock Ownership Plans (ESOP) which handed over only the marketing service to the employees. Lease, a single transaction but added USD 172 million to the magnitude of the country's privatisation programme which formed 39.66 per cent in the total privatisation proceeds.

Restitution is a privatisation method where assets that were formerly in the private hands and were seized by the government following nationalisation, are now restituted back to the former owners (Dhameja and Sastry, 1998:79-80). There were thirteen transactions of this type as Ethiopia is one of the countries of transition after a seven years communism. This study includes only a restitution of business enterprises despite the fact that there were more than 400 houses and other properties on restitution. Eventually, there were only13 transactions of this type—applicable to this study—contributed USD2.23 million, accounting 0.51 per cent in the total proceeds.

The above discussions on modalities may not conclude the implementing issues vested in privatising. It is the post-privatisation monitoring which concludes the whole process in privatising a PSU. Hence, it can be said that the transformation aims not only just handing over the PSU, but also sees whether the ultimate buyers is genuine to the extent that the intended objectives of handing over is being fulfilled. It is also understood from this study that there was a limit on the evaluation since the agency cannot ask why there was no provisions for immediate profit, employment of many workers, training or advertisement of the enterprise. However, the evaluation includes those objectives to the extent of assessing how much effort the investor practically shown as indicated in the business plan; how far he has adjusted himself with the appropriate method of the proposed business activity; to what extent he has participated in the free market competition and how far the buyer had led the business and administration effectively.

Post Privatisation Process

The post privatisation department of the Agency, which is responsible for these evaluations, seeks information about the performance of the privatised enterprise. For this reason, the department sends them the evaluation form (Appendix IX) for ascertaining the post-privatisation performance. But, the response from those privatised enterprises was found low on the financial and labour matters which handicapped the Agency to ascertain whether or not the commitments have been fulfilled as agreed upon. However, the Agency de-privatised four enterprises, owing to a complete failure in obliging to the agreed business plan and failure to pay the remaining price of the enterprise on time.

The foregoing discussions on the transformation issues reveal that the transformation process is carried out on the case-by-case approach to privatisation. The Agency attempted to adhere to those international practices for privatising, but the inherent economic and political conditions ruled out the notion that the country moves faster towards a market-led economy. Many flaws found in the identification to valuation of the PSUs discouraged the buyers who are found to have turned lower to the privatisation initiative of the government. Many medium sized enterprises went for the second attempt of tender, showing the buyers' interest in buying the floated enterprises.

It is also known that asset sale method became widely used in the country since the public offerings cannot be done owing to the absence of stock exchanges. Even in the presence of stock exchange, asset sale method has been preferred by many countries in the context that it is a quicker option to execute. However, the country's poor financial and capital market, coupled with absence of security market left no chance for other modalities except the asset sale.

SIZE AND SPEED ISSUES

Measuring the privatisation is the most crucial task before assessing its impact on any variable be it economic or social. No doubt, the privatisation proceeds help in this regard to judge as to how much the scale of privatisation is in a given country. But, it would not reveal the real magnitude of privatisation unless it is related to the output of the country. Keeping this in mind, the magnitude of privatisation is the sum of privatisation proceeds collected during the year, as a share of GDP which is used to measure the size of the privatisation. This measurement is used as privatisation variable through out this study which is almost same as the privatisation variable used by Cook and Uchida (2003) and Plane (1997).

Data set for the Ethiopian privatisation is summarised in Table 8. They indicate that the country privatised two hundred and twenty enterprises over 1994/95-2003/04, including thirteen restitutions of PSUs taken place in the country as an outcome of political change. Restitutions were strongly included to measure the size and speed of the privatisation in the country because they could play a big role in the privatisation process of the country.

Table 8
Magnitude of Privatisation Transactions, 1994/95-2003/04

Year	*No. of Privatisations*	*Privatisation Proceeds (PP) (USD Millions)*	*GDP (USD Millions)*	*PP/GDP (In Percen0 tage)*
1994/95	14	29.54	5,779	0.51
1995/96	116	51.46	6,393	0.8
1996/97	26	18.72	6,725	0.28
1997/98	9	193.1	6,647	2.9
11998/99	21	89.12	7,067	1.26
1999/00	16	45.87	7,451	0.61
2000/01	1	12.97	8,106	0.04
2001/02	1	0.76	8,326	0.009
2002/03	3	0.56	6,638	0.008
2003/04	3	1.60	7,408	0.021
AnnualAverage	22	43.37	6,277	0.21

Source: EPA (2003) and World Bank (2004).

Table 8 reveals that the privatisation was started with fourteen maiden-transactions, contributed on an average USD43.37 million a year, and the volume rose up to USD51.46 million in the following fiscal year 1995/96 with 116 transactions. The reason for the radical jump in the number of transactions owed to the initial tranche in which many of the small scale (petty) enterprises were slated. Privatisation proceeds collected during the first phase, 1994/95-1998/99 were more lucrative than the second phase, 1999/00-2003/04. Of the total proceeds, 88.07 per cent were collected during the first phase which was a good sign of progress, where as, in the second phase, it was only 11.93 per cent which shows a poor show of the privatisation of the country.

It is also observed that the earlier phase was, hence, considered a boost, owing to the proceeds received during the fiscal year 1997/98 which was the peak moment in the Ethiopian privatisation history that yielded USD193.1 millions, constituting 45 per cent in the total proceeds collected during the privatisation period. Since then, there has not been any commendable progress in the privatisation revenues. In total, the programme yielded USD433.7 million. Nellis (2003) finds that the size of privatisation in the country over the period constitutes only 4.7 per cent of the total sale proceeds received in the whole African region.

Figure 2
Privatisation Proceeds, 1994/95-2003/04

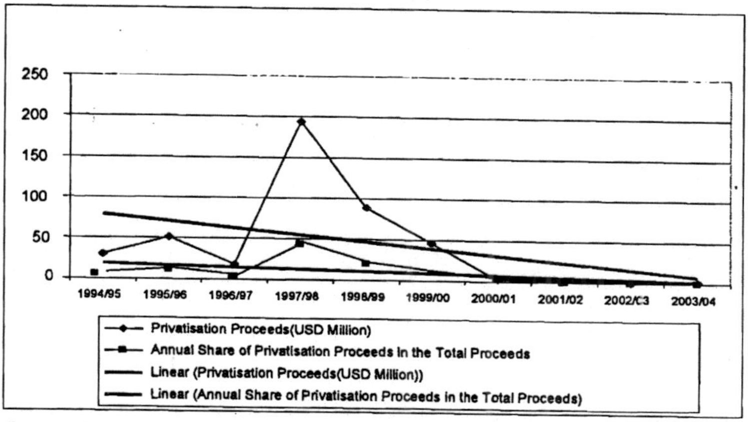

Source: Finance and Administration Department, EPA (2004)

Figure 2 shows an outright fall of privatisation revenues after the fiscal year, 1997/98, shrinking the net magnitude of the privatisation. Further more, there was a high degree of uncertainties on privatisation proceeds—measured by the standard deviation (s = 0.88) of the flow of privatisation proceeds as a share of GDP—fluctuating highly during the study period. It is distressing to note from the findings that PP/GDP has not reached a three per cent figure over the period. The only impressive year was that 1997/98, bagging a two per cent PP/GDP due to the sale of a mining enterprise— the most expensive sale ever in the Ethiopian privatisation history.

Whereas, the analysis after the fiscal year 1997/98 shows a declining trend of 1.26 and 0.61 per cents of PP/GDP for 1998/99 and 1999/00 fiscal years respectively. The size reached the lowest record level even after these fiscal years with an average of 4.25 transactions per year, particularly the fiscal years 2001/02, 2002/03 and 2003/04 which evidenced the sale of only 1, 3 and 3 transactions respectively. As a result, the average PP/GDP during the study period became too little, accounting for 0.21 per cent which fell on the lowest amongst those poorly performing countries. The chi-square test on the speed of privatisation indicates that there is a vast different between the expected and observed speed because the calculated χ^2 value 473.0 is robustly significant, confirming the slowness of privatisation.

Figure 3 shows the speed waves over the study period. It is evidenced that the speed at which the enterprises sold over the period shows a linear relationship with the size of enterprises. Out of 129 retailing enterprises, 128 enterprises—79.8 per cent of these enterprises fell below the value of USD 250,000—were sold out during the first phase of privatisation, 1994/95-1998/99. Hotel and Tourism—85 per cent of them range below the value of USD250,000—cleared its 75 per cent of sale during the first phase. Hence, the analysis proves that 54.54 per cent of total enterprises which carried a value of less than quarter of a million was sold out within the first phase of privatisation. However, the selection of enterprises at each and every fiscal year may not be ruled out because many small enterprises were opted at first for privatising.

Figure 3
Speed of Privatisation

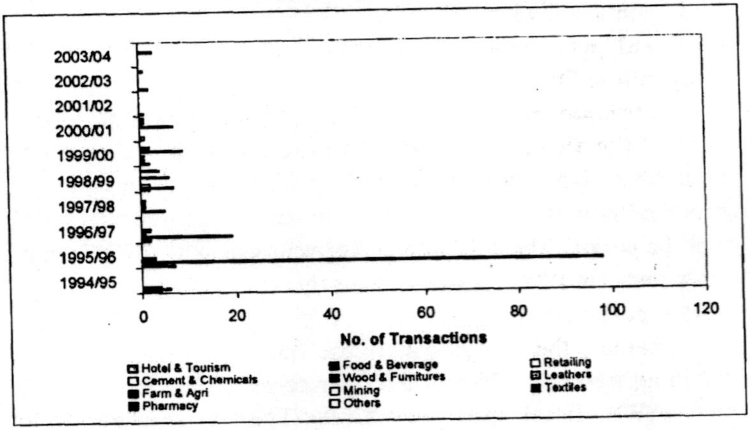

Source: EPA (2004)

Table 9 indicates that the size of privatisation based on the sector. It shows that the retailing business dominates more in the number of business transaction which constituted 58.64 per cent in the total

Table 9
Pace of Privatisation: Sector Wise

Year	Business Sector											
	H & T	*F &B*	*Retail-ing*	*C & C*	*W & F*	*Leathers*	*Farm & Agri*	*Mining*	*Textiles*	*Phar-macy*	*Others*	*Total*
1994/95	4	6	4	nil	nil	nil	nil	nil	nil	nil	nil	14
1995/96	7	5	98	3	3	nil	nil	nil	nil	nil	nil	116
1996/97	2	2	19	1	nil	2	nil	nil	nil	nil	nil	26
1997/98	nil	nil	5	nil	1	1	1	1	nil	nil	nil	9
1998/99	2	7	2	nil	nil	nil	6	nil	nil	4	nil	21
1999/00	2	1	1	nil	1	nil	9	nil	2	nil	nil	16
2000/01	1	1	nil	nil	nil	nil	7	nil	1	nil	1	11
2001/02	1	nil	nil	nil	nil	nil	nil	nil	nil	nil	nil	1
2002/03	2	nil	nil	nil	nil	nil	nil	nil	nil	1	nil	3
2003/04	nil	nil	nil	nil	nil	nil	3	nil	nil	nil	nil	3
Total	21	22	129	4	5	3	26	1	3	5	1	220

number of transactions. This finding reveals the absolute size of the country's privatisation. Farm and agriculture accounted for 11.82 per cent, followed by the food and beverage with 22 per cent. It is also found that hotel and tourism with a lot of development potentialities stood third in the number, constituting 9.5 per cent. Having five transactions each, wood and furniture and pharmacy shared 2.27 per cent each. Cement and chemicals contributed for 1.82 per cent, followed by leathers and textiles with three transactions each represented 1.36 per cent in the total number of transactions. The least was mining which had only one transaction accounting for lesser than half per cent.

Table 10 attempts to explain the size of the country's privatisation in another direction. For the purpose of analysis, the range of value was taken into consideration. The ranges then classified into six: less than a quarter of a million; between a quarter and half million; between half and one million; between one million and two and half a million; between two and half a million and five million and at last above five million.

The result based on the above range of value shows that 63.18 per cent of the total transactions fell in the value of less than a quarter million which is nothing, but 139 PSUs of the total PSUs were sold not more than USD quarter a million each. Out of these transactions, 103 transactions—74 per cent belonged to the retailing business, followed by the hotel and tourism industry accounting 12 per cent.

The analysis also reveals that 9.09 per cent of the enterprises ranged between a quarter million and half a million. Between half a million and one million category, there were 13 enterprises constituting 5.91 per cent. The major portion of the total privatisation proceeds came from the categories of above one million in which 21.82 per cent of the total enterprises put their prints, particularly about nine per cent of the enterprises sold over the value of USD5 million.

It is interesting to note that over USD5 million category, seven food and beverage enterprises as well as six farm and agricultural enterprises were found, indicating their size and contribution not only in the size of privatisation, but also in the total economic activity of the country. The last two ranges yielded about three quarter of the proceeds collected during the study period.

Table 10
Size of Privatisation: Sector Wise

Value (in millions)	*Business Sector*											
	H & T	*F &B*	*Retail-ing*	*C & C*	*W & F*	*Leathers*	*Farm & Agri*	*Mining*	*Textiles*	*Phar-macy*	*Others*	*Total*
Less than 0.25	17	3	103	nil	1	1	8	nil	nil	5	1	139
0.25-0.5	1	2	9	nil	nil	nil	7	nil	1	nil	nil	20
0.5-1.0	2	nil	7	nil	nil	nil	4	nil	nil	nil	nil	13
1.0- 2.5 Millions	1	6	10	1	3	1	1	nil	1	nil	nil	24
2.5-5.0 Millions	nil	4	nil	2	nil	nil	nil	nil	1	nil	nil	4
Above 5 Millions	nil	7	nil	1	1	1	6	1	nil	nil	nil	20

Table 11
Privatisation: Sector Distribution

Business Sector	*Proceeds (Million USD)*	*Share in Total Proceeds (in %)*
Hotel & Tourism	5.18	1.20
Food & Beverage	74.06	17.14
Retailing	30.52	7.06
Cement & Chemicals	14.97	3.46
Wood & Furniture	8.83	2.04
Leathers	26.58	6.15
Farm & Agro	96.68	22.00
Mining	172.00	39.81
Textiles	4.16	0.96
Pharmacy	0.64	0.15
Others	0.08	0.02
Total	433.70	100.00

Source: EPA (2004).

Table 11 shows an inverse relationship between the number and size of privatisation. Looking at the number of retailing enterprises, it is assumed that it would fetch a substantial sale proceeds, but surprisingly, these transactions accounted for only 7.06 per cent in the total proceeds collected over the study period. Next to retailing, the farm and agriculture constituted—many are large sized enterprise—26 in the number of transactions, but contributed 22 per cent in the total proceeds. Food and beverage stood third in the number as well as in the contribution. Food and beverage with 22 transactions yielded USD74.06 million which accounted for 17.14 per cent in the total proceeds.

It is also found that that hotel and tourism—an emerging service sector in the country—with 21 transactions fetched up 1.20 per cent in the total proceeds, where as the mining sector with one transaction contributed 39.81 per cent in the total proceeds. Leathers, cement and chemicals, wood and furniture, textiles and pharmacy contributed 6.15 per cent, 3.46 per cent, 2.04 per cent, 0.96 per cent and 0.15 per cent respectively for the total privatisation proceeds.

The foregoing discussions and analyses reveal and confirm that a case-by-case approach was applied in privatising the PSUs. The privatisation programme commenced in the country with a moderate speed in the initial period, but radically slowed down later on, particularly after 1998/99 fiscal year. The size and speed contributed negatively to each other and hence, brought almost a stand still in the privatisation programme.

The discussion also pictures out the buyers response over the study period which was found far from satisfactory. Medium and large sized enterprises were pushed to the second tender as well as third tender. Processing consumed a long time to convert a PSU into private one, and many buyers complained about the price of the enterprise. It is found in the study that the Agency was not fully autonomous. As a result, the Agency's independence on privatisation activities were much questioned. Nonetheless, risks on the business environment, regulatory and legal framework and transformation were not much lessened even in the latter years of privatisation.

In addition to these, two other important causes may be said for such steep falling which shrunk the privatisation programme in general: the first cause is the capacity of potential buyers and second cause is their willingness in buying those slated enterprises. The weak financial capacity and poor entrepreneurial attitude of local investors can be said as the major reason for the slow-down. Second, the war clouds with Eritrea in 1998/99 fiscal year is the main reason why the willingness to come forward, particularly from the foreign investors, was not so favourable, and subsequently may have acted negatively towards the privatisation in the fiscal years from 2000/01 to 2003/04. The war coupled with a sort of economic instability—it is though diluted—has been persisting as a strong obstacle that still works against the privatisation in the country.

As a result, the buyers' interest on acquiring PSUs became so poor so as to cause a few enterprises to be sold out during the end of the study period. Moreover, the pre-conditions set for privatisation were considered obstacles, owing to the absence of a master plan to guide the programme. Policy issues that need to be resolved before privatisation—for example what level of foreign participation is acceptable –missing in the privatisation programme of the country.

Privatisation in Ethiopia has yet to go a long journey. As a matter of fact, the government has still got a lion share in the nation's economic activity, the holding of which is partly known for two reasons. First, the government wants to retain the most profitable and strategic enterprises such as Ethiopian Airlines, Ethiopian

Telecommunications and Ethiopian Electricity and Power Corporations. Second, no other way except the 'unwanted' retention because many slated enterprises were pending till the end of study period for the want of potential buyers.

Apart from these discussions on what went on so far in the country, it can be said that large industrial and financial enterprises should have been privatised to bring a larger investment, but so far little was done to sell out these enterprises. Sale of these enterprises has been successfully experimented in many developing countries, particularly through public offerings. Sticking only to direct sale may fail when the foreign investors and other industrial enterprises are not interested in acquiring the PSUs which was observed in this study. Lack of experience in privatising, coupled with inadequate savings of the general public may have also contributed its share in the poor show of privatisation.

REFERENCES

Balema, A.A. (2003), *"Economic Development and Democracy in Ethiopia"*, A PhD Thesis Submitted to Erasmas University, Rotterdam, Rotterdam: Erasmas University, pp. 322-24.

Bhardhan, P. (1998), "Economies of Market Socialism and the Issue of Public Enterprise Reform in India", in Basu, K., Majumdhar, M. and Mitra, T. (eds) *Capital, Investment and Development: Essays in Memory of Sukhamoy Chakravarthy.* New Delhi: Oxford Printing Press, p. 212.

Cook, P. and Uchida, Y. (2003), 'Privatisation and Economic Growth in Developing Countries', *The Journal of Development Studies,* Vol. 39, No. 9, pp. 121-54.

Donaldson, D. & Wagle, D.M. (1995), "*Privatisation Principles and Practices: IFC Lessons of Experience Series No. 15007,* Washington, D.C.: World Bank/IFC, pp. 1-22.

EPA (2002), "Privatisation News", Published by the Public Relations Department of the EPA, Vol. 5, No.1, pp. 1-21.

EPA (2003), "Privatisation", Viewed on 06/11/2003 in the EPA Website, http://www.telecom.net.et/~epa/Privatise/index.html.

EPA (2004) "Ethiopian Privatisation Proceeds", Department of Finance and Administration, Addis Ababa: EPA.

Gareth and Smith, C. (1998), *Economic Development.* New York: Palgrave, pp. 118-9.

Gibbon, H. (1996), *"A Guide for Divesting Government-Owned Enterprises"*, How to Guide No. 15, July, Reason Foundation, pp. 1-15.

GoE (1994) "Negarit Gazeta of the Transitional Government of Ethiopia: Ethiopian Privatisation Agency Establishment Proclamation No. 87/ 94", February, Addis Ababa: GoE, pp. 292-95.

GoE (1997) "Negarit Gazeta of the FDRE: Federal Rural Land Administration Proclamation No. 89/97", December, Addis Ababa: GoE, pp. 628-31.

GoE (1998) "Negarit Gazeta of the FDRE: Privatisation of Public Enterprises Proclamation No. 146/98", 5th Year No. 26, December, Addis Ababa: GoE, pp. 933-41.

Gómez-Ibáñez, J.A. and Meyer, J.R (1993) *Going Private: The International Experience with Transport Privatisation.* Washington, D.C., : The Brookings Institution, pp. 22-35.

Kebede, G. (1993), *"Privatisation of Public Enterprises: Modalities and Sequencing"*, A Paper Submitted for the Workshop on Public Enterprises Reforms and Privatisation in Ethiopia, July 1-3, Nazareth: EEA and USAID: (Ethiopia), pp. 1-30.

MoFED (2004) Ethiopia: Private Sector Development Capacity Building Project, Report No. 30639, Addis Ababa: MoFED.

Mugerwa-Kayizzi, S. (2002), *"Privatisation in Sub-Saharan Africa: On Factors Affecting Implementation"*, Discussion Paper No. 2002/12, January, Helsinki: UNU-WIDER(United Nations University-World Institute for Development Economics Research), pp. 1-21.

Nellis, J. (2003), *"Privatisation in Africa: What has happened? and what is to be done?"*, Working Paper No. 25, Centre for Global Development, pp. 6-9.

Nankani, H. (1988), *"Techniques of Privatisation of State Owned Enterprises"*, Vol. II, Selected Country Case Studies, World Bank Technical Paper No. 89, Washington, D.C.: IBRD/WB, pp. 1-69.

Pirie, M. (1988), *Privatisation.* England: Wildwood House Ltd., pp. 1-69.

Plane, P. (1997), "Privatisation and Economic Growth: An Empirical Investigation from a Sample of Developing Market Economies", *Applied Economics,* Vol. 29, No. 2, pp. 161-78.

Sach, J.D. (1992), *"Accelerating Privatisation in Eastern Europe: The Case of Poland"*, The Proceedings of the World Bank Annual Conference on Development Economics 1991, Washington, D.C.: IBRD/WB, pp.15-43.

Sach, J.D. (2005), Interview with the Special Advisor to the Secretary General, UN, on Hard Talk, BBC World, Watched on 14th April, 2005, GMT 6.00 p.m. – 6.30 p.m.

Sadar, F. (1995), *"Privatising Public Enterprises and Foreign Investment in Developing Countries, 1988-93"*, Washington, D.C.: IFC/WB, pp. 1-45.

Shirley, M. and Nellis, J. (1991), *"Public Enterprise Reform: The Lessons of Experience"*, Washington, D.C.: IBRD/World Bank, pp. 16-62.

UNDP (1989), "A Study of the Experience with Privatisation of Public Enterprises in Developing Countries", November, New York: UNDP, p. 29.

Vuylsteke, C. (1988) *"Techniques of Privatisation of State Owned Enterprise"*, Vol. I, Methods and Implementation, World Bank Technical Paper No. 88, Washington, D.C.: World Bank, pp. 1-134.

Welch, D. & Frémond, O. (1998), *"The Case-by-Case Approach to Privatisation: Techniques and Examples"*, WB Technical Paper No. 403, (A Joint Production of the WB and the Inter-American Development Bank), Washington, D.C.: IBRD/World Bank, pp. 1-51.

World Bank (2001), "Ethiopia: Foreign Investment Promotion Strategy Framework", Foreign Investment Advisory Service (FIAS), Washington, D.C.: World Bank, pp. 1-62.

World Bank (2002), "Investment Climate Surveys in Ethiopia", Viewed on 12th March, 2005, http://rru.worldbank.org/InvestmentClimate/Exploreeconomies/Snahshot.aspx?

CHAPTER - 5

Economic and Political Issues in Privatisation

The previous chapter analyses the processing issues in privatisation. The results reveal that the business environment, and regulatory and legal framework—the major pre-conditions—were not made to a level satisfactory for privatisation. Many flaws in the transformation process starting from planning to implementation may capture a cautionary note as to whether the intended objectives of privatisation be accomplished. It is because of the reason that the business environment, legal and commercial framework, transformation process and the size and speed issues determine the success of privatisation. In a nutshell, it can be said that processing issues are pre-requisites for the accomplishment of objectives slated for privatisation.

This chapter dovetails the economic and political issues—can also be called yardsticks—for measuring the success of privatisation in Ethiopia. The success of any privatisation programme can only be measured in terms of the objectives that motivated it. It is clearly stated in the privatisation proclamation that the country implemented privatisation for the accomplishment of many economic objectives (GoE, 1998). The major objective underlying privatisation in the country is to generate revenue required for financing development activities and to promote economic development. The success of any privatisation activity depends on how better these objectives are accomplished. Hence, the purpose of this chapter can be put in a question form to know whether privatisation has brought any positive change on the economic and political issues.

This chapter attempts to analyse at first the impact of privatisation on individual economic and political variables over the privatisation period, followed by an empirical testing and analysis of these variables with reference to privatisation. The earlier one enables us to know through descriptive statistics the changes and impacts which privatisation has brought onto the individual economic and political variable. Whereas, the latter one helps substantiate the results and discussions to empirically prove as to whether the privatisation has brought any progress or development in the economy.

ECONOMIC GROWTH AND ECONOMIC DEVELOPMENT ISSUES

Economic growth can be defined most simply as the ability of a nation to expand its capacity to produce the goods and services its people want. In simple terms, the economic growth expands a country's production possibilities (Milner and Greenaway, 1979). Gross domestic product (GDP) and its components are taken for this study to measure the impact of privatisation on these variables, owing to the reason that the most widely reported measure throughout the world of a nation's economic performance is GDP (Tucker, 1997).

Table 1
GDP and its Components

Year	*Agriculture*	*Industry*	*Services*	*GDP*
1994/95	3.4	8.1	7.05	6.1
1995/96	14.7	1.6	7.4	10.6
1996/97	3.4	6.7	7.1	5.2
1997/98	-11.2	2.4	9.53	-1.2
1998/99	3.8	8.6	6.7	6.3
1999/00	2.2	1.8	9.0	5.4
2000/01	11.5	5.0	4.85	8.9
2001/02	-3.1	5.8	4.5	2.7
2002/03	-12.6	4.6	2.5	-3.7
2003/04	18.9	6.9	6.95	11.6
Annual Average	3.1	5.2	6.56	5.2

Sources: MoFED (2004) and (World Bank, 2002)

Table 1 shows that the GDP grew at an annual average of 5.2 per cent, where as agriculture grew at 3.1 per cent over the privatisation period. It also indicates that a significant variation in the economic performance is particularly attributed to the fluctuation in the agricultural output. It is because the country has a high dependence on agriculture, accounting for an annual average of 45.8 per cent in the total output over the study period. Any shock in agriculture reflects in the total output of the country. The growth achieved its moderate achievement despite the negative performance in the fiscal year 1997/98 as well as the poor show in the 2002/03.

This study discloses that the reason for 1997/98 set back was the war climate with Eritrea. After that dismaying experience, the economy picked up immediately as real GDP grew by 6.3 per cent in 1998/99 and subsequently by 5.4 per cent and 8.9 per cent respectively in 1999/00 and 2000/01. But, the fiscal year 2001/02 was a deceiving year with the lower growth rate of 2.7 per cent, and the 2002/03 fiscal year was the worst. It recorded a negative growth rate of GDP at 3.7 per cent. The economy again grew very positively and strongly at 11.6 per cent in 2003/04.

When the growth rate is analysed, the importance of agriculture in the national economy can be learned. A simple fluctuation in agriculture affects the total production of the country. It is more evident in 1996/97, 2001/02 and 2002/03 fiscal years where agricultural production was not up to the mark, recording negative 11.2, 3.1 and 12.6 per cents respectively. This poor performance was attributed not only to the war with Eritrea, but also to the drought conditions. The soothening factor was that industry and services grew at an annual average growth rate of 5.52 per cent and 6.56 per cent respectively over the study period.

The above findings on economic growth in the country—agriculturally dependent and fluctuating—cannot be a stimulus for economic development. A long standing growth always ensures economic development through the diversification of economic activities than what it used to produce in the past. This statement was in much vague in the country because this study finds little evidence on economic development as three things are found unsupportive: first, the industrialization in the country is absolutely slow in progress with a few agricultural products, particularly coffee and hide—coffee's share in total export earnings as of 2003/04 fiscal year stood at 37.2 per cent; second, Ethiopia was then a major importer even for the basic and necessary raw material for its industrial sector and finally, the technological advancement in Ethiopia was poorer than any other Sub-Saharan African (SSA) countries. It can, therefore, be said that privatisation, which was expected to expand and diversify an economy through its vigorous private sector development, was found to be failed in these two economic aspects.

In addition to these three points, one strong objection comes when poverty is taken as an indicator to measure the economic development in which these economic reforms have not brought any change as a number of people are living below USD one dollar is 81.9 per cent as of 2001/02 (UNDP, 2003). However, the consoling factor is inflation was under control during these two periods, showing 1.26 (negative) and 2.5 per cent respectively. It is found that the reason for moderate effect of inflation in the country is due to the resources, especially food which is self-provided and fulfills the needs of maximum number of mass living in the rural areas.

The country took many efforts to increase economic growth after the implementation of economic reforms. Privatisation initiative cannot be denied as one among them as many countries succeeded in increasing the total output of the product through an intensive private sector participation and development. Privatisation proceeds as a share of GDP—the standard measure indicating privatisation magnitude—is used as a predictor to examine its impact on the growth of GDP, agriculture, industry and services through a simple correlation analysis. The result, shown in Figure 5.1, indicates that there is little negative correlation between privatisation and GDP growth (correlation coefficient is -0.308). The similar results are found for agriculture (correlation coefficient is -0.378) and industry (correlation coefficient is -0.320) which are exhibited in Figures 2 and 3 respectively. The correlation behaved differently for services, showing a positive correlation (correlation coefficient is 0.664), significance of which is as obviously exhibited in Figure 4.

The derived result on services can be justified from the privatisation data that no single year was left without selling either retailing or hotel and tourism enterprises which usually account for under services. The sale of agricultural and industrial enterprises was not found in the beginning years of privatisation and moreover, their transactions were not regular and continuous over the period despite which they yielded substantial proceeds. Nonetheless, it should

Figure 1
Correlation between Privatisation and GDP

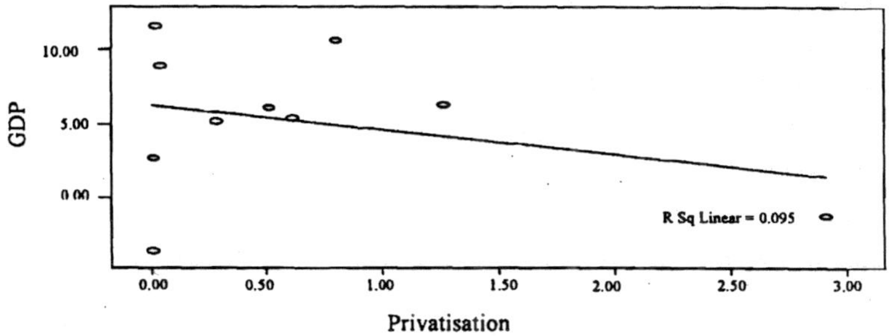

Figure 2
Correlation between Privatisation and Agriculture

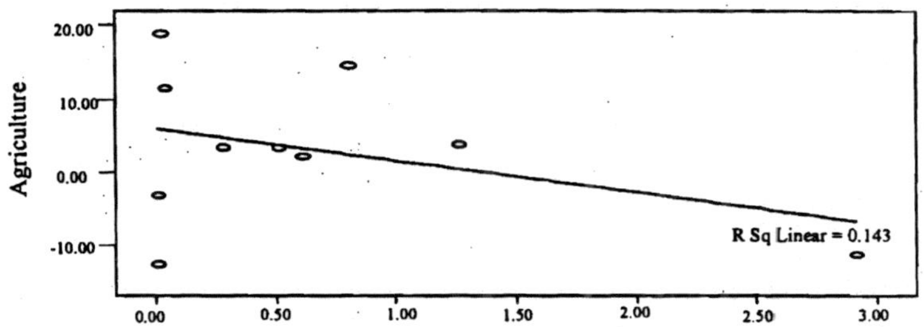

Figure 3
Correlation between Privatisation and Industry

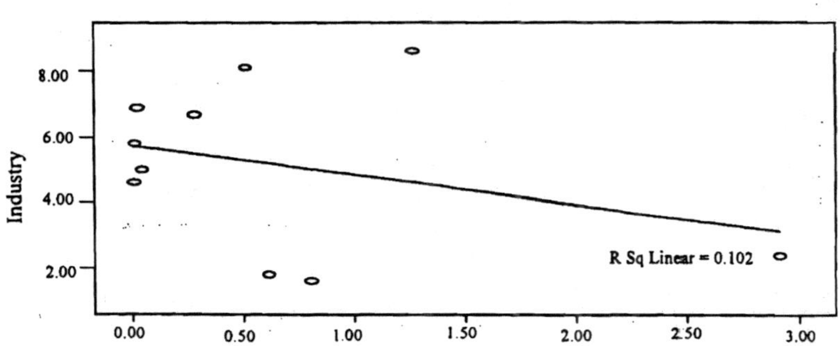

Figure 4
Correlation between Privatisation and Services

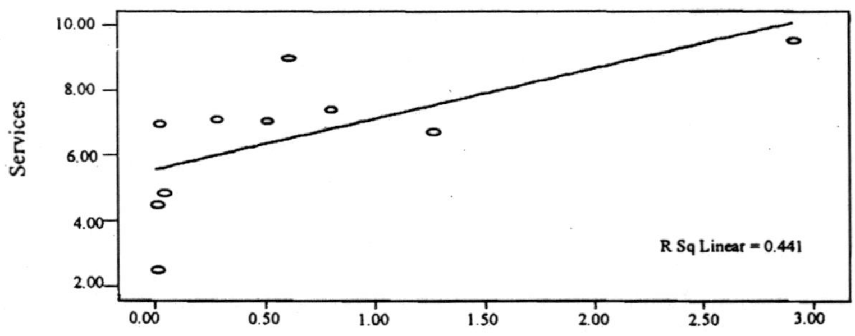

carefully be noted that this simple correlation does not eliminate the possibility of these correlations occurring out of many unexplained reasons.

BUDGET DEFICIT AND EXTERNAL DEBT ISSUES

Budget deficit and external debt have perennially been at the centre of economic policy debates in many developing countries. In these countries, the operations of PSUs are a significant component of the government budget. The role of PSUs expanded in many cases and the economic role of the state was perceived to be important both for ideological reasons as well as owing to the alleged productivity of public goods. However, PSUs have become a drain on the budget in many countries, partly as a result of poor investment, the collapse in terms of trade and various structural problems. Privatisation, in many cases, has become an attractive way to help cope with budget deficit (Agénor and Montiel, 1999).

Budgetary Deficit

Ethiopia is no exception to this theory of other developing countries. Many PSUs in the country were found working at the poor growth rate. The annual report of MoFED (2004) indicates that the annual production performance and sales performance accounted for 2.05 and negative 0.13 per cent respectively which shows a dismaying performance of PSUs over the study period. These indications confirm that the PSUs may also contribute its negative share in the budget deficit.

However, it should be carefully noted that the fiscal effects of privatisation is that they are not generally equal to privatisation proceeds, especially because measuring fiscal effects in that way fails to take into account the positive or negative effects on the government's budget of keeping the enterprises.

Table 2
Budget Deficit and its Share in GDP

Year	*Budget Deficit (USD Million)*	*Budget Deficit/ GDP (in Percentage)*	*PSUs Share in Budget Deficit (in Percentage)*
1994/95	214	3.7	2.20
1995/96	333	5.21	1.74
1996/97	98	1.46	4.23
1997/98	194	2.92	3.30
1998/99	462	6.54	1.36
1999/00	764	10.25	0.9
2000/01	350	4.32	1.27
2001/02	555	6.67	1.48
2002/03	435	6.55	5.12
2003/04	528	7.13	1.0
Annual Average	393	5.48	2.00

Source: World Bank (2004a) and MoFED, (2004).

Table 2 shows that the budget deficit to GDP, which stood at 3.7 per cent in the first fiscal year of the privatisation period, 1994/95, was raised to 7.13 per cent in 2003/04, the last fiscal year of the study period. It grew at an annual average of 5.48 per cent over the period. The deficit was very low only in the fiscal years of 1996/97 and 1997/98. But the post war effect on budgetary deficit was observed in the fiscal year 1998/99 and 1999/00 which recorded 6.54 and 10.25 per cents respectively. The observed rising phenomenon in the budgetary deficit, particularly after the war continued throughout the study period. Furthermore, the deficit fluctuated rapidly over the period ($\sigma = 2.29$ per cent) as exhibited in Figure 5.

The share of PSUs in budget deficit shows no improvement over the privatisation period. Privatisation should have reduced the deficit in the budget not only by its privatisation proceeds, but also by reducing the fund allocated to the PSUs, especially to the weak. But in contrary, Table 2 shows that the budget allocated to PSUs grew at annual average of two per cent (σ = 1.42 per cent) over the privatisation period.

Figure 5
Budgetary Deficit

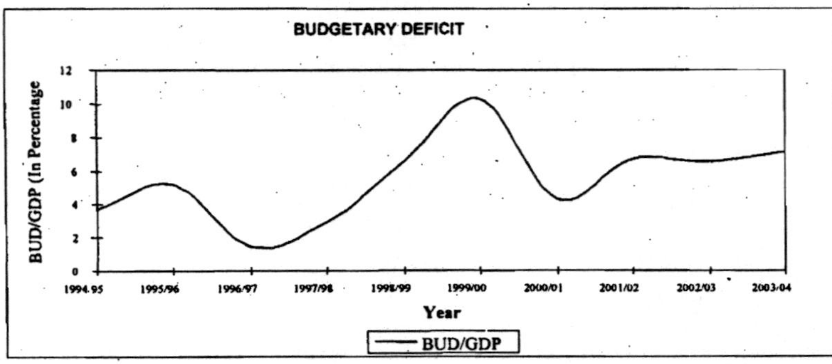

For the preliminary analysis, the effects of privatisation variables are linked to the size of the government budget deficit since privatisation may have been implemented as a quick solution to a budgetary problem in the country. In order to examine this effect, a simple correlation is applied. The result shows that there is a weak correlation (correlation coefficient is -0.268) found between privatisation and budgetary deficit (Figure 6).

Figure 6
Correlation between Privatisation and Budgetary Deficit

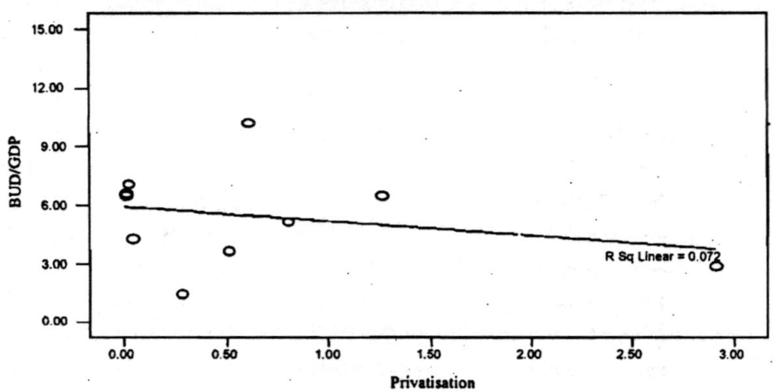

There may be two reasons which justify this no effect phenomenon: first, the privatisation proceeds brought by the size of privatisation are too small to bring effect on the budgetary deficit and second, the retaining of major PSUs by the government may leave the budgetary deficit no link to the privatisation. However, the tendency of government's budget deficit reduces investment spending which is otherwise called a crowding effect. Reduced investment spending implies a slower capital formation and lower economic growth. This adverse effect of budget deficit on economic growth is probably the most important cost deficit and a major reason why economists strongly advise governments to minimise this deficit.

Having tested the effect of privatisation on the budget deficit, this study attempts to examine the debt which bears a high degree of impact on a national economy. In recent years, the government's revenues exceeded expenditures, a situation that official forecasts say will continue through the next decades (Tucker, 1997:423).

External Debt

The distinction between deficit and debt can be explained in such a way that the debt at a given time is the sum of all past budget deficits. That is, the debt is the cumulative excess of past spending over past receipts. Thus in a year with a deficit, the debt goes up; in a year with surplus, debt goes down. In the total debt, the most undesirable and threatening is external debt. In the case of its increasing, the future generation certainly bears a burden, because its consumption level is reduced by an amount equal to the loan plus the accrued interest that must be sent to foreign lenders. Not surprisingly, much of the analytical and empirical work by economists in the last decade has, therefore, been concerned with various aspects of debt issues (Lal, 2001). Privatisation aims at improving economy is expected to help the economy to reduce the debt burden which have been observed in many developing countries. Hence, this study entails an analysis of external debt and its change of magnitude to the tone of privatisation.

The forthcoming analyses on external debt, debt servicing and debt to export, help this study assess their magnitude during the privatisation period. The analysis of debt-servicing enables this study to measure the nation's current debt burden. Debt servicing refers to a nation's external debt relative to its current export earnings which is considered a more reliable measurement. Changes in this debt-to-export ratio indicate whether a nation's debt burden is rising or falling in relation to its ability to pay. Carbough (1995) says that from the late 1973 to 1987, the ratio of developing nation's external debt-to-export ratio rose from 133 per cent to 161 per cent. This implies that the external debt exceeded, and grew more rapidly than export revenues over this period. By 1993, the debt-to-export ratio had moderated to 113.4 per cent.

Ethiopia is one of the highly indebted poor countries (HIPC) according to the World Bank Classification (World Bank, 2002a: 362-3). As a privilege, the country comes under HIPC Debt Initiative[1]. This status came to the country owing to its poorest economic conditions and high indebtedness. Table 5.3 shows that country's external debt as a percentage of GDP which, otherwise, refers to the size of the country's debt in relation to the size of its economy. In general, a high debt to GDP is an indication of future debt burden, whereas debt-to-servicing and debt to export indicate the present debt burden of the country.

Table 3
External Debt and Debt Servicing

Year	*External Debt/GDP (In Percentage)*	*Debt Service (In Percentage)*
1994/95	178.37	8.07
1995/96	157.64	10.82
1996/97	149.81	8.67
1997/98	155.66	9.15
1998/99	78.45	12.83
1999/00	73.56	11.13
2000/01	69.26	14.65
2001/02	78.07	14.47
2002/03	98.69	5.52
2003/04	97.19	5.68

Source: World Bank (2004a) and MoFED (2004).

As it is seen in Table 3, the external debt to GDP moved down from 178.37 per cent in 1994/95 to 97.16 per cent in 2003/04 which results in the reduction of indebtedness of the country. However, as of 2003/04, 97 cents in every Ethiopian Birr of GDP was required to liquidate the debt. As a consequence, every Ethiopian's moral responsibility (actual burden as of 2000/01 was low) to liquidate the debt recorded for USD103 (USD 7,200 million is divided by 70 million population) despite the fact that there was a reduction in the total external debt, thanks to the waiving off USD4,321 million in the fiscal year 1998/99 (World Bank, 2004b). It can be observed that after the debt reduction by the donors, the external debt to GDP reduced from 155.66 per cent to 78.45 per cent. This result may, therefore, rule out the contribution of privatisation robustly in the debt reduction.

While analysing, it is observed that debt-to-service was reduced from 8.07 per cent in 1994/95 to 5.68 per cent in 2003/04 (Table 3). This result reveals a fact about the increase of export over the privatisation period, resulting in a decrease of debt servicing, ceteris paribus. The fiscal years between 1998/99 and 2001/02 shows that the country increased its debt servicing, where as in the fiscal years 2002/03 and 2003/04 witness a diminishing trend despite an increase in exports over the period.

Table 4
External Debt to Exports

Year	*External Debt to Export (In Percentage)*
1994/95	1275
1995/96	1224
1996/97	996
1997/98	997
1998/99	607
1999/00	557
2000/01	586
2001/02	712
2002/03	574
2003/04	535

Source: MoFED (2003a), MoFED (2003b), MoFED (2003c) & World Bank (2004a)

Table 4 indicates that the external debt to export was reduced from of 1275 per cent in 1994/95 to 574 per cent in 2003/04 over the privatisation period. The result supplements the fact that the reduction arrived at not only owing to the debt forgiveness, but also owing to an increase in exports. Furthermore, this analysis shows that the country's ability to pay was considerably increased and eventually the possibility of reducing the debt burden was increased over the period. Nonetheless, the country's present value of debt was in danger since it ran out of safe ratio. The universally acceptable safe ratio is around 150 per cent (Diwan, 2004).

The foregoing analysis reveals that the country was severely indebted despite the privatisation programme implemented to aim at its reduction. The standard World Bank definitions (World Bank, 2004c) reveals that any country where the present value of debt to GDP reaches above 50 per cent or present value of debt to export exceeds 275 per cent it is called a severely indebted country. On these two indicators, the study indicates an absolute poor position on debt of the country.

To assess whether external debt captured any effect from privatisation, a simple correlation is done. The correlation analysis proves that there is a correlation between privatisation and external debt in the country (Figure 7). But it is insignificant with the coefficient of 0.382. However, the result on debt-to-service and debt to export were found satisfactory, leaving a notion that the condition on indebtedness may reverse. This reverse on the indebtedness may also be expected from the policy considerations of the WB and other donors.

Figure 7
Correlation between Privatisation and External Debt

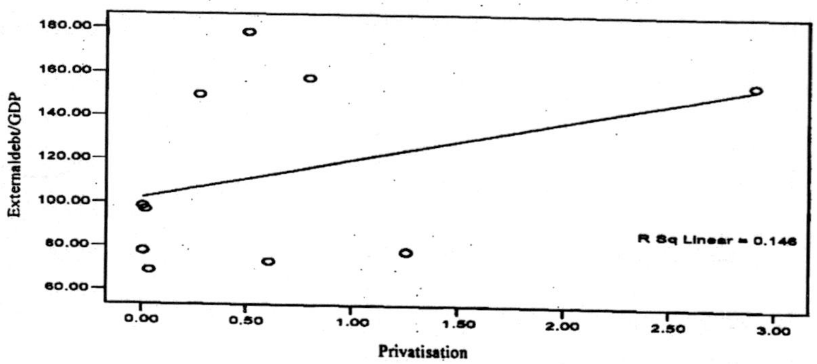

INTERNATIONAL TRADE AND CURRENT AND TRADE ACCOUNT DEFICITS ISSUES

Openness and export orientation are the main policy variables affecting the growth. Many developed countries have made extensive use of privatisation as a policy tool in support of liberalisation (Sadar, 1995: 33) which, in turn, inculcated in them a high degree of export orientation in their economies. As a result, they raised their hopes on the current and trade accounts, showing either a less debit balance or surplus. Thirwall in his study (2004:640) finds that there is a positive relation between openness and economic growth.

Table 5 shows that the openness of the country during the privatisation period. Openness started with 18.74 per cent in the beginning of privatisation period and ended with 28.9 per cent. Openness was relatively better in the fiscal years of 2002/03 and 2003/04. However, the annual average openness shown over the period was 20.91 per cent with a standard deviation ($\sigma = 4.27$). Hence, the country failed to hold the openness high because minimum 30 per cent is required to be achieved to call a country moderately open at this globalised economy. For instance, The Netherlands is considered an extremely open economy because its openness accounts about 50 per cent (Baumol and Blinder, 1997).

Table 5
Openness (Liberalisation)

Year	*Imports*	*Exports*	*Im+Ex/2*	*GDP*	*Openness (In Percentage)*
1994/95	808	1,357	1,083	5,779	18.74
1995/96	823	1,731	1,277	6,393	19.97
1996/97	1,011	1,378	1,195	6,725	17.77
1997/98	1,037	1,653	1,345	6,647	20.23
1998/99	914	1,873	1,394	7,067	19.73
1999/00	984	1,960	1,472	7,451	19.76
2000/01	957	1,992	1,475	8,106	18.2
2001/02	912	2,004	1,458	8,326	17.51
2002/03	1,140	2,431	1,786	6,638	29.91
2003/04	1,347	2,936	2,142	7,408	28.9
Annual Average	993	1,932	1,475	7,054	20.91

Source: World Bank (2004a).

Openness is normally favourable provided the export dominates more than import despite the latter is an inevitable engine for a faster growth. There are two indicators taken into account for measuring the export orientation of the country: export to import and export to GDP, which are furnished in Table 6.

Export to import, which stood at 59.54 per cent in the first year of privatisation, 1994/95, was reduced to 45.88 per cent in 2003/04. Import started to exceed exports particularly after 2002/01 which reveals a mixed signal: First, the country has been seen coming out of an inward oriented structure, and second, trade and current account balances may pose a high danger. The earlier outcomes are considered feasible as an outward economy is required to meet the growing needs of the private sector which requires enormous foreign technology and infrastructure, whereas the latter outcome is dangerous unless and otherwise the country has got ample foreign reserves.

Table 6
Export Orientation

Year	*Export to Import*	*Export to GDP*
1994/95	59.54	13.61
1995/96	47.54	13.23
1996/97	73.36	15.80
1997/98	62.73	15.80
1998/99	48.80	14.19
1999/00	50.20	15.40
2000/01	48.04	15.08
2001/02	45.51	15.20
2002/03	46.89	17.10
2003/04	45.88	16.78
Annual Average	52.20	15.17

Source: World Bank (2004) and MoFED (2004).

Nonetheless, the export in per cent of GDP shows an increase over the period. It was 13.61 per cent in the first fiscal year of privatisation—facing less fluctuation—raised to 16.78 per cent at the end of the privatisation period. Ethiopian export is predominantly influenced by coffee, constituted 37.2 per cent in 2003/04 in total export earnings. MoFED (2004) reports that coffee alone brought foreign exchange earnings of USD 224 million. As it is already mentioned in this study, the country has not increased the number of items which the country produces and imports during the post reform period and therefore, any change or fluctuation in the coffee market affects the trade and current account balance very severely.

Table 7
Trade and Current Account Balances

Year	*Trade Balance to GDP (In Percentage)*	*Current Account Balance to GDP (In Percentage)*
1994/95	-9.25	-1.5
1995/96	-14.60	-7.4
1996/97	-5.74	-6.5
1997/98	-9.38	-5.1
1998/99	-14.90	-7.8
1999/00	-15.27	-5.1
2000/01	-16.31	-4.0
2001/02	-18.20	-6.0
2002/03	-19.45	-4.7
2003/04	-19.8	-13.24
Annual Average	-14.29	-7.6

Source: World Bank (2004), NBE (2003) and NBE (2004).

Trade and current account balances are the direct outcomes of these openness and export orientation, ceteris paribus. These balances may be negative for the poor economies like Ethiopia in which the export is found to be lesser than import. Table 7 illustrates the trade balance and current account deficits over the privatisation period. It indicates that the trade deficit increased slowly over the period, whereas the current deficit increased but with a little fluctuation. This trend of increase in the export to GDP was expected to have smoothened the trade and current account balance over the period, but the analysis over export to import prevented the expectation from yielding a positive effect on these balances.

As it is discussed earlier, the export to import is found unfavourable toward these balances. The study also finds that the current account balance (deficit) was increased but not proportionately to the increase of trade account deficit. The reason is that the international reserve in the country has been raised remarkably from USD20 million to USD433 million over the period, acting as a soothing effect (World Bank, 2003a).

Figure 8
Trend: Export, Trade and Current Deficits

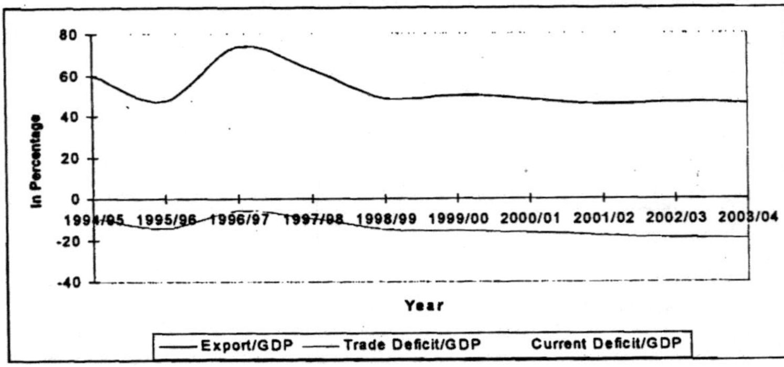

Figure 8 exhibits the relationship between these export to import and deficits. The decreasing trend in the export to import pushed the deficit lines down the zero point, whereas the increasing trend in the export pulled back the deficit lines from further going down the zero point. It shows that any increase in export to import causes a decrease in the trade and current deficits. The analysis after the fiscal year 1998/99 shows that the export to import slowed down, owing to an increase in imports.

The above discussion shows that the country improved moderately its openness over the study period. Export to GDP increased, but much slowly. Trade balance became wider because the export to import ratio slowed down during the study period. Current account deficit was under control—though it increased suddenly in the fiscal year, 2003/04—which was due to the reason that the international reserves served a balancing effect.

While analysing all these effects, the most important variable evolves these is export. If export increases, the export to GDP and export to import increase, where as the trade balance and current account deficit decline. But the question is that to what extent privatisation brought changes in these variables. Not all variables were linked to privatisation to find a simple correlation, but export to GDP is considered a central theme for all effects in this regard. The result reveals that there is no correlation between privatisation and export which may presumably be true on other variables as well.

Figure 9
Correlation between Privatisation and Export Orientation

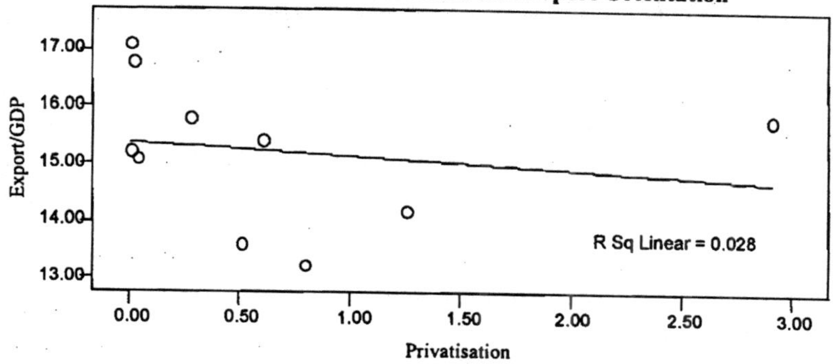

The result may be substantiated to the extent that privatisation seldom touched the coffee processing industries which constitute a major portion in the export. But the result may be argued on two important factors: first, export revenues from leather and service sectors may not be ruled out because many of these industries were privatised over the study period, and second, the export orientation of the enterprises that was considered one of the important criteria for selecting buyer might have its own impact on the possibility of involving exports.

The foregoing discussion and analysis reveal that there has been an improvement in the openness, export orientation and current account deficits. But attributing this development to privatisation is highly questionable because those fields, which are not touched by privatisation, dominate much in export earnings and other reason is obviously the size of privatisation which, in fact, failed to have effect on exports.

INVESTMENT ISSUES

Creating and improving the investment climate is a top priority for the modern world, particularly for the developing African countries because investment is considered an engine for economic growth, and even for poverty reduction in the long run. The task of attracting a sizable investment in this regard for many African countries is indispensable, and should be pursued multifaceted that investment leads not only to a simple growth but also creates sustainable jobs and opportunities for citizens and entrepreneurs.

Ethiopia, which is one of the fiscally grave-positioned in the Sub-Saharan, is now an investment driven and felt country where it is believed that investment helps to reduce the cost of goods consumed by poor people, and improves the living conditions of them directly. It, moreover, contributes to an expanding tax base than indirectly enhancing the government's interest in improving health, education and welfare of the people.

Ethiopia ranking one of the highest in poverty (World Bank, 2004) and the lowest in the human resource development index (UNDP, 2003) had realised a decade ago the paramount importance of investment after the installation of the new government in 1991. Commencing with the Investment Code Reform No. 15/1992, the government established the Ethiopian Investment Authority (EIA), followed by the establishment of the Ethiopian Privatisation Agency (EPA) in 1994. Furthermore, the Investment Code Amendments in 1996 and 1998 and their re-enactments with the broader objectives in 2002 are worth-mentioning to enrich the Ethiopian investment drive, calling the potential domestic and foreign investors to exploit and develop the immense natural resources (GoE, 2002).

Investment climate after a series of proclamations and reforms provides incentives for development related investment, reduces capital entry requirements for joint ventures and technical consultancy services, permits the duty free entry of capital goods (except computers and vehicles), opens the real estate sector to expatriate investors, extends the losses carried forward provisions, cuts the capital gains tax from 40 to 10 per cent, full repatriation for foreign investors and gives priority to investors in obtaining land for lease.

Since 1991, any investment that supplements the attempts of creating an openness economy has been well privileged on the payment of duties and other taxes (GoE, 1992). The guarantee is extended to investors that no asset will be expropriated or nationalised except in accordance with the regulations of the government, and upon the payment of adequate compensation. To change the negative opinion about the judiciary system, particularly among foreigners, the country signed the World Bank Treaty "International Convention on Settlement of Investment Disputes between States and Nationals of other States".

It is also observed that neither under the Transitional nor the present government, any act of expropriation or a thought of re-nationalisation was found to have occurred or was deemed to be imminent. Encouragement came from all angles opening the country to the private investors. The foreign participation in the most profitable energy and financial services was, however, restricted, posing obstacles to the privatisation and investment climate.

Table 8
Investment and its Share in GDP

Year	*Gross Public Investment/ GDP (%)*	*Gross Private Investment/ GDP (%)*	*GDI* or GFCF/GDP (%)*	*FDI/GDP (%)*
1994/95	7.5	8.9	16.4	0.14
1995/96	7.5	9.4	16.9	0.16
1996/97	8.3	8.7	17.0	0.89
1997/98	7.4	9.8	17.2	0.11
1998/99	8.1	8.8	16.9	1.92
1999/00	5.2	10.7	15.9	0.68
2000/01	8.5	9.3	17.8	0.64
2001/02	11.5	9.0	20.5	0.00
2002/03	11.6	8.9	20.5	0.22
2003/04	na**	na	22.6	0.02
Annual Average	8.18	9.26	18.06	0.27

Note: *Gross Domestic Investment(GDI) and Gross Fixed Capital Formation (GFCF) can be interchangeably used.**Not available.
Source: World Bank (2004) and MoFED (2004).

Table 8 shows the performance of gross domestic investment—public and private—and foreign direct investment during the privatisation period. It indicates that there was a considerable share of private investment in the total GDI, comparing to the public investment. Although the difference of annual average rate between the public and private investment in per cent of GDP was too narrow—the difference between the private and public investment was only 1.8 percentage points (Table 8), the achievement on the private investment may not be underestimated.

While analysed for such a meagre difference, the reason may be nothing but the country's transition from the socialism to capitalism, finds always difficulties to withdraw its stake from the business in a short period of time. And also, the withdrawal of state intervention from the economy has carefully been carried out in the country which is contrary to those Latin American and Eastern European Blocks where the withdrawal was fast and vast (Thobani, 1994: 9).

It is also found that FDI as a share of GDP increased but insignificantly from 0.14 per cent to 0.21 per cent over the period. It is due to the fact that foreign investors are pragmatically more sensitive than the domestic investors to the prevalence of the economic and political conditions which they always see and analyse in a microscopic view because the only reason they invest is to enhance their welfare, whatever they perceive it to be (Ambrosio, 1976: 15). Nonetheless, the meagre flow may have its own share in increasing GDI on a fact that there is a direct positive linear between FDI, domestic investment and the growth of GDP (Thirwall, 2004: 592-93).

Whatever be the case, the country's performance on private investment compared to other Sub-Saharan Africa (SSA) was far from satisfactory as the latter were able to achieve an annual average of 13.5 per cent (World Bank, 2004a) during the study period. It is important to note that GDI in SSA has been lower than in other developing regions (Griffin, 2001: 21). In a nutshell, the Ethiopian's performance in attracting private investment directly or through privatisation initiatives was not robust compared to its Sub-Saharan neighbours, and was very little relative to other developing countries in the world (International Finance Corporation (IFC)/World Bank, 2001) despite the country's investment climate-creating efforts.

When analysing the causes for failure in attracting a significant amount of investment, it may owe it to the economic and political instability, weak openness, slow and small privatisation and poor commercial framework. Most significant variables to attract investment are the rate of growth and openness. Economic growth and openness are positively associated and in turn correlate with investment (Alesina, 1998). But the growth was found low and unstable in the country with a lot of fluctuation and uncertainties amidst a significant increase of the output during the privatisation period and so was openness. Bräutigam (1998) proves in his empirical study that if there is difficulty in maintaining macroeconomic stability, it will lead to a sharp decline in the investment. The inflows of investment are thus a consequence of successful development, not a cause of it.

Slow privatisation always resists investment, causing damage to many African countries with significant FDI potential (Eden, 1996). A weak capacity and poor entrepreneurial attitude of the locals, coupled with the processing constraints, may also be the reasons for the poorer show of privatisation and capital accumulation. No doubt, the capacity to purchase and invest primarily correlates with the saving pattern, but it was, however, a soothing effect. Gross domestic savings as a share of GDP over the first phase of privatisation accounted for 7.64 per cent which was declined to 4.74 per cent over the study period (World Bank, 2004a).

The annual average real interest rate, which was 9.5 per cent over the period (MoFED, 2004), was considered a moderate rate for the borrowers. Inflation found over the period was moderate, recording 3.61 per cent. However, it fluctuated highly and had risen to even 15 and 9 per cents in 2002/03 and 2003/04 respectively which might cause a low profile for those potential investors to make long term investment decision leading to a lower rate of capital formation. On the other hand, such conditions develop a pattern of investment biased in favour of projects with a quick pay off (Griffin, 2001: 17). Nonetheless, a mild inflation, up to 5.8 per cent, is positively beneficial for growth (Thirwall 2004), particularly in developing countries.

The war with Eritrea in 1998 has, however, caused a lot of damage to the Ethiopian investment climate, impinging investors' attitudes towards investing. The war—though now diluted—coupled with a sort of uncertainty in the economic and regulatory policy have been persisting as strong obstacles that still work against the privatisation and investment of the country.

Ethiopia, which is with a poorer market potentiality and high risks associated with the security of property rights and poor consumer preferences, should over-perform to convince investors to receive a steady flow of investment. The need of such task is very urgent due to the following reasons: Land issue is the most haunting one in the country since the investors can buy only the factory infra-structures and business, but not the land. Many existing as well as the potential investors were not at ease on land issue which was found to have adversely affected their further investment on modernisation and expansion. Although concrete efforts were taken, the judiciary system was found to be far from satisfactory.

Above all, micro problems such as administration of tax rates, electricity, customs and trade regulations, corruption, anti-competitive or informal practices and commercial and regulatory uncertainty have been found as major hindrances in attracting investment inflows. Tax rates and its administration are the most dislikeable ones to the potential investors (Investment climate Survey, World Bank, 2002b). The survey, which was conducted in the country, found that the commercial conduciveness and infra-structure and service facilities existing in the country were rated poor by the investors and firms. Corruption and diseases prevail—which are though found everywhere, particularly in all developing countries—but economic isolation (Sach, 2005) is the special phenomenon in the African continent. Ethiopia is no exception to this isolation.

Empirical Analyses on Economic Issues

The empirical analysis is conducted with a view to testify the above discussions and descriptive analyses. Four different econometric models are developed for major economic issues which are expected to have drawn effects from privatisation. The first model which is developed to see the impacts of privatisation on the economic growth (GDP or output) of the country; second, to test the effect of privatisation on budgetary deficit and external debt; third, to find whether openness of the country captures any effect from privatisation, and last to prove any significant relativity between investment creation, particularly private investment and privatisation. The empirical results in this connection are given in the respective tables.

The results of the effect of privatisation on growth, which are tested at 5 per cent significance level, are presented in Table 9.

The empirical findings underscored the fact that privatisation proved no impact on the economic growth of the country with the model's explanatory power of 0.992 R^2. The privatisation variable, as expected, has insignificant association with the economic growth of the country which may be substantiated with a fact that privatisation as proved in the previous chapter was slow and small for the economic growth to capture the effect. However, a robust positive result is obtained for agriculture because of its viable growth record over the privatisation period.

Table 9
OLS Result: Effect of Privatisation on the Economic Growth

Variable	*Coefficient*	*T-statistic*	*Significance*
Constant	7.053	4.18	0.009
Agriculture $[A]_t$	1.005	22.665	0.000
Industrial Output $[R]_t$	0.049	1.138	0.307
Investment $[I/Y]_t$	-0.114	-2.504	0.054
Privatisation $[PRIV/Y]_t$	0.04	0.808	0.456
R^2	0.992		
Adjusted R^2	0.985		
F-statistic	148.537		
Significance (F-statistic)	0.000		
D/W statistic	2.859		

Note: Dependent variable: $[y]_t$

The result on agriculture is the expected one despite the fact there has been many peaks and troughs of agriculture fluctuating about an upward line. The result obtained for industrial output is insignificant and positive because its contribution to the total output of the country was observed as very much minimal. In contrast, the result on investment is completely significant but negative which may be said to have been influenced from privatisation, contributing little to the investment climate of the country.

The results of the effect of privatisation on budgetary deficit, which are tested at 5 per cent significance level, are presented in Table 10.

Table 10
OLS Result: Impact of Privatisation on the Budgetary Deficit

Variable	*Coefficient*	*T-statistic*	*Significance*
Constant	-21.580	-4.214	0.014
GDP $[y]_{t-1}$	-0.795	-2.030	0.112
Inflation $[p]_t$	-0.538	-1.700	0.164
Interest $[r]_t$	1.127	3.173	0.034
Privatisation $[PRIV/Y]_t$	0.160	0.599	0.582
R^2	0.733		
Adjusted R^2	0.467		
F-statistic	2.749		
Significance (F-statistic)	0.175		
D/W statistic	2.893		

Notes: Dependent Variable: $[Def/Y_t]$

Table 10 reports the result of the heterodox specifications, estimated using OLS. The results indicate that the GDP growth of the country contributed inversely to budgetary deficit, i.e. a positive impact, indicating the insignificance of instability of the growth on the reduction of budgetary deficit. However, the fact underlying the result may not be underestimated, owing to the relative better performance of the economy over the study period. Privatisation is insignificant on budgetary deficit which is not surprising because of the magnitude—analysed in the previous chapter—is too small to have any effect on the deficit.

The test result indicates that the growth rates are stationery at 5 per cent significance level. The results of OLS model are presented in Table 11.

Table 11
OLS Result: Impact of Privatisation on External Debt

Variable	*Coefficient*	*T-statistic*	*Significance*
Constant	164.255	5.393	0.001
Budgetary Deficit $[Df/Y]_t$	0.623	2.262	0.058
Privatisation $[PRIV/Y]_t$	0.215	0.780	0.461
R^2	0.506		
Adjusted R^2	0.365		
F-statistic	3.591		
Significance (F-statistic)	0.084		
D/W statistic	1.175		

Notes: Dependent Variable: $Debt/Y_t$

The results are impressive, particularly between external debt and budgetary deficit which indicate that an increase in the budgetary deficit led to an increase in the external debt. This empirical result matches with the normal expectation that almost all countries irrespective of their economic status borrow outside of their purview to finance their budgetary deficit. Ethiopia is no exception to this phenomenon. But it is surprising to note the robustly significant and direct relationship between budgetary deficit and external debt in the country despite much of the external debt was waived off by the WB and other Western countries. Privatisation is insignificant on the variable of external debt, owing to its small sized proceeds to repay the external debt.

Privatisation through its private sector development effort is believed to increase the rate of openness of any country. The time when privatisation is implemented, the government of any country attempts to globalise its economy through increasing its share in the total imports and exports i.e. openness. The openness—otherwise called as the worth of international trade to a nation—is defined as the average of imports and exports, expressed as a share of GDP which is always expected by the result of privatisation a positive and significant effect. Week (2001) cites in his study on Macro economic policy for growth that the share of imports and exports is assumed to be functions of the real exchange rate.

It is further noted from the heterodox model that the import share increases with the rate of growth, and holding the exchange rate constant, export rise with an improvement in the terms of trade[TT][2] boosting further investment. Studying openness is avoided because some of the I variables become redundant and mixed. Here, an attempt is made to see independently whether the privatisation improved import and export conditions in the country in Ethiopia.

Table 12
OLS Result: Impact of Privatisation on Imports

Variable	*Coefficient*	*T-statistic*	*Significance*
Constant	4.096	11.323	0.000
GDP Growth $[y]_{t-1}$	-0.882	-2.623	0.047
Exchange Rate $[er]_{t-1}$	-0.586	-1.727	0.145
Privatisation $[PRIV/Y]_t$	-0.24	-0.695	0.518
R^2	0.620		
Adjusted R^2	0.393		
F-statistic	2.724		
Significance (F-statistic)	0.154		
D/W statistic	2.578		

Note: All variables in logarithmic form; Dependent Variable: Imports $(N/Y)_t$

Table 12 reveals the result of the impact of privatisation on the imports of the country tested at 5 per cent significance level. The result of GDP growth on imports is robust, but negatively contributed. It shows that the trend in the country's total output may not be an encouraging factor in importing as much goods as possible. Exchange rate is insignificant, the reason to which is further probed due to its non-monetised nature. Privatisation is also found to be insignificant and negative, indicating its inability to facilitate the country to become an outward oriented economy. Hence, this study rules out an existence of friendly environment for making the country more outward and open oriented even after privatisation.

Table 13
OLS Result: Impact of Privatisation on Exports

Variable	*Coefficient*	*T-statistic*	*Significance*
Constant	*2.168*	*1.097*	*0.334*
GDP Growth $[y]_{t-1}$	-0.757	-2.325	0.081
Exchange Rate $[er]_{t-1}$	0.342	0.524	0.628
Terms of Trade $[TT]_t$	0.055	0.192	0.857
Privatisation $[PRIV/Y]_t$	-0.26	-0.686	0.531
R^2	0.729		
Adjusted R^2	0.458		
F-statistic	2.691		
Significance (F-statistic)	0.180		
D/W statistic	1.982		

Note: All variables in logarithmic form; Dependent Variable: Exports $[X]_t$

The results of OLS estimation given in Table 13 indicate the GDP's failure to create a conducive climate for export. Other variables are insignificant, in which exchange rate and TT are positive, where as privatisation is negative. It shows that the influence of these three variables on export is very fragile or inactive. It indicates, particularly, TT and privatisation failed to boost the export climate in the country.

As a series of analysis of the impact of privatisation on economic issues, the study focuses on (domestic) private investment and FDI as well. It is because of the reason that privatisation as policy gears up the general investment climate of the country. Two OLS models are constructed with a view to analysing the impact of privatisation on private investment and FDI. The models are similar on general parameters justified for investment whether it is domestic or foreign excepting a few alterations in order to capture the real effects. The results of impact of privatisation on private investment tested at 1 per cent of significance level are given in Table 14.

The performance of model is not impressive as far as privatisation variable is concerned. The empirical findings in the model underscores the fact that privatisation is insignificantly negative on the investment of the country. The result is not surprising as the privatisation programme in the country has suffered a serious setback owing to the weak institutional framework, poor processing, small size and slow pace. Moreover, the economic reforms in general, which are supposed to supplement or facilitate the privatisation, are not up to the mark. Such flaws, as seen in the previous discussion, are found ample on tax rates and its administration, property rights and commercial framework in the country.

Table 14
OLS Result: Impact of Privatisation on Investment

Variable	*Coefficient*	*T-statistic*	*Significance*
Constant	1.761	3.666	0.044
GDP Growth $[y]_{t-1}$	-0.195	-0.603	0.589
Savings $[S/Y]_t$	0.360	1.019	0.383
Inflation $[p]_t$	0.213	0.338	0.758
Real Interest Rate $[r]_{t-1}$	0.236	0.438	0.691
Privatisation $[PRIV/Y]_t$	-0.982	-2.607	0.080
R^2	0.835		
Adjusted R^2	0.559		
F-statistic	3.031		
Significance (F-Statistic)	0.195		
D/W	2.729		

Note: All variables in logarithmic form; Dependent Variable: Private Investment $[PK/Y]_t$

The estimation also shows that a positive but statistically insignificant result is obtained for GDP which is in contrary to the outcomes of many developing countries where it has had a significant impact on the investment (Weeks, 2001). This result may be justified from the point that the country failed to stabilise the economic growth despite its moderate achievement on the growth rate over the privatisation period.

Theories of economic growth gives its own practical literature that economic growth is not simply an increase of productivity over a period, but it is concerned with the long run trend rise in output rather than its fluctuation (Pentecost, 2002). So, it can be said that a country cannot take advantage of investment if there has been instability despite a growth.

The result, moreover, indicates that savings is positive but insignificant. The result can be substantiated from the fact that the country has got the lowest record of savings, comparing to other SSA countries. In the same line, inflation and real interest rates are also insignificant on the investment. The insignificance of inflation may be attributed to the reason that the inflation was found to be low profile over the privatisation period, many private investors are assumed to have invested on those short-run and non-productive investments. In this case, for these people, the effect of inflation is considered insignificant and secondary. Real interest rate may be caused by the weak credit demand of the investors (World Bank, 2003b).

Table 15
OLS Result: Impact of Privatisation on FDI

Variable	*Coefficient*	*T-statistic*	*Significance*
Constant	2.353	1.287	0.289
GDP Growth$[y]_{t-1}$	-1.130	-6.923	0.006
Inflation$[p]_t$	0.271	1.339	0.273
Real Interest Rate$[r]_{t-1}$	0.645	3.352	0.044
Private Investment$[PK/Y]_t$	-0.256	-1.646	0.198
Privatisation$[PRIV/Y]_t$	-0.147	-0.894	0.437
R^2	0.974		
Adjusted R^2	0.931		
F-statistic	22.485		
Significance (F-Statistic)	0.014		
D/W	1.989		

Note: All variables in logarithmic form; Dependent Variable : FDI $[FDI/Y]_t$

The estimation of this equation in Table 5.15 indicates that privatisation is not an important element in the FDI decision. It reveals that the foreign investors never perceived privatisation as a signal indicating a general improvement in the investment climate in the country. The co-efficient is, as expected, negative and insignificant.

This result went contrary to Sadar (1995) who found privatisation significantly contributed to FDI in the developing countries. The model's explanatory power increases substantially with an R^2 of 0.974 compared to that of estimation on private investment (R^2 = 835). GDP is robustly negative with significant effect which sounds the foreigners concern over the economic growth of the county. Inflation is insignificant, resembling the estimation of private investment. Real interest is robustly positive with a significant effect which indicates its viability to attract FDI.

Table 16
Summary of OLS Modeling Results on Economic Issues

Variable	*Impact*	*Result*
GDP Growth	Insignificant & Positive	Not Rejected*
Budget Deficit	Insignificant & Positive	Not Rejected*
External Debt	Insignificant & Positive	Not Rejected*
Export and Import	Insignificant & Negative	Not Rejected*
Private Investment	Insignificant & Negative	Not Rejected**

FDI Insignificant & Negative Not Rejected*
Note: *Tested at 0.05 level **at 0.01 level

To conclude, the impact of privatisation on all the selected economic issues is fragile and insignificant. The aforementioned analyses failed to empirically support privatisation toward any single economic variable discussed and analysed for this study. Privatisation on investment in the constructed model appears to be somewhat sensitive (though insignificant), but is found negative. It can be said if analysed, the privatisation programme in the country achieved zero in convincing investors, particularly the foreign investors. However, the effects on debt directly or indirectly, capacity to repay the debt may not be underestimated.

It can be understood that privatisation alone cannot achieve the expected objectives set forth for it, but the whole economic reforms should facilitate the privatisation. Unfortunately, the economic reforms have not been implemented in all spheres of economic activities which posed a lot of obstacles to the privatisation programme's smooth sailing. What has so far been discussed is the result from one face of privatisation, and the second face is political which has also got issues to be confronted by privatisation in determining its overall success despite its less severity in the country. The forthcoming discussion, therefore, deals with the political issues of privatization.

POLITICAL ISSUES IN PRIVATISATION

Privatisation is adopted by the world economies for different reasons, particularly for economical and political depending upon their perspectives. The manifesto of privatisation in a country normally depicts why privatisation is? Many countries irrespective of their economic status have launched a privatisation programme with a different mixture of these reasons. There are many strong evidences that the developed countries have accelerated privatisation equally for economical and political purposes (Esser, 1998) and (Aharoni, 1988 and 1991), whereas in the developing countries, privatisation stands more for economical and the least for political, targeting only the economic growth (Donaldson and Wagle, 1995). Economies of transition are, however, a notable exception having a political reason at first with an objective of moving from a centrally planned communist system to a market economy (Selvam et al., 2005).

Ethiopia is one of the transition countries where privatisation as a strong reform measure confronted not only by economic issues, but also by political issues. While privatisation is adopted, the implementing country should be very cautious about the public opinion, trade unions' resistance, exertion of external pressure, foreign dominance (sovereignty) and distribution of ownership. These issues are considered as political issues vested in privatisation which need to be handled cautiously.

Against all odds, the issues such as public agitation and trade union's resistance in the form of strikes were not found against the privatisation programme of the country. The reasons could be attributed to a sense of non-interest and illiteracy of public towards major economic programmes of the country. As a result, the fortune came to privatisation implemented without any ill-opinion in the form of agitation or demonstration either from public or political parties which has widely been observed in many countries. In India, the opposition parties have repeatedly expressed outrage at the move to privatise—privatisation in India called as disinvestment, carries behind a political agenda—government stake in companies that were built at enormous cost over a long period (Frontline, 2003). Tagema (2002) reports that public opinion in Tanzania turned against privatisation programme in the country when the government attempted to privatise those strategic organizations in the country.

Resistance from labour unions was not observed against privatisation, but they showed a kind of resentment against retrenchment in connection with privatisation. The resistance was not at all a shock to privatisation in the country since these unions (labour confederations) serve as semi-governmental organisations with little collective bargaining. In this regard, unlike other African countries, the privatisation in the country confronted almost no resistance from public and trade unions. In South Africa, ideological and political opposition towards privatisation became an obstacle, limiting the methods, extent and pace of privatisation, particularly from trade unions on perceived threats to jobs (Economic Perspective, 2001).

The aforementioned political issues are, therefore, found less prone to privatisation in the country, but for the external pressures, foreign dominance and ownership distribution. These issues are considered important not only ideologically, but also their prevalence and application raise many questions to judge the success of privatisation. This section of the study assess these issues underlying privatisation in the country.

External Pressure Issues

Privatisation has been critically debated for more than two decades in the context of a measure forced by the West or the International Financial Institutions such as the World Bank and IMF. World Bank (1995) contains strong evidence for having privatisation as an important feature in the Bank's adjustment lending from the mid-1980s. This reflected both the concurrent ideological shift in favour of private ownership as well as the Bank's long, and painful experience with failed attempt in reforming PSUs.

Abu Shair (1997) states in his empirical literature that privatisation is an invention of the industrialised countries. Bayliss (2000) reveals in her study that the World Bank has played a key role in the implementation of privatisation in low-income countries attaching privatisation to aid disbursements and promoting a pro-privatisation culture. It is also widely observed that those economies, which are highly indebted, have been directed to adopt privatisation as one of the structural adjustment programme. Furthermore, in recent years, donors and multinational agencies have made privatisation a key conditionality. Indeed, more African countries undertook privatisation in an effort to assuage donor fears over domestic reform commitment than out of ideological or economic conviction (Mugerwa-Kayizzi, 2002).

The World Bank has keenly supported privatisation in Africa. As a result, Ethiopia, which is one amongst 42 (out of 52) African countries, started privatisation in 1994. The country is one of the highly indebted poor countries in the world which may leave room to go against the argument that privatisation in the country is by its own conviction. It can also be said that the country receives a substantial assistance and aid from the World Bank and other western donors for its poverty reduction programme. As result, knowingly or unknowingly, the country is obliged towards these externalities' conditions, particularly, the WB's private sector development (World Bank, 2004d) for poverty eradication—though it is highly criticised by the intellects—may link to the birth of privatisation in the country.

The analysis made in the earlier chapter of this study reveals that there was sufficient evidence on the weak financial performance and under capacity utilisation of PSUs. It is, therefore, understood that privatisation is not the sole outcome of those external pressures. However, the externalities (external pressures) on privatisation of the country may not be ruled out since there have been evidences about the country's high dependency on external loan and aid. Such financial problems in the county may be a force which cannot be easily underestimated as well. The extent of external pressures, in addition to general debt and aid, is determined with a parameter of structural adjustment loans (SAL), particularly offered by the World Bank. It should be mentioned that this SAL is meant for the whole structural adjustment programme of the country in which privatisation also shares its substantial account.

Table 17 discloses that the WB showed its highest interest in the country's privatisation programme. It is evidenced that in the first fiscal year of privatisation, the Bank sanctioned USD254 million towards the structural adjustment programme. Of which, around USD one million was spent only for studying feasibilities for implementing the privatisation programme in the country. Afterwards, there has not been any loan towards Structural Adjustment Programme (SAP) until 1999/00. This occurrence may be correlated with the political instability raised out of the War with Eritrea. It can also be interpreted that the Bank might have been disappointed of the pace of privatisation programme because the Bank imposed a pre-condition to have the programme completed almost by the fiscal year 2000/01.

Table 17
Structural Adjustment Loans from the World Bank

Year	*SAL (USD Million)*	*SAL/GDP*
1994/95	254.0	4.4
1995/96	nil	0
1996/97	nil	0
1997/98	nil	0
1998/99	nil	0
1999/00	nil	0
2000/01	144.7	1.79
2001/02	195.6	2.35
2002/03	132.8	2.00
2003/04	30.7	0.41
Annual Average	75.78	1.03

Source: World Bank (2004d) and MoFED (2004)

A simple analysis is made below to see whether there is a positive relation between privatisation and structural adjustment programme. The magnitude of the WB's SAL is calculated in the same manner as the privatisation indicator (i.e., the amount of the WB's SAL during the particular fiscal year is divided by the GDP of the same year). The main purpose of this analysis is to eliminate the chances of capturing privatisation variable by the SAL variable. It is because of the reason that the empirical analysis in this study supports that the country adopted privatisation as an initiative of the poor financial performance of PSUs rather than as an blind compulsion of the external agencies.

As it is expected in this study, there is no correlation found but an inverse trend (correlation co-efficient is -0.388) exist between privatisation and SAL variables (Figure 10) which may otherwise be concluded that no strong evidence is found on the outright pressure and motivation of the WB behind the country's privatisation. This result is also substantiated by the WB official that "*the WB does not use privatisation as a condition for supporting the GoE's development programmes or projects; what it does is encourage or help the GoE to privatise where it is useful to do so.....................*"

However, the WB's intention towards active privatisation cannot be covered up. It is found that after being disappointed upon the privatisation programme, the WB directed the loan 1999/00 towards other structural adjustment programme but privatisation. This result

Figure 10
Correlation between Privatisation and SAL

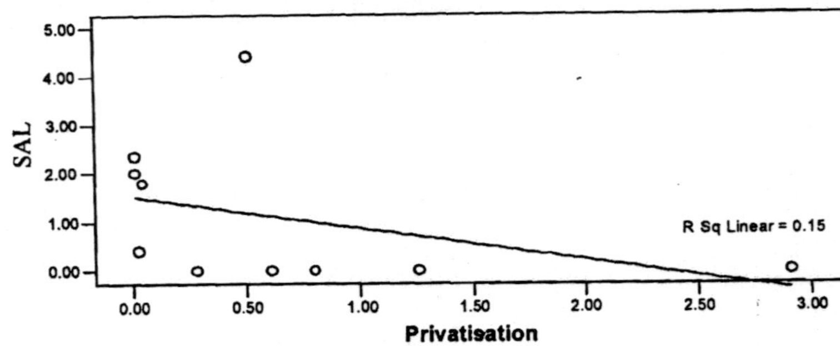

can supplement the argument that the dependency on the WB may cause a greater possibility of initiating a country to privatise, but the continuation of the privatisation programme depends on the success and the will of the country to continue it. The country was then with a huge PSUs share, but stagnated the privatisation to indicate that there was no hard and fast rule from the WB for the country to be an active privatiser.

Foreign Dominance Issues

The meaning of privatisation in practice depends on a nation's position in the world economy. In the wealthier countries, it is easy to treat privatisation purely as a question of domestic policy. But where the likely buyers are foreigners, as in the Third World, privatisation of PSUs often means denationalisation—a transfer of control to foreign investors or managers. Since the state ownership often originally came about in an act of national self-assertion, privatisation appears to be a retreat in the face of international pressure. The more dependent a nation is on foreign investment, the greater the likelihood that privatisation will raise the prospects of diminished sovereignty, and excite the passions of nationalism in Starr (1989).

The above mentioned literature cannot be taken for granted in the case of Ethiopia, where foreign dominance was found more prevalent. Table 18 shows the foreign dominance over the number of privatised enterprises which is categorized on sector wise. It indicates that foreign dominance was on a small number of enterprises, mounting on a few sectors.

Table 18
Foreign Dominance Sector Wise

Sector	*Domestic*	*Foreign*	*Total*
Hotel & Tourism	20 (95.24)	1 (4.76)	21 (100)
Food & Beverage	11 (50.00)	11 (50.00)	22 (100)
Retailing	128 (99.23)	1 (0.77)	129 (100)
Cement & Chemicals	3 (75.00)	1 (25.00)	4 (100)
Wood & Furniture	5 (100)	Nil (0.00)	5 (100)
Leathers	Nil (0.00)	3 (100)	3 (100)
Farm & Agriculture	19 (73.08)	7 (26.92)	26 (100)
Textiles	3 (100)	Nil (0.00)	3 (100)
Mining	Nil (0.00)	1 (100)	1 (100)
Pharmacy	5 (100)	Nil (0.00)	5 (100)
Others	1 (100)	Nil (0.00)	1 (100)
Total	195 (88.64)	25 (11.36)	11.36 (100)

Note: Figures in parentheses indicate percentages to totals.
Source: EPA (2004)

The study reveals that over the number of privatised enterprises, the foreign dominance occupies only 11.36 per cent. However, its target was observed on a few sectors such as mining, leathers, food and beverage, farm and agriculture and cement and chemicals. As far as mining and leather are concerned, it got 100 per cent since respectively one and three transactions were acquired by foreigners. The number of food and beverage industries was equally shared between foreigners and locals with 1:1 ratio. Farm and agriculture and cement and chemicals transacted for foreigners respectively for 26.92 per cent and 25.00 per cent. Hotel and retailing were the least to foreign dominance, followed by wood and furniture, textiles and pharmacy with no foreign purchase.

Table 19 shows the magnitude of foreign dominance over the sector wise privatisation and these sectors were relatively large sized ones with unaffordable indicative price by the domestic investors. The earlier analysis of foreign dominance over the number of privatisation is not correlating with its magnitude. Foreign dominance of 11.36 per cent over the number of transactions captured 75.08 per cent of the total value of privatisation. Mining sector alone, which was a huge indicative price gone to a foreigner, constituted 39.66 per cent in the total value of privatisation. Food and beverages and leather industries are also of same pattern with more indicative sale price which offered room only for the foreigners.

Table 19
Magnitude of Foreign Dominance

Sector	*Domestic*	*Foreign*	*Total*
Hotel & Tourism	3.84 (65.16)	1.34 (34.84)	5.18 (100)
Food & Beverage	16.30 (22.00)	57.76 (78.00)	74.06 (100)
Retailing	30.34 (99.40)	0.18 (0.60)	30.52 (100)
Cement & Chemicals	12.52 (83.61)	2.45 (16.39)	14.97 (100)
Wood & Furniture	8.83 (100)	nil (0.00)	8,83 (100)
Leathers	nil (0.00)	26.58 (100)	26.58 (100)
Farm & Agriculture	31.37 (32.45)	65.31 (67.55)	96.68 (100)
Textiles	4.16 (100)	nil (0.00)	4.16 (100)
Mining	nil (0.00)	172.00 (100)	172.00 (100)
Pharmacy	0.64 (100)	nil (0.00)	0.64 (100)
Others	0.08 (100)	nil (0.00)	0.08 (100)
Total	108.07 (24.92)	325.63 (75.08)	433.70 (100)

Note: Figures in parentheses indicates percentages to total column.
Source: EPA (2004)

While probing the foreign dominance, the dominance emerged not as a result of the most competitive manner. As it is revealed, the expensiveness of PSUs prevented many local investors from purchase which restricted these sales only to foreigners who are relatively with a higher financial capability. Moreover, the foreigners were much advantaged since their money bought the most profitable ones such as agro and farm, food and beverage and leather industries. In this regard, the local investors lost opportunities to keep their nation's most strategic and profitable ones except small retailing and hotel enterprises. Table 19 authenticates it that 99.4 per cent and 65.16 per cent of retailing and hotel enterprises were purchased by the local investors because of the advantage that they were not expensive ones.

The further probing reveals that the saving level in the country was one of the lowest in the world which recorded only 3.53 per cent to GDP over the study period (World Bank, 2004). This scenario may have worsened the situation which cut off many large sized PSUs, going into the hands of locals. The study made by Price Warehouse (2003) pinpoints that for the acquisition of then 114 enterprises intended to be privatised required between USD350 million and

USD700 million which was twice the total annual savings of Ethiopians. It shows nothing but it is very difficult for local investors to purchase. Unless, some arrangements are made, the forthcoming larger enterprises would continue beyond the financial capacity of local entrepreneurs.

Whatever be the causes, the foreign dominance is profound in the privatisation of the country. One cannot deny the fact that foreign investment drives an economy to grow as evidenced in many empirical studies. But there is enough evidence to indicate that it may solve the current economic crisis in the short run, whereas in the long run, it has the potential to lay down the foundation for the domination of the national economy by foreign capital, considering the present structural weaknesses of the country. Such a scenario is not only found in the country, but in the whole of the African region (Mujaju, 1990).

But there should always be a limit to have its dominance which needs to be well monitored despite this there is no nationalism or protectionism found in the country against the selling of PSUs to foreign investors. It is surprising to note that the country, which was never colonised before, was found to have no such anti-foreign attitude as it has been observed in other countries. The magnitude of such an attitude is articulated by Starr (1989:20-1),

> *"Throughout the world, the privatisation of strategic enterprises raises especially sensitive questions of sovereignty and security. In most oil producing companies, for example, no government is likely to try to privatise the stale oil companies because of the likely domestic political reactions. Even in Great Britain, the prospective sale of a helicopter company to an American company caused a political stir........................... Like national interests, the more parochial concerns of politically dominant racial and ethnic groups may also confound privatisation plans. In many countries, ethic minorities, such as Indians in East Africa, make up disproportionate numbers of the potential domestic buyers of public assets. When a country's bureaucratic and entrepreneurial classes differ in ethnic composition, privatisation may be understood as a transfer of wealth and power from one group to another and be politically resisted for that reason."*

This study also attempts to investigate the distribution of foreign dominance over various nationalities. It is done with a view to knowing the nature and extent of nationalities' distribution as a share of percentage over the foreign transactions of USD 325.63.

Figure 11 exemplifies that 91 per cent in the foreign share was dominated by Saudi nationalities through purchasing 23 large sized transactions. The second share goes to Yemenis who held 6 per cent of the foreign share with only one transaction. French, the only European, purchased a single transaction, holding 3 per cent in this value.

Figure 11
Distribution of Foreign Dominance over Nationalities

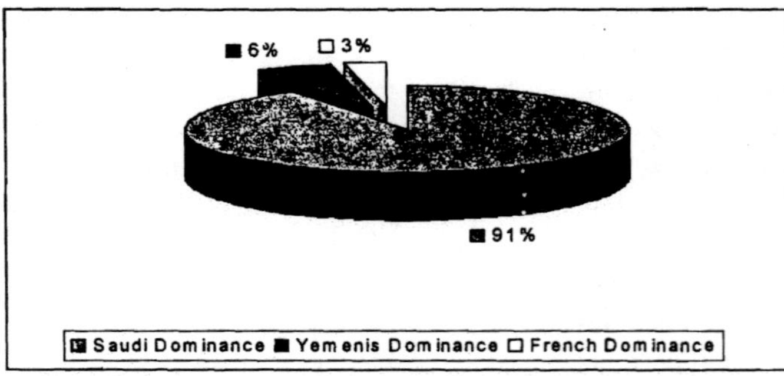

An additional probe into this foreign dominance reveals that in Saudi dominance, a single person held his share, accounting for 92.6 per cent—for 63.47 per cent in the total privatisation proceeds—, creating an impression among the public that privatisation in the country is nothing, but a single man show. Not only is his domination found in the privatisation, he shares as much as 69 per cent of all FDI in the country (World Bank, 2001) reports that this scenario of such single man's dominance cannot be taken for granted as it may cause a market imperfection ruled by a single market leader. Furthermore, such foreign dominance is considered the least political desirability.

The analysis, therefore, indicates that there is little wider distribution of foreign ownership over nationalities. This finding, however, reveals the distribution of foreign ownership, but unless, the overall ownership distribution is analysed, it is very difficult to conclude about the political agenda of privatisation which is to switch over from a centralized to a decentralised economy.

Ownership Distribution

Ethiopia, a transitional economy, has used privatisation for one of its political objectives of distributing the ownership of PSUs to the public. It is believed that such distribution enables the country to move logically towards a competitive perfect market. In addition to this, wide share ownership has important consequences in helping changes from a centralised to a decentralised economy. The wider ownership extends the stake in capitalism itself as well as in privatisation as a policy. Furthermore, it involves more people to understand the role of investment and profits, and there would be less likelihood to be deluded by false attacks on business.

In the privatisation programme of many countries, the wider share ownership distribution was included as one of the objectives for promoting people's capitalism (Cook, 1998). This political cum economic objective can be achieved only if many of the public get ownership through privatisation. The analysis in the previous chapter has already ruled out the possibility of extensive ownership distribution. It is because of the reason that the privatisation programme used sale of assets as a modality of sale for selling many of its PSUs. Sale of asset, if adopted, is difficult to bring a wider ownership unlike public offerings.

But it is unfortunate to observe that no public offering was made owing to the non-existence of stock market. It may be argued that the public offerings, particularly in LDC—though desirable politically—may be the hardest to achieve because of the state of the capital market in the country concerned. As a result, the only modality which may be able to accomplish the task are sales to corporate and to trade purchasers irrespective of its likeability.

Table 20 shows the ownership distribution against the number of transactions in the country. It also examines the ownership creation efficiency of privatisation which is arrived at by dividing the number of owners created by the number of transactions. This calculation indicates the efficiency of each privatisation transaction in creating the number of owners. It is understood that 1,579 new owners were created out of 220 transactions over the study period.

The analysis also reveals that in many fiscal years, the efficiency ratio was below one. It is because of the reason that many buyers were repeated ones in purchasing PSUs. The fiscal year 1995/96 shows the unprecedented highest owners creation ratio of 12.83 which came in as a result of 48 MEBO transactions. It is also found that over the study period, overall owners' creation efficiency ratio stood at 7.17.

Table 20
Ownership Creation Efficiency

Year	*No. of Privatisation*	*No. of Owners created**	*Ownership Creation Ratio*
1994/95	14	14	1.00
1995/96	116	1489**	12.83
1996/97	26	24	0.92
1997/98	9	5	0.55
1998/99	21	14	0.66
1999/00	16	14	0.87
2000/01	11	9	0.81
2001/02	1	2	2.00
2002/03	3	4	1.33
2003/04	3	3	1.00
Total	220	1578	7.17

Note: *includes single and corporate purchasers **transactions out of MEBO.
Source: EPA (2004).

The analysis and discussion on political issues show that the privatisation is not so successful in approaching political issues. As far as the external agencies' pressures are concerned, the study failed to find a strong evidence but the country's external indebtedness may not rule out these agencies' pressure exertion on the privatisation programme. Foreign dominance is found high and concentrated in a few hands which signals a negative climate toward market. Furthermore, privatisation has failed to create as much owners as possible among the public, owing to the non-existence of stock market. A lesser favourability of capital market is also a reason why it failed to create many owners in the country.

To conclude on the economic and political issues of privatisation, there are not robust empirical evidences in this study to prove that privatisation achieved what was actually expected for. The country even after privatisation remained in a poor state with instable growth rate, increasing budgetary deficit and relatively weak private capital accumulation. External debt burden was reduced, but no evidence was found owing to privatisation. External pressures were not openly found, but cannot be ruled out, owing to the higher indebtedness to them. Foreign dominance was enormously found, and at the worst, resting in a few hands. Owners creation was fragile, creating a confusion over moving from the centrally planned to the decentralised with popular capitalism.

NOTES

1. The Heavily Indebted Poor Countries (HIPC) debt initiative was proposed by the World Bank and IMF, and agreed to by governments around the work in the fall of 1996. It was the first comprehensive approach to reduce the external debt of the world's poorest, most heavily indebted countries, and represented and important step forward in placing debt relief within an overall framework of poverty reduction. While the initiative yielded significant early progress, multinational organization, bilateral creditors, HIPC governments and the civil society have been engaged in an intensive dialogue about the strengths and weaknesses of the programme. A major review in 1999 has resulted in a significant enhancement of the original framework, and has produced a HIPC initiative which is deeper, broader and faster (see African Development Indicators, World Bank (2002).
2. Terms of Trade refers to the measure or relative movement of export and import prices. This series, which is included in the study, is taken from the WB indicators. It is calculated as a ratio of a country's export unit values or prices to its import unit values or prices. It shows changes over a base year (1995) in the level of export unit values as a percentage of import unit values (World Bank, 2004:147).

REFERENCES

Abu Shair, O.J.A.R. (1997), *Privatisation and Development*. London: Mac Millan Press Ltd., pp. 86-7.

Agénor, P.R. and Montiel, P.J. (1999), *Macroeconomic Development*. New Jersey: Princeton University Press, pp.186-88.

Aharoni, Y. (1991), "On Measuring the Success of Privatisation", in Ramamurthi, R. and Vernon, R. (eds) *Privatisation and Control of State Owned Enterprises*, Washington, D.C.: World Bank, pp. 73-84.

Alesina, A. (1998), "The Political Economy of High and Low Growth", in Pleskovic, B. and Stiglitz L. Joseph (eds) *The Annual World Bank Conference on Development Economics 1997*, Washington, D.C.: World Bank, pp. 217-37.

Ambrosio, D.C. (1976), *Principles of Modern Investment.* Chicago: Science Research Associates, pp. 15-6.

Balema, A.A. (2003), *"Economic Development and Democracy in Ethiopia"*, PhD Thesis, Rotterdam, Erasmus University, pp. 322-45.

Barro, R. and X. Sala-i-Martin (1995), *Economic Growth.* New York: McGraw-Hill, pp. 1-49.

Baumol, J. W. and Blinder, A.S. (1997), *Macro Economics.* New York: Dryden Press, p. 28.

Bayliss, K. (2000), *"The World Bank and Privatisation: A Flawed Development Tool"*, November, London, Public Services International Research Unit, University of Greenwich, pp. 1-14.

Bräutigam, D. (1998), "Comment on What can Developing Countries Learn from East Asia's Economic Growth? by Takatoshi Ito", in Pleskovic, Boris and Stiglitz L. Joseph (eds) *The Annual World Bank Conference on Development Economics 1997*, Washington, D.C.: World Bank, pp. 201-6.

Carbaugh, R.J. (1995), *International Economics.* Ohio: South-Western College Publishing Co., pp. 472-75.

Cook, P. (1998), "Privatisation in the UK: Policy and Performance", in Parker, D. (ed) *Privatisation in the European Union: Theory and Policy Perspectives.* London: Routledge, p. 219.

EPA (2003), "Privatisation Proceeds", Dept. of Finance and Administration, Addis Ababa, EPA.

Diwan, I. (2004) *Interview with the Country Representative of the World Bank in Ethiopia*, Reporter, Vol. VIII, No. 399, pp. 14-5.

Economic Perspective (2001) "Focus Article: Privatisation in South Africa", Fourth Quarter, pp.1-7.

Eden, L. (1996) "Whither WIR?", *Transnational Corporation*, Vol. 5, No. 2, pp.145-55.

Esser, J. (1998), "Privatisation in Germany: Symbolism in the Social Market Economy?" in Parker, D. (ed), pp. 101-21.

Frontline (2003) "Disinvestment: Indian Oil Corporation Ltd. (IOCL), The Next in Line", Vol. 20, No. 21, pp. 125-6.

GoE (1998), "Privatisation of Public Enterprises Proclamation No. 146/ 1998", Federal Negarit Gazeta of the Federal Democratic Republic of Ethiopia, Addis Ababa, GoE, pp. 933-41.

Gómez-Ibáñez, J.A. and Meyer, J.R. (1993) *"Going Private: The International Experience with Transport Privatisation"*. Washington, D.C: The Brookings Institution, pp. 22-35.

Griffin, K. (2001), "Macroeconomic Reform and Employment: An Investment-led Strategy of Structural Adjustment in Sub-Saharan Africa" in Mclinely Terry (ed) *Macro Economic Policy, Growth and Poverty Reduction.* New York: Palgrave, pp. 16-45.

IFC/WB (2001), "Ethiopia: Foreign Investment Promotion Strategy Framework", World Bank, Washington, D.C., p. 16.

Lal, D. (2001), "International Capital Formation and Economic Development" in Scott, M. and Lal, D. (eds) *Public Policy and Economic Development: Essays in Honor of Ian Little.* Oxford: Larendon Press, pp. 231-73.

MoFED (2003a) Economic Indicators, Department of Policy Analysis, Addis Ababa, MoFED.

MoFED (2003b), Economic Indicators, Department of National Accounts, Addis Ababa, MoFED.

MoFED (2003c), "Annual Report on Macroeconomic Development in Ethiopia, September, Addis Ababa, MoFED.

MoFED (2004), "Annual Report on Macroeconomic Development in Ethiopia, 2003/04", September, Addis Ababa, MoFED, pp. 1-42.

Mugerwa-Kayizzi, S. (2002) *"Privatisation in Sub-Saharan Africa: On Factors Affecting Implementation",* Discussion Paper No. 2002/12, January, Helsinki, UN/WIDER (UN World Institute for Development Economics Research), pp. 1-21.

Mujaju, A. (1990) "A Public Sector without a Public Philosophy: The Case of Uganda" in Chole, E., Mlay, W. and Oyugi, W. (eds) *The Crisis of Development Strategies in Eastern Africa.* New Delhi: OSSERA, pp. 153-190.

NBE (2003) Annual Report, 2002/03, Addis Ababa, NBE.

NBE (2004) Annual Report, 2003/04, Addis Ababa, NBE.

Oyugi, W.O. (1990), "Privatisation in Africa: Promises and Prospects" in Chole, E, Mlay, W. & Oyugi, W.O (eds) *The Crisis of Development Strategies in Eastern Africa.* OSSERA(Organsiation for Social Science Research in Eastern Africa): New Delhi, pp. 188-90.

Pierre-Richard, A., Nihal, B. and Karine El, A. (2005), *"Roads out of Poverty? Assessing the Link between Aid, Public Investment, Growth and Privatisation",* Policy Research Working Paper 3490, Washington, D.C.: World Bank, pp.1-46.

Sadar, F (1997), *"Privatising Public Enterprises and Foreign Investment in Developing Countries, 1988-93",* Foreign Investment Advisory Service Occasional Paper 5, Washington, D.C., World Bank, pp. 1-45.

Sach, J. (2005). Interview with the Special Advisor to the Secretary General, UN, on Hard Talk, BBC World, Watched on 14th April, 2005, GMT 6.00 p.m.-6.30 p.m.

Selvam, J., Iyappan, T. and Rajan, M.S. (2005) *"Ethiopian Privatisation Paradigm and its Effect on Investment"*, A Paper Presented at the Third International Conference on Ethiopian Economy, June, 2-4, 2005, UNECA Centre, Addis Ababa.

Starr, P. (1989), *"The Meaning of Privatisation"*, Yale Law and Policy Review, Vol. 6, pp. 6-41.

Tagema, H. (2002), *"Who's for Privatisation"*, New African, July/August, No. 409, p. 17.

Thirwall, A.P. (2004), *Growth and Development: With Special Reference to Developing Economies*, London: Palgrave, pp. 561-93.

Tucker, I. B. (1997), *Macroeconomics for Today*, New York: West Publishing Co., p. 122 & 338-427.

Thobani, M. (1994), *"The Privatisation Experience of Latin America"*, Public Policy for the Private Sector, December, 1994, pp. 9-12.

UNDP (2003), "Human Development Report: Millennium Development Goal Indicators", New York, UNDP, p. 200.

Week, J. (2001), "Macroeconomic Policy for Growth with Reference to Africa South of the Sahara" in Mckinley, T. (ed) Macroeconomic Policy, Growth and Poverty Reduction. New York: Palgrave Publishers Ltd, p. 58.

World Bank (1995), "Structural and Sectoral Adjustment Lending: World Bank Experience (1980-1992)", Operation and Evaluation Department, Washington, D.C., World Bank, p. 56.

World Bank (2001), "Ethiopia: Foreign Investment Promotion Strategy Framework", Washington, D.C., World Bank, p. 8.

World Bank (2002a), African Development Indicators (Drawn from the World Bank Africa Data Base), Washington, D.C., World Bank.

World Bank (2002b), "Investment Climate Surveys in Ethiopia", Viewed on 12/03/05, *http://rru.worldbank.org/InvestmentClimate/Exploreeconomies/Snahshot.aspx?*

World Bank (2003a), "Global Development Finance: Striving for Stability in Development Finance (Summary and Country Table)", Washington, D.C., World Bank, p. 212.

World Bank (2003b), "Ethiopia: Letter of Intent, Memorandum of Economic and Financial Policies, and Technical Memorandum of Understanding", July, 22, Washington, D.C., World Bank, p. 2-10.

World Bank (2004a), African Development Indicators, Washington, D.C., World Bank.

World Bank (2004b), "Global Development Finance: Harnessing Cyclical Gains for Development (Summary and Country Table II)", Washington, D.C.: World Bank.

World Bank (2004c), "World Bank List of Economies", July, Washington, D.C., World Bank.

World Bank (2004d), "Structural Adjustment Credit: Private Sector Development", Washington, D.C., World Bank.

CHAPTER - 6

Socio-labour and Managerial Issues in Privatisation

The discussions and analyses in the previous chapter leave no significant empirical evidence in favour of privatisation toward the economic and political issues set for the privatisation programme of the country. However, the facts on many implications underlying the real economic growth of the country remain in question as long as the approaches of privatisation towards socio-labour issues are not attended by the study.

Privatisation, which is the logical corollary steps to free economy and enhancing competitiveness at macro and micro levels, involves complex social and labour issues. Hence, this chapter attempts to study those selected social and labours issues, revealing what impact privatisation brings forth in social and labour issues of the country. Moreover, this chapter discusses some of the managerial issues which are one of the direct objectives of privatisation. Managerial issues are those issues which are—unlike other issues of the study—micro issues found at those privatised enterprises. This chapter is divided into two sections. The first section deals with social and labour issues of the privatisation, and second section handles managerial issues of privatised enterprises.

SOCIAL ISSUES

Most of the macro economic policies of the government aim at economic, political and social objectives. However, many of these policies are evaluated only in terms of economic and political objectives, ignoring social ones. Many times, the impacts on these actors, importantly the public and the labour, have been underestimated despite the fact they are considered the ultimate beneficiaries of any policy. As a result, the evaluation of these policies fails to render a holistic and comprehensive feedback and result.

Empirical evidences indicate that privatisation is also one of the major economic policies expected to bring changes not only in economic and political scenario, but also in the social aspects of the country. In many developing countries, privatisation proceeds have been used for social sector development activities (Thobani,1994), and eventually improved social welfare (Aharoni,1991). In contrary, Jauch (2002) argues against privatisation, impinging even the existing social services offered to the poor. So, it is confusing to say assertively whether privatisation helps improve the welfare services of a country. Regarding Ethiopia, there has been a dearth of empirical evidences which examined the relation between privatisation and social issues. Hence, the forthcoming discussion section analyses the impact of the Ethiopian privatisation on social issues at first, followed by the labour issues. The social indicators selected for this analysis are GDP per capita, education, health, road construction, social welfare and poverty of the country in which the expenditure on education, health and social welfare are called as social infra-structure, whereas the expenditure on road construction is referred to economic infrastructure.

Privatisation and Income Per capita

GDP growth as discussed in the previous chapter may not reveal an accurate picture of the economic growth of the country as long as population growth is not inducted in the estimation. Although GDP rises, per capita GDP has remained constant or fallen because the population has grown just as rapidly or more quickly. So, it can be said that the actual economic growth lies not exactly in the rise of GDP, but lies more in the per capita GDP. The reason why per capita GDP is put under social issues in this study, is the right measure of people's well being. For this study, per capita GDP is substituted by per capita income (GNI per capita) for the accurate results.

It is believed that privatisation increases the nation's productivity capacity and so does per capita GDP. Table 1 shows about GDP, population growth and per capita income over the study period.

Table 1
GDP Growth, Population Growth and Per Capita Income

Year	*GDP Growth (In Percentage)*	*Population Growth (In Percentage)*	*Per capita Income (In USD)*
1994/95	6.1	5.47	110
1995/96	10.6	3.24	110
1996/97	5.2	2.6	100
1997/98	-1.2	2.54	100
1998/99	6.3	2.47	100
1999/00	5.4	2.13	100
2000/01	8.9	2.62	100
2001/02	2.7	2.28	100
2002/03	-3.7	2.3	90
2003/04	11.6	1.41	100
Annual Average	5.2	2.56	101

Source: World Bank (2004) and MoFED (2004).

Table 1 indicates the dynamics between GDP growth, population growth and per capita income over the study period. Although GDP grew at the rate of 5.2 per cent over the period, there was no improvement in uplifting per capita income, causing a standstill in the standard of living of people of the country. Contrary to what is expected from privatisation programme, per capita income stood only at USD101 which is considered one amongst the lowest per capita GDP recorded in the poorest countries in the World. What is more surprising is that the per capita income even declined from USD110 in 1994/95 to USD100 in 2003/04 despite the fact the population grew only at 2.56 per cent. Abu Shair (1997: 145) points out that in a country where annual average population growth rate is 3.5 per cent, GDP growth needs to be at least 5.0 per cent in order to maintain the people's standard of living. In the Ethiopian case, amidst convincible record of GDP and population growth, per capita income remains a haunting one which needs to be elaborately studied.

Coming to privatisation's effect on per capita income, a simple correlation analysis shows that there is no correlation (correlation coefficient is 0.143) between these two variables (Figure 1). This result is also substantiated from the fact that when privatisation fails to have a positive effect on GDP, nothing more could be expected on per capita income, ceteris paribus (correlation coefficient is -0.308,

Figure 1
Correlation between Privatisation and Per capita Income

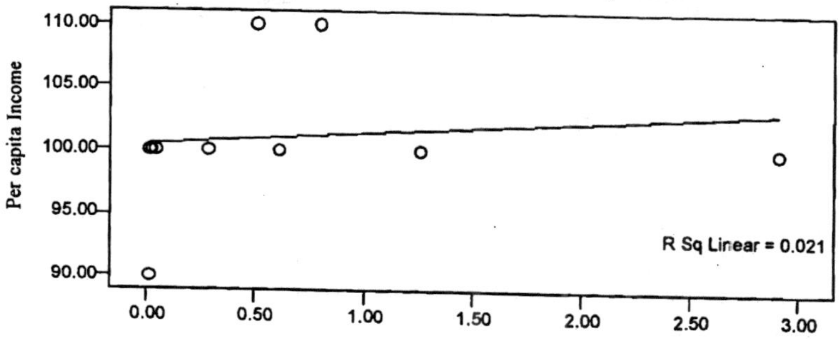

as seen in the previous chapter, between privatisation and GDP growth). This simple analysis confirms that privatisation may be insignificant to per capita income. Nonetheless, the advantage of slowness in increase of population, and substantial growth in industries and service sector may not be underestimated to picture out a different scenario if the relationship between privatisation and per capita income is thoroughly analysed.

Privatisation and Education

Education plays a key role in offering individuals with the knowledge skill and competencies to participate more effectively in society. A well educated and well trained population is important for the social and economic well being of countries and individuals. Technological advances and hence the rising skill needs of labour markets underscore the importance of continuous development of skill levels. The level of educational attainment in a population is an indicator of the stock of human capital (The Hindu, 2001: 20).

Ethiopia is the second most populous country in SSA, but with a 56.2 per cent of illiteracy among the adult population in 2003/04. As far as the education attainment is concerned, the country improved over the study period because the illiteracy stood at 71 and 64 per cents respectively in the fiscal years of 1990/91 and 1996/97 (World Bank, 2004). Other indicator of primary school gross enrollment ratio also improved from 37 per cent in 1994/95 to 64 per cent during the end of the study period, where as the pupil/teacher ratio increased from 38 to 55 over the study period, owing to the rapid number of students going to schools. But the number of schools was not increased proportionately. CSA statistical abstracts in 1999, 2002 and 2004 report that the number of government schools, which stood at 10,148 in 1994/95, rose to only 12,217 in 2003/04, where as the number of students admitted increased from 3.2 million to 8.7 million over the period.

As it is anticipated privatisation improves educational spending of a country, this study attempts to see whether there is any connectivity between privatisation and improvement in the education over the study period. Before investigating the relations between privatisation and education, Table 2 shows the details of education expenditure during the privatisation period. For the analysis, the magnitude of education is expressed in terms of expenditure in per cent of GDP.

Table 2
Spending on Education

Year	*Education Expenditure (USD Million)*	*Education/GDP (In Percentage)*
1994/95	19.65	0.34
1995/96	23.00	0.36
1996/97	25.40	0.38
1997/98	29.05	0.44
1998/99	24.51	0.35
1999/00	29.09	0.39
2000/01	29.29	0.36
2001/02	39.74	0.48
2002/03	49.73	0.75
2003/04	56.02	0.76
Annual Average	30.81	0.44

Source: GoE (1993), GoE (1994), GoE (1995), GoE (1996),GoE (1997), GoE (1998) and MoFED (2004)

Table 2 shows that the country improved its stand on education by increasing its expenditure share on education. The education expenditure increased from USD19.65 million in 1994/95 to USD56.02 million in 2003/04, recording an average spending of USD31 million over the study period. Spending on education relative to GDP gives a measure of how much a country invests in human capital. Education in per cent of GDP also rose over the period, climbing from 0.34 per cent to 0.76 per cent, accounting for an annual average of 44 per cent over the period. A simple correlation analysis reveals that there is insignificant negative correlation (correlation coefficient is -0.312) between privatisation and educational spending (Figure 2).

Figure 2
Correlation between Privatisation and Education Spending

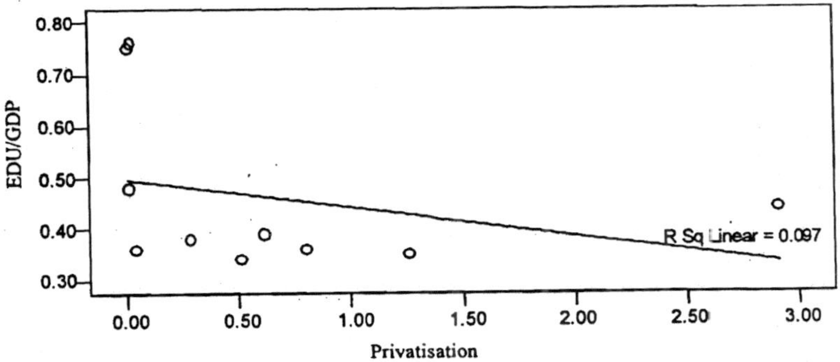

Privatisation and Health

The attainment of a healthier society depends on how much the government spends on health. Health coupled with education determines the quantity and quality of manpower available in a country. Health facilities in Ethiopia were in a bad condition since its national income could not afford to provide as much health facilities as possible to the public. Looking at the statistics of population per hospital bed rose from 4,141 in 1994/95 (World Bank, 1996) to 6,561 (CSA, 2004) in 2003/04. As of 2003/04, the country had 83 hospitals and 2,013 clinics, manned with only 1,301 doctors and 9,228 nurses.

Table 3 shows the health expenditure over the study period. It indicates that the health expenditure declined by almost half the amount over the period. In 1994/95, it recorded USD17.55 million, but reached at the end of the study period, only USD7.45 million despite an alarming increase of HIV/AIDS infections in the country. Unprecedently, the fiscal years 1996/97 and 1997/98 received relatively a huge share, but afterwards, it is found that there was a steep decline in the health expenditure.

Table 3
Spending on Health

Year	*Health Expenditure (USD Million)*	*Health/GDP (In Percentage)*
1994/95	17.55	0.30
1995/96	19.46	0.30
1996/97	88.33	1.31
1997/98	74.48	1.12
1998/99	13.21	0.19
1999/00	8.12	0.11
2000/01	10.74	0.13
2001/02	7.22	0.09
2002/03	8.03	0.12
2003/04	7.45	0.10
Annual Average	16.03	0.23

Source: GoE (1993), GoE (1994), GoE (1995), GoE (1996), GoE (1997), GoE (1998) and MoFED (2004)

A simple correlation analysis shows that there is a moderate correlation (correlation coefficient is 0.523) between privatisation and health expenditure (Figure 3), but the inference on this case may not be positively concluded since as per the analysis the health expenditure decreased rapidly over the period.

Figure 3
Correlation between Privatisation and Health Spending

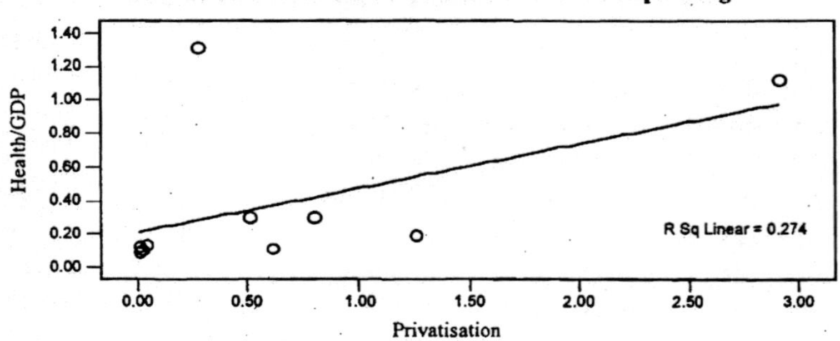

Privatisation and Road Construction (Rc) and Social Welfare (Sw)

In line with education and health, road construction and social welfare are the critical ones. Expenditure on road construction—one of the economic infra-structure—plays a vital role in the development of any country, particularly in alleviating poverty. Having more than 80 per cent of the population living in rural areas, the country has realised the importance of roads, connecting villages to main towns and capital cities. Roads not only bring people together, but also the rural commodities for their livelihood. Expenditure on social welfare determines the friendliness and concern of the government towards the society. Social welfare includes safety net programme for the labour, family planning programme and food security.

Table 4 shows the expenditure on road construction and social welfare activities over the study period. It pictures out that the expenditure on road construction increased rapidly, where as the spending on social welfare declined over the study period. The spending on road construction, which accounted for USD17.95 million in 1994/95, rose to USD140.83 millions in 2003/04, constituting an annual average of USD69.8 million over the period.

Table 4
Spending on Road Construction and Social Welfare

Year	*Road Construction (Rc) (USD Million)*	*Social Welfare (Sw) (USD Million)*	*Rc/GDP (in percentage)*	*Sw/GDP (in percentage)*
1994/95	17.95	17.27	0.31	0.30
1995/96	13.12	14.06	0.21	0.22
1996/97	15.34	67.69	0.23	1.01
1997/98	21.1	52.36	0.32	0.79
1998/99	77.68	0.03	1.10	0.0003
1999/00	79.25	0.20	1.06	0.0026
2000/01	94.32	0.06	1.16	0.0007
2001/02	116.53	nil	1.40	nil
2002/03	121.87	0.42	1.84	0.006
2003/04	140.83	1.26	1.90	0.017
Annual Average	69.8	17.03	0.71	0.031

Source: Source: GoE (1993), GoE (1994), GoE (1995), GoE (1996), GoE (1997),GoE (1998) and MoFED (2004)

It is also observed that Rc/GDP increased from 0.31 per cent to 1.90 per cent, establishing an annual average of 0.71 per cent over the study period. The reasons are not known for the reduction of social welfare spending, but the spending on road construction may have resulted in improving the well being of the people. Dercon (2002) also find that the market connectedness efforts through road infrastructure during the reform period improved the well-being of the people.

It is also drawn from Table 6.4 that the spending on social welfare declined from USD17.27 million in 1994/95 to USD1.27 million in 2003/04. The lowest spending was found at the aftermath of the war, particularly in the fiscal years 1998/99 and 2001/02. Spending on social welfare on an annual average stood at USD17.03 millions, accounting for 0.031 per cent in terms of GDP over the period.

A simple correlation analyses on the variables of road construction and social spending reveal that there is a negative correlation (correlation coefficient is -0.508) observed with road construction (Figure 4), whereas a positive relationship (correlation coefficient is 0.469) with social welfare spending (Figure 5). Both these results

Figure 4
Correlation between Privatisation and Road Construction Spending

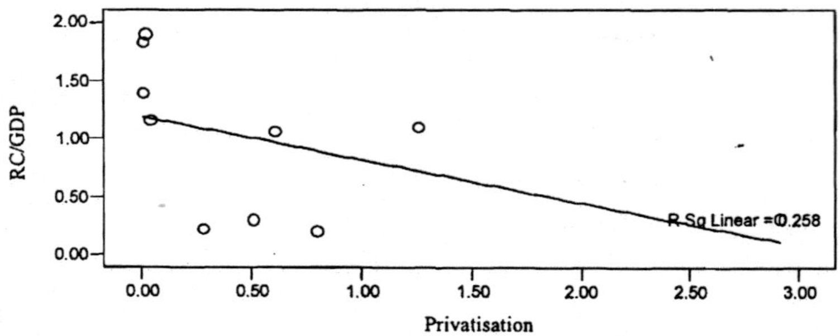

Figure 5
Correlation between Privatisation and Social Welfare

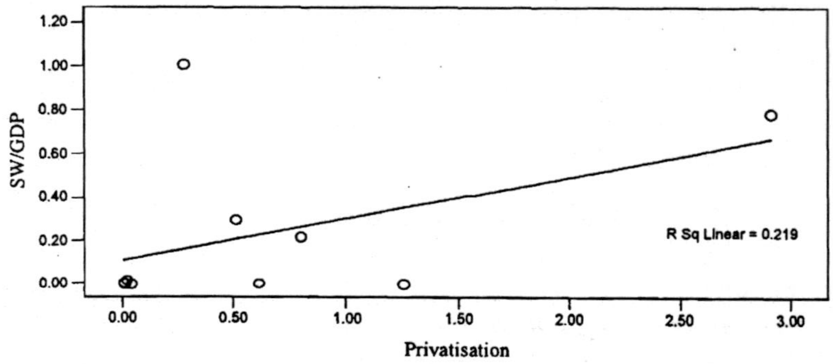

may also be interpreted in such a way that the direction of their magnitude counts a lot to determine their correlation. As it is already learned that the magnitude of privatisation shrunk over the period relates inversely with the spending on road construction which increased over the period, while directly relating with shrinking pattern of social welfare spending.

Privatisation and Poverty

Assessing the impact of privatisation in Ethiopia is much complicated, owing to the privatisation's objectives, complicated further by the priority given to poverty reduction. However, an attempt is made here to discuss the link between privatisation and poverty reduction. Having already discussed about the per capita income—revealing an annual average of USD101 per capita income over the study period, the country remained to be one of the poorest countries in the world. As a result, poverty reduction has become one of the major objectives behind the economic reforms and privatisation efforts in the country. The government committed to these reforms either by voluntarily or forcibly for poverty reduction within a framework of macro-economic stability because most of the policy framework of the World Bank links even privatisation with poverty eradication (World Bank, 2003).

While observed, during the initial period of implementation of privatisation programme, 45.5 per cent of the population was under absolute poverty, meaning unable to meet the minimum requirements for subsistence. In this rate of national poverty, the rural constituted 47.0 per cent, whereas the urban accounted for 33.3 per cent (MoFED, 2002). Looking at the UN definition of poverty, the population living below USD1 a day was 81 per cent in the same period which stagnated over the study period, showing no further improvement. However, the "absolute poverty" declined from 45.5 per cent in 1993/94 to 44.2 per cent in 2002/03, resulting in a decrease of rural poverty by 4.26 per cent.

In the line with poverty, the human development index which is the weighted average of five indices (UNDP, 2003:244)—life expectancy, education, population, GDP at market prices and GDP per capita index is a more comprehensive measure of the social status of the people. The country moved from the HRD index of 0.252 HRD (UNDP, 1998) in the fiscal year of 1994/95 to 0.359 in 2002/03, resulting in an increase of a marginal percentage point of 0.107. However, the rank remained 169th out of 174 countries taken into consideration.

As far as access to an improved water sources, 15 per cent of the rural population had access in 1994/95 which unfortunately declined to 12 per cent as 2002/03 (UNDP, 2003). This decline of facilities correlates with the observed decrease of the government expenditure on health and social welfare, particularly in rural areas. On the other hand, in urban areas, it was increased from 66 per cent to 81 per cent over the same period.

It can be said that the national poverty and HRD index were reduced but insignificantly over the study period. The rural showed the positive effect in which there is, however, no strong evidence to have linked with privatisation, owing to non-availability of time series data on poverty. Christiaensen et al. (2002), however, links this poverty reduction, through their international cross-sectional growth regression, with the macro economy policy improvement in the country. Whatever be the case, it is found that the facilities offered to the rural were found declining. If it were the case, the effect may no longer hold good.

It is unfortunate to see that the country over a decade with these economic reforms including privatisation has been unsuccessful in stimulating recovery. Weeks (2001) acknowledges that such failure was only rampant in SSA. It is because of the reason that these countries lack a growth-focused macroeconomic policy which is essential to a new policy consensus. The first step toward poverty reduction strategy is faster growth. No matter, how often it is asserted, deficit cutting, exchange rate liberalisation and high real interest rates do not cause a growth strategy. This is true in the case of Ethiopia where a lot of reforms were made towards these determinants. Inflation and interest rates were not so harmful, but no effect was found in poverty reduction. The problem in the country was that slow growth, with a lot of uncertainties. Unless the focus is showered on this aspect, the expected changes of these reform policies may not be imminent.

The above discussions on social issues reveal that the country remained in the same condition as far as the standard of living is living concerned and so is poverty. The data on per capita income and poverty proves this statement. It is also found that the government spent substantially on education and road construction to improve the quality of human stock, and enhance the market connectivity. However, the spending on health and social welfare was reduced over the study period against all odds that privatisation improves the expenditure on social over heads.

Empirical Analyses on Social Issues

The empirical analysis is conducted with a view to testify the above discussions and descriptive analyses. Five different econometric models given below are developed for the selected social issues which are expected to have drawn effects from privatisation. The models are designed in such a way to see the impacts of privatisation on the per capita income, and also in relation to spending on education, health, road construction and social welfare. The purpose is to see whether these variables capture any effect from privatisation.

Furthermore, these models are constructed, and expected to assume those results based on the perspectives of heterodox approach as it is carried out for economic issues. Any result obtained from this regression that exhibits a significant level of multi-collinearity (that is, a regression showing that a variance inflation factor (VIF) is greater than 10) is discarded from these results. Moreover, the results are adjusted for the presence of auto-correlation. Durbin-Watson is used to detect the autocorrelation and also the analysis is ensured that homoscedasticity is met.

Table 5 reports the results of impact of privatisation on social variables. The hypotheses are tested at 5 per cent significance level excepting the health variable which is tested at 1 per cent significance level.

The results in Table 5 indicate that privatisation contributed significantly to per capita income, confirming the side by side effects of a steady increase in industrial sector coupled with a slow growth of population. The model explanatory power is R^2 of 0.76. While such results always have to be interpreted rather carefully, the coefficient indicates that each per cent increase in privatisation provided an additional 63 cents in the per capita income of the country. Having much subsistence on agriculture, the country benefited out of growth in agriculture which in turn contributed positively to the

Table 5
OLS Results on Social Issues

Variable	*Coefficient*	*T-statistic*	*Significance*
Constant	4.635	90.798	0.000
GDP Growth$[y]_{t-1}$	0.442	2.480	0.056
Population $[POP]_t$	0.324	1.298	0.251
Privatisation $[PRIV/Y]_t$	0.587	3.359	0.02
R^2	0.865		
Adjusted R^2	0.784		
F-statistic	10.659		
Significance (F-statistic)	0.013		
D/W statistic	2.053		

Note: All the variables in the logarithmic form Dependent Variable: GYP

Variable	*Coefficient*	*T-statistic*	*Significance*
Constant	-0.698	-8.705	0.080
GDP Growth $[y]_{t-1}$	-0.69	-4.517	0.043
Privatisation $[PRIV/Y]_t$	-0.481	-3.151	0.018
R^2	0.868		
Adjusted R^2	0.825		
F-statistic	19.806		
Significance (F-statistic)	0.002		
D/W statistic	2.286		

Note: All the variables in the logarithmic form Dependent Variable: $[Edu/Y]_t$

Variable	*Coefficient*	*T-statistic*	*Significance*
Constant	-0.462	-0.692	0.515
GDP Growth $[y]_{t-1}$	-0.282	-0.887	0.409
Privatisation $[PRIV/Y]_t$	0.664	2.089	0.082
R^2	0.429		
Adjusted R^2	0.239		
F-statistic	2.258		
Significance (F-statistic)	0.186		
D/W statistic	1.541		

Note: All the variables in the logarithmic form Dependent Variable: $[H/Y]_t$

Variable	*Coefficient*	*T-statistic*	*Significance*
Constant	-0.696	-1.201	0.275
GDP Growth $[y]_{t-1}$	-0.112	-0.353	0.736
Privatisation $[PRIV/Y]_t$	-0.621	-1.96	0.098

Variable	*Coefficient*	*T-statistic*	*Significance*
R^2	0.433		
Adjusted R^2	0.243		
F-statistic	2.287		
Significance (F-statistic)	0.183		
D/W statistic	0.774		

Note: All the variables in the logarithmic form Dependent Variable: $[Rc/Y]_t$

Variable	*Coefficient*	*T-statistic*	*Significance*
Constant	-1.464	-0.519	0.623
GDP Growth $[y]_{t-1}$	-0.28	-0.693	0.514
Privatisation $[PRIV/Y]_t$	0.137	0.339	0.746
R^2	0.078		
Adjusted R^2	-0.229		
F-statistic	0.225		
Significance (F-statistic)	0.783		
D/W statistic	1.508		

Note: All the variables in the logarithmic form Dependent Variable: $[Sw/Y]_t$

per capita income and a slight improvement in the poverty incidence. Khan (2001) supplements that for poverty alleviation, the overall growth in per capita income should be consistent with a high growth of rural GDP. Privatisation is also found insignificantly positive for health expenditure. Whereas on education, privatisation is significant, but negatively contributed, while showing insignificant and fragile coefficients to road construction and social welfare.

Table 6
Summary of OLS Modeling Results on Social Issues

Variable	*Impact*	*Result*
Per Capita Income	Significant & Positive	Rejected*
Education	Significant & Negative	Rejected*
Health	Insignificant & Positive	Not Rejected**
Road Construction	Insignificant & Negative	Not Rejected*
Social Welfare	Insignificant & Positive	Not Rejected*

Note: *Tested at 0.05 significance level **Tested at 0.01 significance level.

The foregoing discussions and empirical analyses are given in Table 6 which exhibit that the approach of privatisation to social issues is mixed. The empirical analysis proves that privatisation is a significant element in per capita income of the country, revealing a surprising note of distinguishing effect of privatisation on GDP growth (proved insignificant in Chapter III), and on per capita income. These variables, sometimes, vary in their re-actions to one another, owing to their sectoral composition and growth. GDP growth may not contribute to the improvement of variables such as per capita income, living standard and poverty of the people if there are adverse distributional changes. However, recapitulating the significant effect of privatisation on agriculture, these variables seemed to be have behaved moderately in the country. Population is insignificant to the per capita income, revealing the unimportance of this variable in the country like Ethiopia where the population was not too large.

As far as social expenditures are concerned, privatisation contributed insignificantly to health expenditure, the same result of which was observed for the road construction and social welfare spending which are considered important elements in poverty reduction. Education received a negative sign from privatisation, indicating its negligible role in the nation's human capital development. Comparing to the results drawn from the economic issues, the above results on social issues are relatively better, but are far from satisfactory.

LABOUR ISSUES

Labour or employee issues are burning issues in privatisation. Unless, these issues are analysed to measure as to what the labour get out of privatisation: carrot or stick, it is somewhat difficult to evaluate the overall performance of privatisation in a country. The labour is the major stakeholders in the society because what they receive, the same the society receives. They are the integral part of the society, determining success or failure of any policy. As far as privatisation is concerned, the labourers have been debated regarding their fate.

Empirical evidences give different ideas about the approach of privatisation towards labour issues, substantiating their own view and findings which are in favour of and against privatisation. The assumption of what does privatisation mean for the labour in Ethiopia has, therefore, urged this part of the study to investigate the issues: communication about privatisation, labourers fear; wage and salary; incentives; work hours and work load; job security, favourability and adherence to labour laws and followed by, more importantly, the issues on employment (job retrenchment or job creation). The forthcoming analyses are made in such a way that it shows the labour conditions not only with overall privatisation, but also sheds light on these conditions between domestic and foreign enterprises after privatisation. Chi-square analysis tests are made, particularly to measure the magnitude of difference on treatment of these labour issues between domestic and foreign privatisation.

Awareness and Communication about Privatisation

Awareness and communication about privatisation are the major issues in the perspective of the labour. Awareness and communication are seen differently in this study. Awareness indicates the labourers' literacy and alertness in what is going on at enterprise as well as at national level. Although privatisation cannot be hidden, it may be possible in varying degrees, particularly in LDCs, at which many may not know their enterprises being privatised until they realise by any condition which they might not have confronted in the PSUs.

Communication about privatisation in this context refers to the organisation efforts in disseminating and discussing with the labours regarding the change of ownership. The labour have the right to information to learn the change of the legal form of enterprise where they have been working. The factor is very clear for this concern because it is learned that the change is not simply the legal form, but the change in ownership, contractual obligation, working conditions and life conditions. However, in many LDCs, the labour are kept away from informing and discussing their fate at the advent of privatising which is assumed to dilute resistance of labour unions. In the series of analysing these two issues, Table 7 reveals how much of awareness the labour got about their enterprises to be privatised.

Perusal of Table 7 reveals that a high majority (95 per cent) of the respondents (labourers), belonging to both the domestic and foreign enterprises, were well aware that their enterprises were going to be privatised. Although there is no vast disparity in terms of percentage between the labour of domestic and foreign enterprises on the awareness about privatisation proceeds, the highest (100 per cent) is found among the labour of domestic enterprises.

Table 7
Awareness on Privatisation

Privatised Enterprise	*Awareness*		*Total*
	Aware	*Unaware*	
Domestic	30 (100.00)	0 (0.00)	30 (100.00)
Foreign	84 (93.34)	06 (6.66)	90 (100.00)
Total	114 (95)	06 (5)	120 (100.00)

Note: Figures in parentheses indicate the percentages to row total.
χ^2 value is 2.106 which is not significant at 0.05 level.
Source: Primary data.

The result of the chi-square test also confirms that there is no significant difference on the awareness about privatisation among the labour working between domestic and foreign enterprises since the calculated chi-square value (χ^2 2.106), which is found insignificant. This shows that the labour, irrespective of the ownership of their enterprise, have a close look at the ownership changes taking place in their enterprise in the near future. Moreover, privatisation since 1994/95 fiscal year as well as reform policy since 1991/92 in the country was found to have spared sufficient time for the labour to be completely aware of their fate sooner or later.

Table 8
Communication about Privatisation

Privatised Enterprise	*Communication*		*Total*
	Communicative	*Non-Communicative*	
Domestic Privatised	24 (80)	06 (20)	30 (100)
Foreign Privatised Enterprises	61 (67.78)	29 (32.22)	90 (100)
Total	85 (70.83)	35 (29.17)	120 (100)

Note: Figures in parentheses indicate the percentages to row total.
χ^2 value is 1.625 which is insignificant at 0.05 level.
Source: Primary data.

The survey results in Table 8 finds that as much as 70.83 per cent of the respondents representing both the domestic and foreign enterprises were well informed about the privatisation proceeds of their enterprise. However, the percentage of respondents informed about the privatization is found more (80 per cent) in domestic enterprises than that of foreign enterprises. The Chi-square test reveals that there is no significant difference on this issue between domestic and foreign enterprises as the calculated χ^2 value 1.625 which is not significant.

It, therefore, indicates that both the domestic and foreign enterprises took effort in communicating the information about privatisation, revealing some efforts of the PSU in discussing the issues pertaining to privatisation with the labour and union. This result gives altogether a different signal that the privatisation in the country maintains a close contact with labour unions with no pretext of confronting a political dispute which is unlikely in many of the developing countries (Hoeven and Sziraczki, 1998: 13-4).

Labourers Fear towards Privatisation

The labour in general are scared of privatisation. There might be numerous reasons: first, the labour are basically injected by the labour confederations or unions in the sense that privatisation reduces their collective bargaining; second, there would be a possibility of mass retrenchment at the aftermath of privatisation if the privatised enterprise prefer down sizing of their labour force; third, their job security is assumed to be at stake as they are required to work at the most challenging situations unlike in PSUs and lastly, a kind of comfort—a kind of blind interest and liking towards PSUs which adopt, most of the times, a free-rein approach towards employees. These are the reasons why the labour community in general was in fear when it was heard of privatising their enterprise irrespective of what would actually happen after privatisation. Table 9 reveals this phenomenon.

The survey shows that a majority (60 per cent) of the respondents of both the domestic and foreign enterprises were afraid about the privatisation of their enterprise. This finding is substantiated by one of the managers, revealing in discussion that *"Workers were shocked at first when they heard that their enterprise is being sold"*. However, the percentage of respondents, who were afraid of the privatising their enterprise, is found more in domestic enterprises as compared to that of foreign enterprises. The result of the chi-square test also confirms that there is a significant difference in the level of fear among labours between domestic and foreign enterprises since the calculated chi-square value (χ^2*value*= 4.627) which lies in the rejection area.

Table 9
Privatisation Fear among the Labour

Privatised Enterprise	Privatisation Fear		*Total*
	Feared	*Not Feared*	
Domestic	23 (76.6)	07 (23.4)	30 (100)
Foreign	49 (54.4)	41 (45.6)	90 (100)
Total	72 (60.0)	48 (40.0)	120 (100)

Note: Figures in parentheses indicate the percentages to row total.
χ^2 value is 4.627 which is significant at 0.05 level.
Source: Primary data.

The result, therefore, indicates that labours working in domestic enterprises were highly afraid about the privatisation of their enterprise. The reason could be attributed to the on-going adverse labour conditions in many domestic private enterprises which were far from the satisfactory level of most of the labour. When these labourers were informed of their enterprises going to be privatised, they might have felt their conditions becoming worse. Hoeven and Sziraczki (1998:13) substantiate such fear that the labour in PSUs has conditions of service equal to or resembling those of civil servants, both in terms of job security and social protection and in terms of regulations relating to union membership and collective bargaining, whereas in the privatised enterprises all these conditions are marginal. Ratnam (1998) also agrees about the fear about privatisation concerning the potential loss of present and future jobs. But the case was different among employees who were transferred to the foreign privatised enterprise, owing to their existing better conditions in the country.

Wage, Salary and Incentives Systems

Privatisation usually entails restructuring and changes in the wage and salary structure and incentive system in the enterprise. It is well expected that private enterprises offer attractive salary as compared to PSUs since they attempt to enhance maximum efficiency and performance (Decenzo and Robbins, 2003) through exploiting the competitive market conditions. Table 10 shows the degree of changes in wage and salary structure in the privatised enterprises.

The survey finds that a single majority (44.17 per cent) of the respondents belonging to both the domestic and foreign enterprises realised more than 20 per cent change in their wage and salary which is the outcome of privatisation of their enterprises. Similarly, 29.17 per cent of the respondents realised between 10 and 20 per cent change in their wage and salary, followed by 13.33 per cent of respondents realised less than 10 per cent change. However, the percentage of respondents who realised the change in their wage and salary after privatisation of their enterprise is found more among the labour in the foreign enterprises than in the domestic enterprises.

Table 10
Magnitude of Change in the Wage and Salary Structure

Privatised Enterprises	*Magnitude of Change in Wage and Salary*				*Total*
	> than 20%	*10% to 20%*	*< than 10%*	*No Change*	
Domestic	09 (30.00)	04 (13.33)	01 (3.33)	16 (53.33)	30 (100.00)
Foreign	44 (48.88)	31 (34.45)	15 (16.67)	0 (0.00)	90 (100.00)
Total	53 (44.17)	35 (29.17)	16 (13.33)	16 (13.33)	120 (100.00)

Note: Figures in parentheses indicate the percentages to row total.
χ^2 value is 54.88 which is significant at 0.05 level.
Source: Primary data.

Furthermore, it is distressing to note that 53.33 per cent of the labour of domestic enterprises reveals that there is no change in their wage and salary structure after privatisation. The result of chi-square test also proves the significant difference prevailed between the labour of domestic and foreign enterprises on the issue of change in their wage and salary as the calculated χ^2 *value* 54.88 which is found lying in the rejection area.

Thus, it may be stated that the labour working in foreign enterprises have monetarily benefited out of privatisation which could be due to the strong financial base, affordability, volume of business, and also the replacement of existing labour by new ones. Whatever be the case, privatisation in the country resulted in an increase of previous pay structure as it is observed in the findings of other studies (Kühl, 1998; Redwood, 1990; Park, 1997). This finding substantiates why there was a lower level of fear among the labour when they were told about their PSUs to be sold to foreign investors. As against usual debating between private and public enterprises on salary issue, this finding initiates a new trend of debate within privatisation as to which type of privatisation benefits a lot to the labour.

Fixing a reasonable wage and salary does not mean the existence and guarantee of performance based incentives in an enterprise. Performance based incentives are otherwise called "payment by results". Private enterprises are famous for such kind of incentives with a view to stimulating employees to work hard. It is well known that in the presence of a good incentive plan, the labour are happier in their work; cooperation and loyalty are more pronounced, productive output is set up, and quality is better. Eventually, the committed labourers are expected to be rewarded in addition to the normal payroll salary or wage, unlike in PSUs where the labour are paid almost the same regardless of individual performance (Prokopenko, 1999: 281).

The survey results in Table 11 shows that a single majority (43.33) per cent of the respondents belonging to both the domestic and foreign enterprises agreed that they received performance based incentives after privatisation of their enterprise, where as 56.67 per cent of the respondents of these enterprises revealed that there was no performance based incentives after privatisation.

Table 11
Performance Based Incentives

Privatised Enterprise	*Performance-based Incentives*		*Total*
	Announced	*Not announced*	
Domestic	10 (33.33)	20 (67.67)	30 (100.00)
Foreign	42 (46.67)	48 (53.33)	90 (100.00)
Total	52 (43.33)	68 (56.67)	120 (100.00)

Note: Figures in parentheses indicate the percentages to row total.
χ^2 value is 1.627 which is insignificant at 0.05 level.
Source: Primary data.

Although the difference exists according to the survey, but owing to its insignificance, the result of chi-square test reveals no significant difference between the labours of domestic and foreign enterprise on the announcement performance based incentives since the calculated

χ^2 value 1.627 which is not significant even at 0.05 level. This indicates that these enterprises especially foreign enterprises did not take serious efforts in implementing performance based incentives despite showing up their interest in revising the wage and at salary structure of labours.

There are different types of incentive plans. The basic principle underlying incentive compensation is that an offer of additional money will motivate workers to work harder and more skillfully (Tripathy and Reddy, 2004). But question arises as to whether it actually motivates or not which in turn depends on the satisfaction of the labour. Hence, a survey among the labour who received incentives was conducted in order to know their satisfaction. The survey results are given in Table 12.

Table 12
Satisfaction of the Labour with Incentives

Privatised Enterprises	*Satisfaction of Labour*			*Total*
	Satisfied	*Not satisfied*	*Indifferent*	
Domestic	10 (100.00)	0 (0.00)	0 (0.00)	10 (100.00)
Foreign	22 (52.38)	11 (26.19)	09 (21.43)	42 (100.00)
Total	32 (61.54)	11 (21.15)	09 (17.31)	52 (100.00)

Note: Figures in parentheses indicate the percentages to row total.
χ^2 value is 7.68 which is significant at 0.05 level.
Source: Primary data.

The study reveals that cent per cent of the labour belonging to domestic enterprise were satisfied with the performance based incentives, whereas only 52.38 percentage of respondents representing foreign enterprise were satisfied with the newly announced incentive scheme. The result of chi-square test also confirms that there is a significant difference in the satisfaction of labour towards incentive schemes between domestic and foreign enterprises. There may be various reasons for the prevalence of dissatisfaction: first, the incentive schemes announced by the foreign enterprises may have many flaws—it may not reward as much as for their sacrifice and second, the labour would have developed a high level expectation which might be more than what they deserve. Such kind of abnormal expectations are common among the labour working in multi-national or transnational or foreign private enterprises.

Job Security

Job security is the most important motivating determinant in administering the labour. Among all job factors, the labour perceive a very high degree of fulfillment in respect of adequate salary and job security, owing to the situation, particularly in LDCs where the labour have not yet crossed the first two lower level needs, if viewed against Maslow's need hierarch theory (Tripathi and Reddy, 2004: 220).

Full employment has traditionally been a primary objective and a characteristic feature of the centrally planned economy. Privatisation is expected to reverse this. This is one of the reasons why the general public opinion is very skeptical about privatisation (Prokopenko, 1999:280). An attempt is made here to find out how the labour perceive their security in the new environment. The survey results pertaining to their perception of job security are given in Table 13.

Table 13
Job Security

Privatised Enterprise	*Job Security*		*Total*
	Ensured	*Not ensured*	
Domestic	15 (50.00)	15 (50.00)	30 (100.00)
Foreign	53 (58.88)	37 (41.12)	90 (100.00)
Total	68 (56.66)	52 (43.34)	120 (100.00)

Note: Figures in parentheses indicate the percentages to row total.
χ^2 value is 0.7 which is insignificant at 0.05 level.

Source: Primary data.

The study reveals that a majority (56.66 per cent) of the respondents of both the domestic and foreign enterprises perceived that their job security was highly ensured after privatisation. Whereas 43.34 per cent of the respondents perceived that their job security was not ensured after privatisation. Since the perceptional difference witnessed between the labour of domestic and foreign enterprises on the job security is marginal, the chi-square test does not rule out the null hypothesis, revealing no significant perceptional differences between the domestic and foreign enterprises' labour on the job security since the calculated χ^2 value 0.7 which is lesser than the critical value 3.841.

However, it can be said that the overall result threatens the job security of many employees working in the privatised enterprises. In the focus group discussion, one of the labour working in pharmacy stressed *"I don't welcome privatisation; you see the job security that I enjoyed previously is no more, but at a great stake. My owner may fire me at any time for his self-interest"*. The finding of this survey, coupled with the distress of the labour as revealed in the focus discussion prove Prokopenko's (1999) positive view about privatisation on job security, and contradicts against the study's finding (Park, 1998: 34) on privatisation's inclination towards job security. But at the same time, for privatisation ensuring job security, the government's effort in guaranteeing labour security in the wake of privatisation which is not overruled in his study.

Working Hours and Load

Privatisation restructures enterprises in terms of working hours and load. It is always said that private enterprises mount a lot of pressure to work hard which may, sometimes, go beyond the maximum physical abilities of a man. Such pressure and environment naturally deteriorate health of many employees. Table 14 shows the changes in the working hours and labour load after privatising their enterprises. The base from which the changes is effected is that the average number of hours over a period is not expected to exceed eight hours per day or forty eight hours per week (GoE, 2004).

As for change in work hours and work load, 46.7 per cent of the labour representing domestic and foreign enterprise opined that there was an increase in the working hours and work load after privatisation, where as 24.1 per cent of the labour of these enterprises opined that there was a reduction in the working hours and work load after privatisation. However, 29.2 per cent of the labour of these enterprises felt that there was no change in the working hours and work load after privatisation of their enterprise. Since there is a significant difference in terms of percentage between the labour of domestic and foreign enterprise on the increase of working hours and load, the result of chi-square test taking the latter rule of 0.01 significance level shows that there is a difference in the change of the working hours and work load of the labour between domestic and foreign enterprises. It can, therefore, be interpreted that the foreign enterprises attempted to draw the maximum work from the labour, utilising the man hours either completely or over time.

Table 14
Change in the Working Hours (WH) and Load (WL)

Privatised Enterprises	*Change in the working hoursand work load*			*Total*
	Increase in WH & WL	*Reduction in WH & WL*	*No change*	
Domestic	08 (26.66)	09 (30.00)	13 (43.54)	30 (100.00)
Foreign	48 (53.33)	20 (22.22)	22 (24.45)	90 (100.00)
Total	56 (46.7)	29 (24.1)	35 (29.2)	120 (100.00)

Note: Figures in parentheses indicate the percentages to row total.
χ^2 value is 5.97 which is insignificant at 0.05 level, but significant at 0.01 level.

Source: Primary data.

The finding of increase in the working hours and load in both enterprises can also be argued that it may attribute to the perception of the labour comparing to their previous environment. Many PSUs would not have utilised the man-hours completely, owing to their capacity utilisation problems. Whereas the decrease in the working hours and load might have caused to their preliminary restructuring which may take some time to bring the enterprise into normalcy.

Adherence to Labour Laws

Adherence to labour laws determines the degree at which the labour rights and employment conditions are protected. If there is a less adherence, the labour rights are at a great risk which damages the industrial relations and peace. The survey results in Table 15 portraits the degree of adherence of the enterprises after privatisation.

The survey finds that only 4 per cent of the respondents belonging both to the domestic and foreign enterprises opined that their enterprises adhered much to the provisions of labour law. Another 30 per cent of the respondents opined that their enterprises were somewhat better in the adherence to labour law. About 41 per cent of respondents strongly believed that their enterprises were disobedient in one way or the other to the labour law.

It should, however be noted that the percentage of respondents agreed to their enterprises' adherence to labour law, particularly with respect to change in the working hours, overtime and holidays which was found the highest in foreign enterprises as compared to that of domestic enterprises.

Table 15
Adherence to Labour Laws

Privatised Enterprise	*Adherence to Labour law*					*Total*
	A	*B*	*C*	*D*	*No Change*	
Domestic	02 (6.66)	0 (0.00)	13 (43.34)	05 (16.66)	10 (33.34)	30 (100.00)
Foreign	03 (3.33)	36 (40.00)	19 (21.11)	13 (14.45)	19 (21.11)	90 (100.00)
Total	05 (4.18)	36 (30)	32 (26.66)	18 (15.00)	29 (24.16)	120 (100.00)

Note: A-More adherence, B- Somewhat adherence, C-Less adherence, D-Not at all adherence Figures in parentheses indicate the percentages to row total. χ^2 value is 18.213 which is significant at 0.05 level.
Source: Primary data.

The result of chi-square test also confirms that there is a significant difference in the opinion of the labour between domestic and foreign enterprises pertaining to the adherence to the labour law since the calculated χ^2 value 18.213 which is statistically significant at 0.05 level. This indicates that the enforcement of labour law was insignificant to the extent that most of the privatised enterprises may violate the provisions in the labour law. Nonetheless, many foreign privatised enterprises were somewhat an exception, revealing the fact that the foreign employer is more obedient than the local employer to the law.

Keeping the major job factors in mind, a survey (Table 16) meant to ascertain the overall favourability of the labour reveals that a high majority, 31 per cent of the respondents agreed that their enterprises became very favourable after privatisation and the rest around 76 per cent of respondents said that their enterprises became somewhat favourable, giving a hint of their partial satisfaction on the work environment of the privatised enterprise. It is interesting to note that no labourer opined it was bad. This result on favourability owes much to the foreign privatised enterprises in which 100 per cent of the labour opinion ranged in the favourability area.

Table 16
Favourability towards the Labour

Privatised Enterprise	*Favourability*					*Total*
	Very Favourable	*Some what Favourable*	*Unfavourable*	*Bad*	*No Change*	
Domestic	08 (26.67)	15 (50.00)	04 (13.33)	0 (0.00)	03 (10.00)	30 (100.00)
Foreign	29 (32.22)	61 (67.78)	0 (0.00)	0 (0.00)	0 (0.00)	90 (100.00)
Total	37 (30.83)	76 (63.33)	04 (3.33)	0 (0.00)	03 (2.5)	120 (100.00)

Note: Figures in parentheses indicate the percentages to row total.
χ^2 value is 18.213 which is significant at 0.05 level.

Source: Primary data.

The result of χ^2 test also confirms the above interpretation that there is a significant perceptional difference between the labour of domestic and foreign enterprises since the calculated χ^2 value 23.09 which is found statistically significant. Thus, it may be stated that the foreign enterprises were labour-friendly enterprises which revealed their supremacy over the domestic enterprises.

Relationship between the Labours and Management

Relationship between labours and management is another issue which needs to be assessed in the wake of change of ownership. It is strongly believed that the labours' relationship with management which sometimes includes that with employer—if the employer manages the enterprise—has been noticeably improving after privatisation.

Perusal of Table 17 reveals that a majority (55.08 per cent) of the respondents of both the domestic and foreign enterprises viewed that their employers have been maintaining cordial relationship with them amidst change in the ownership. Whereas 38.15 per cent of the respondents viewed that there was no change in the relationship with their employer after privatisation. However, the percentage of respondents viewing a healthy relationship with their employers was found the highest (58.88 per cent) in foreign enterprise as compared to that of domestic enterprises.

Table 17
Relationship with Management

Privatised Enterprises	*Relationship with employer*			*Total*
	Healthy Relationship	*No Change*	*Worse*	
Domestic	12 (42.85)	10 (35.72)	06 (21.43)	38 (100.00)
Foreign	53 (58.88)	35 (38.88)	02 (2.24)	90 (100.00)
Total	65 (55.08)	45 (38.15)	08 (6.77)	118 (100.00)

Note: Figures in parentheses indicate the percentages to row total.
χ^2 value is 14.75 which is significant at 0.05 level.
Source: Primary data.

The analysis is substantiated by the result of chi-square test which reveals that there is a significant difference found on the views of the labourers regarding improvement of employer employee relationship between domestic and foreign enterprises as the calculated χ^2 value 14.75 which is statistically significant. Thus, it may be stated that employers of foreign enterprise have been creating a conducive work atmosphere by maintaining cordial relationship with their employees. Not only is this statistical analysis, a manager of one of the foreign privatised breweries during the focus group discussion for this study said, *"My relationship with the owner after privatisation has been as much smooth and transparent, and happy to find him to be easily approached*". Irrespective of the difference between the domestically and foreign owned, Sampson (1999) in his case study proves that post-privatisation brings improved changes in the employee and employer relations.

Privatisation and Employment

Privatisation as a policy is expected to generate employment within a country. It is believed that it generates employment in the short run, if not at least in the long run. Not necessarily deemed it as a major objective, but with other economic, political and social objectives, the country privatised more than 60 per cent of PSUs. But leaving employment issues uncared for may cause a kind of unrest in the whole society. It is well observed that there was no major agitation against privatisation, particularly for the cause of employment which does not mean that the society seldom bothers about privatisation.

The silence among the labour is not that they liked privatisation, but their weak bargaining, owing to the Unions' tie-up with the government.

Table 18
Employment by Sector

Sector	*Before Privatisation*	*After Privatisation*	*Employment in Number*	*Net Effect in Percentage*
Hotel and Tourism	187	152	-35	-18.7
Food and Beverages	6,690	5,750	-940	-14.05
Retailing	603	686	83	13.76
Cement & Chemicals	757	644	-113	-14.93
Wood and Furniture	858	696	-162	-18.9
Leathers	1,284	1,200	-84	-6.54
Farm and Agriculture	4,286	3,666	-620	-14.47
Mining	625	655	30	4.8
Textiles	3,880	4,213	333	8.58
Pharmacy	20	22	02	10.0
Total	19,190	17,684	-1,506	-7.56

Source: EPA (2002) and (EPA) 2004.

Table 18 shows the employment conditions of the privatised enterprises. The conditions on sectoral classification throw light on the positions of each and every sector whether they generated or reduced jobs over the study period. PSUs, which held 19,190 jobs just before privatisation, reduced their jobs to 17,684 after taking the legal form of private enterprise. Thus, privatisation in general reduced the jobs by 1,506 with a total job loss of 7.6 per cent over the study period.

Except retailing, mining, textiles and pharmacy, other sectors reduced their employment while privatising. Job losses by sectors are as follows: hotel and tourism by 18.7 per cent; food and beverages by 14.05 per cent; cement and chemicals by 14.93; wood and furniture by 18.9; leathers by 6.54 and farms and agriculture by 14.47 per cent (EPA, 2004). It is because of the reason that many privatised enterprises downsized their labour force in the name of structural adjustment which includes scale-down or closure of dormant plants. It is unfortunate to observe that these job losses were due from the sectors which are considered high potential to generate employment, particularly hotel and tourism, food and beverages, leather and farm and agriculture. These enterprises were found viable in the economy of the country.

The findings in Table 18 also signal a caution that their position on job creation may get worse unless and otherwise they expand their business vertically and horizontally. The government should also look into this net effect of employment which is harmful to the society in particular and the country in general. These job losses may be minimised at least in long run if government encourages these privatised enterprises through various business incentives such as free entry to expand or diversify their business, cutting tariffs and reducing the constraints in Exim (export and import).

Table 19
Employment by Ownership Origin: Domestic and Foreign

Classification of Privatisation	*Employment*		
	Newly Generated Jobs	*Retrenched Jobs*	*Net Employment*
Domestic Privatisation	248 (29)	689 (29.4)	-441(29.3)
Foreign Privatisation	595 (71)	1,660 (70.6)	-1,065 (70.7)
Total	843 (100)	2,349 (100)	-1,506 (100)

Note: Figures given in the parentheses indicates percentages to column total.
Source: EPA (2002) and EPA (2004).

Table 19 explains the above conditions in terms of domestic and foreign privatisation, that is, in terms of to whom either local or foreigner, PSU is sold out. It analyses the employment generation and losses from the view of ownership which helps this study to have a broader insight into this issue.

The inference in Table 19 reveals that the domestic privatisation created 248 new jobs, while retrenching 689 existing labours. Net employment result accounted for negative 441 jobs, constituting negative 29.3 per cent in the total job losses. It can also be interpreted that domestic privatisation got an equal share of about 29 per cent in the total creation as well as loss of jobs after privatisation. Foreign privatisation added 595 jobs while downsizing 1,660 jobs which accounted for 71 per cent of addition in the total jobs generated while recording the same per cent of downsizing in the total job losses.

Foreign privatisation created more new jobs comparing to domestic privatisation, but the severance of foreign privatisation in the total retrenchment overruled this minimum advantage. Out of 1,506 net job losses, the foreign privatisation constituted 71 per cent which shows their deliberation in scaling down the labour force. Two reasons may be said for this phenomenon: first, those newly created jobs were done to replace as much of unskilled labour, and second, the mechanisation and sophisticated production techniques might have substituted many existing jobs.

Although domestic privatisation performed less in new job creation, it relatively slowed down in retrenching the labour force. Controversial views might arise on this interpretation. One could argue that neither the intention to retain the existing labour nor the improved capability to retain as much labour as possible may be found among the domestic enterprises. The distinction may owe to the number of employees that the enterprises had during their privatisation. Looking at this point of view, the PSUs bought by the foreigners were large in size, presumably with the larger number of personnel. However, the damage done towards employment by the foreign privatisation was very high, owing to their inherent style of cost effectiveness through downsizing labour force.

Whatever be the case, the down sizing should not be out rightly seen as a bad-effect. Gebeyehu (2002) argues that maintaining an optimal combination of labour and capital through reducing the number of workers has a long-run societal benefit over and above its direct effect on improving efficiency of privatised enterprises. He also said that although measures taken by the foreign privatised enterprises might affect the well-being of some workers in the short-run, larger number of people would benefit from their spill-over effect of their efficient operation in the long run. Hoeven and Sziraczki (1998) say that privatisation usually involves immediate job losses since the introduction of more capital-intensive technique in a period of slow growth—a characteristic of the general setting in which privatisation many privatisation exercises take place—will lead to less demand for labour.

A thorough insight into the above discussed labour issues reveals two different results in terms of micro and macro aspects. Micro labour issues are issues raised among the labour retained in the privatised enterprises. These issues are very much internal as well as limited in their scope, requiring more of bargaining and negotiation, whereas macro issues are those issues concerned with employment generation and retrenchment which go somewhat outside the enterprises, affecting the society in particular and economy in general.

The foregoing results on micro results reveal a satisfactory approach of privatisation towards labour issues. The issues such as the right of labour to know their transfer to another legal form of enterprise, and communication with the labour and unions were well handled by privatisation. Fear towards privatisation as expected was highly prevalent among the labour, but it was surprisingly lower among them transferred to foreign enterprises.

Another interesting finding was that overall wage and salary structure and incentive plans were relatively improved, but contrarily, the labour in domestic enterprises was more satisfied as compared to the labour in foreign enterprises. Job security, the major job factor, was perceived to be uncertain since a little less than half the total number of labour felt themselves insecure in their jobs. As far as working hours and load are concerned, many viewed that there was an increase, particularly in the foreign enterprises. The study also reveals that there was less adherence to labour law, attributing to the failure in the enforcement, but the foreign enterprises were proved to be better ones, comparing to the domestic enterprises. However, it leaves a strong cautionary note for the government authorities to take necessary steps, if not things may become worse within a short period of time. The most important finding is that no single labourer viewed their post-privatised working conditions bad. Rather many deemed it favourable. And the finding on relationship with the employer was found to be encouraging which also holds privatisation better in the micro-labour issues.

The effects of privatisation on the macro issues are, however, negative since the labour was reduced by 7.56 per cent in the name of re-structuring. Had they not created job opportunities for 843 new labourers, the number of the labour would have been reduced by 12 per cent. It is haunting to note that the most potential sectors recorded a much higher downsizing which threatens the future employment potentialities of the Ethiopian manpower. In the total retrenchment, the enterprises that had gone to foreign buyers shared more than two-thirds, signaling their intensive structural adjustment despite they shared the higher share in new job creation. Hence, it can be concluded that the approach of privatisation on the issue of micro issues has been mixed, but the privatisation proved as much ineffective on macro issues putting the future employment in a big question.

MANAGERIAL ISSUES

New market oriented management practices naturally demand new managerial outcomes and styles which demand a complete organisational change. Of course, it is more difficult to change the managerial practices and outcomes which had been vested traditionally for a long time with the PSUs. Changes of the managerial issues in private companies are becoming more noticeable as PSUs move towards private ones. Changes in these issues are common when privatisation involves restructuring and changes in management and enterprise behaviour, all with far-reaching effects on productivity, profitability, liquidity, capacity utilisation, management philosophy, orientation and development of the labour, retention policy, work freedom, relationship with the labour. This section of the study deals with these issues to measure to what extent privatisation brought changes in the managerial outcomes and issues of the privatised enterprises.

The analysis on managerial issues attempts to gives more of micro insights into the enterprises which have been privatised. It is not a simple task to provide a crystal picture about the internal performance, particularly finance where most of the organisations were reluctant to show a fair and correct view of the financial affairs. Nonetheless, there are some observable effects for discussion. Table 20 serves this purpose with a view to investigate the performance of selected enterprises after privatisation.

Production growth in Table 20 shows that it declined by 14.21 per cent over the post privatisation period. There were many reasons which justified this reduction: first, while transferring, many privatised enterprises were vested with worn out machines, coupled with the shortage of raw materials. Shortage of raw materials is not a new problem over the post privatisation, but it has been a chronic worry to the industrial sector in the country; second, the restructuring took much of the time of the employer and management to spend time on improving production, third, the employees who were afraid may have resulted in the reduction of their productivity.

Table 20
Performance Variables

Performance Variables	*Pre-Privatisation*	*Post Privatisation*
Production	20.61	17.68
Sales	23.67	17.57
Liquidity	3.05	3.21
Net Profit Ratio	0.087	0.279
ROI	0.029	0.015
Capacity Utilisation	58.62	71.09
Fixed Assets per Person	0.012	0.009

Note: Production and Sales are given in the per cent of change.
Fixed Assets per Person is measured in USD Million.
Source: Post-Monitoring Department, EPA (2004).

Liquidity is measured only in terms of the current ratio. Current ratio shows the enterprises' ability to cover its current liabilities with current assets. Many financial statement users consider 2:1 to be an acceptable level; however some industries may require more or less (Edmonds et al., 2000). This rule is based on the logic that in a worse situation, even if the value of current assets becomes half, the enterprise will be able to meet its obligations. The analysis reveal that the liquidity increased from 3.05:1 in pre-privatisation period to 3.21:1 in the post privatisation period, representing an increase, and hence, a vast margin of safety for creditors. But such a ratio may not be considered a healthy symptom, indicating the poor management of stocks and investment opportunities in relation to current operational requirements. Furthermore, it may arise out of over accumulation of stocks, owing to the poor planning of production and sales activities.

Profitability is one of the major managerial issues which portraits the efficiency of the total management system. An efficient management system aims at improving the profitability of the enterprises. For the calculation of profitability, the profit after tax (EAIT) was taken into consideration. As it is perceived and experienced, the major purpose of privatisation, particularly at micro level is to increase the profitability. Table 6.20 shows also an interesting finding that profitability ratio was increased from 0.087 in pre-privatisation period to 0.279 in post privatisation period. This result goes much in favour of privatisation in the country irrespective other political issues raised against it. Gupta (2005) says that whether or not accepting privatisation is purely a political issue, but the most important thing in it that the PSUs after privatisation are profitable.

The privatised enterprises' profitability was observed to improve continuously after privatisation albeit some decline in the return on investment (ROI). The reason for such inverse relationship between profitability and return on investment may take place when the enterprise retains a substantial portion of profit as retained earnings for the development of business. The analysis over this result, therefore, indicates that the efficiency of the management was relatively improved because they might be able to use the existing machineries effectively with new methods. Furthermore, the increase of salaries of the retained employees as is found in the previous analysis would have also contributed to this improvement.

Capacity utilisation or technical efficiency improved from 58.62 in the pre-privatisation period to 71.09 per cent in the post privatisation period. The result is satisfactory because it was said to be one of the major reasons for implementing privatisation in the country. The increased capacity utilisation would have contributed to the increase of profitability over the post privatisation period. Nonetheless, the gap between the actual and optimum capacity was so wide as to be filled within a short period of time. One major causal factor might be the obsolescent or moribund nature of machinery and equipment which most privatised enterprises acquired during the transfer of ownership. The finding of this study contradicts with Gebeyehu (2000) who found the technical efficiency among the privatised enterprises declining. However, his suspicion as to whether the decline in technical efficiency in these enterprises had started before privatisation cannot be ruled out.

Fixed asset per person indicates the attitude of private enterprises which usually scale down the labour. Table 20 also reveals that the fixed assets per person reduced from 0.012 in pre-privatisation period to 0.009 in the post privatisation period, proving the labour reduction strategy which is already proved in the previous analysis.

Management Philosophy

Management philosophy is one of the managerial issues which determine the efficiency of an enterprise. It includes many derivations, but the most important component that offers is the style in which authority is executed. Execution of any task through authority is a careful task which needs a right philosophy for directing the people. There are different models recommended by various schools: Autocracy (more production oriented and dictatorship); democracy (consideration and support), and free-rein (consideration, support and lenient). No single method is considered to be the best one, but can be made to be the best considering the situation and type of labours. However, the labour prefers the management to follow either democratic or free-rein where they may have a lot of freedom and support. But the philosophy of autocracy is disliked by the labour since many may not like to work under high pressure and dictation.

The assumption behind this analysis is that the managers of PSUs are politically appointed which gives them enormous power, coupled with political influence. They obviously convert themselves sooner or later into authoritarian. While privatising, it is expected that private enterprises switch over from autocratic to democratic philosophy as they know well that it gets work done effectively. The application of free-rein is more lenient than democratic and cannot be applied in all situations and to all people. It, therefore, restricts its wider application. Table 21 shows the shift of management philosophy which indicates from which direction to which direction the privatised enterprises moved on.

The study finds that as low as 35 per cent of the respondents perceived that their enterprises, after privatisation, shifted its management philosophy from autocracy to democracy, and about 8 per cent of respondents viewed that the philosophy moved from autocracy to free-rein, revealing 43 per cent of the total move from autocracy to varied degree of democratic philosophies. Where as, 22.5 per cent of the respondents perceived that management of their enterprise shifted from democracy to autocracy.

Further, change in the management philosophy from autocracy to democracy was found high (56.67 per cent) in domestic enterprises, while democracy to autocracy was found high (26.67 per cent) in foreign enterprises. Similarly, shift in the management from autocracy to fee-reign was found only in foreign while democracy to free-reign was found comparatively higher in domestic enterprises. However, as low as 18.33 per cent of respondents perceived no shift in the management philosophy in either of the enterprises after privatisation.

Table 21
Shift in the Management Philosophy

Privatised Enterprises	*Shift in the Management Philosophy*					*Total*
	Autocracy to Democracy	*Democracy to Autocracy*	*Autocracy to free rein*	*Democracy to free rein*	*No Change*	
Domestic	17 (56.67)	03 (10.00)	0 (0.00)	09 (30.00)	02 (3.33)	30 (100.00)
Foreign	25 (27.78)	24 (26.67)	10 (8.33)	19 (15.83)	21 (23.33)	90 (100.00)
Total	42 (35.00)	27 (22.5)	10 (8.33)	19 (15.83)	22 (18.33)	120 (100.00)

Note: Figures in parentheses indicate the percentages to row total.
χ^2 value is 19.98 which is significant at 0.05 level.

Source: Primary data.

The result of the χ^2 test also reveals that there is a significant difference between domestic and foreign enterprise in the shift in the management philosophy since the calculated χ^2 value 19.98 which is higher than the critical value of 6.635. This indicates that some of the domestic and foreign enterprises changed their style of management from autocracy to democracy to ensure decentralization and delegation as well as participation. To pinpoint, the domestic enterprises were found largely exercising the expected philosophy of a varied degree of democracy as compared to the foreign enterprises. Nonetheless, the fact which cannot be denied is that as much 38 per cent perceived that their philosophy in their previous PSUs was nothing but either democratic or free-rein management philosophy.

Work Freedom

Management philosophy and work free are much correlated. If the management exercises more of democratic or free-rein management philosophy, it definitely leaves a lot of work freedom to the labours working in the organisation. Whenever the freedom is taken into consideration, it should be seen that it is not, at any point, lavishly offered with absolutely no control from the management. But at the same time, the lenient type of freedom style is also considered ineffective which may prevent the labour from the state of satisfaction.

Table 22 shows the perception of the labour towards how much of freedom they received from the management after privatisation. As it is expected on the management philosophy, the same effect is anticipated from this analysis which is nothing but that the private enterprises prefer the labour to work at a balanced freedom—lying between more freedom and less freedom.

Table 22
Work Freedom

	Work Freedom					*Total*
	More Freedom	*Moderate Freedom*	*Less Freedom*	*No Freedom*	*No Change*	
Domestic	01 (3.33)	17 (56.67)	03 (10.00)	06 (20.00)	03 (10.00)	30 (100.00)
Foreign	10 (11.11)	61 (67.78)	12 (13.33)	07 (7.78)	00 (0%)	90 (100.00)
Total	11 (9.17)	78 (65.00)	15 (12.5)	13 (10.83)	03 (2.5)	120 (100.00)

Note: Figures in parentheses indicate the percentages to row total.
χ^2 value is 13.28 which is significant at 0.05 level.
Source: Primary data.

The analysis reveals that a majority (65 per cent) of the respondents perceived work freedom moderately after privatisation of their enterprises. However, the percentage of respondents perceived work freedom moderately was found more among foreign enterprises than the domestic enterprises. It is also noticed that 30 per cent of the respondents belonging to domestic enterprises perceived that there was no freedom on their work after privatisation.

Further probe has been made through χ^2 test to find out perceptional differences between the labour of domestic and foreign enterprise on their work freedom. The result of the χ^2 test shows that there is a significant difference between the labour of domestic and foreign enterprises on their work freedom after privatisation since the calculated χ^2 value 13.3, which is found significant. Thus, it may be concluded that the labour belonging to foreign enterprises perceived better work freedom which reveals a strange result if the previous result is taken into consideration.

According to the expectation, the domestic enterprises which enjoyed the higher degree of democratic philosophy of management should have enjoyed relatively more work freedom. On the contrary, the foreign enterprises went upper hand in offering work freedom, disclosing a unique result of segregation between the management philosophy and work freedom. Therefore, it cannot be said that the presence of democratic management philosophy—seen variably by these two privatisations—ensures a high degree of work freedom.

Orientation and Training and Development

Orientation and training and development are considered the major managerial issues which are given different dimension after the market-led economy. Formally it was thought that the training of the labour was unnecessary on the ground that the new employee would gradually pick up all the particulars on the job. After the wake of market-led economy, the changes in production techniques and the functional areas of management are much faster and frequent. These changes urge the management to keep the labour updated to the changing complicated environment. It is also increasingly realised that the formal training is important not only for new recruits, but also for the existing employees. Training function, in fact including orientation and development, has become the corner stone of sound management.

In the line of analysis of this managerial issue, an attempt is made here to see at first whether the labour was properly oriented towards the new environment, and followed by the management policy on training and development. Two survey results given below help this study to bring out results on these two crucial managerial issues.

Orientation aims at gradually changing the attitudes of the labour from public oriented to business service so that they become the most dynamic business oriented people in the long run. Orientation in this context does not mean the orientation after their induction into the new situation, but is also considered a continuous process to the emergence of new things into the enterprise. Orientation normally depicts how alert and dynamic the management is for getting the labour ready for any new assignment. Moreover, orientation links deliberately the values, mission and new culture to the work of the time, in discussion with managers. Table 23 shows the style of management on orientation after privatisation.

Table 23
Orientation on New Environment and Changes

Privatised Enterprise	*Orientation on new environment and changes.*		*Total*
	Oriented	*Nor oriented*	
Domestic	16 (53.33)	14 (46.67)	30 (100.00)
Foreign	76 (84.44)	14 (15.56)	90 (100.00)
Total	92 (76.63)	28 (23.37)	120 (100.00)

Note: Figures in parentheses indicate the percentages to row total.
χ^2 value is 13.28 which is significant at 0.05 level.
Source: Primary data.

The survey reveals that a majority (76.63 per cent) of the respondents belonging to both the domestic and foreign enterprises were oriented towards the new environment after ownership change. It is further distressing to note that 46.67 per cent of the respondents belonging to domestic enterprises were not oriented towards new organisational environment and changes which is the resultant factor of ownership change. It is worth to mention that the percentage of respondents oriented towards new environment was found more in foreign enterprises than the domestic enterprises.

The result of chi-square test also proves this finding that there was a significant difference between domestic and foreign enterprises in providing orientation to their employees towards new environment since the calculated χ^2 value 12.17 which is statistically significant. This indicates that foreign enterprise took the lead in orienting their employees towards new environment after the ownership change. Fernando (1999:243) substantiates this finding that privatisation is a simple political issue but it has tremendous effects on the people who are required to do work in a totally new environment. The labour have to change from working as public service employees in a centrally planned enterprise to working as employees of business oriented enterprises where productivity and quality are necessary for survival.

The above analysis reveals that there was an expected positive change on orientation after privatisation, but the existence of the same attitude of management on training and development is a question. It is because of the reason that each and every training and development effort is considered complex and money and time consuming ones. However, many enterprises after privatisation committed to their organisational development strategy that will produce a workforce able to achieve the enterprises' objectives (Hinds, 1999). This strategy is being implemented through measures, particularly like training and development. In this regard, Table 24 explains how committed these privatised enterprises were on training and development after privatisation.

The result over analysis given in Table 24 finds that only 50 per cent of the respondents representing both the domestic and foreign enterprises imparted professional training and development after ownership change. However, the percentage of respondents that imparted professional training and development was found the highest (65.55 per cent) in foreign enterprises as compared to that of domestic enterprises. Further, 96.67 per cent of respondents belonging to domestic enterprises were not at all imparted professional training and development after ownership change which shows the lethargic tendency of the management.

Table 24
Training and Development

Privatised Enterprise	*Training and Development to the labour*		*Total*
	Imparted	*Not imparted*	
Domestic	01 (3.33)	29 (96.67)	30 (100.00)
Foreign	59 (65.55)	31 (34.45)	90 (100.00)
Total	60 (50.00)	60 (50.00)	120 (100.00)

Note: Figures in parentheses indicate the percentages to row total. χ^2 value is 34.82 which is significant at 0.05 level.
Source: Primary data.

Supplementing this, the result of chi-square test shows that there was a vast difference between the domestic and foreign enterprises on the training and development conduciveness. Thus it may be concluded that foreign enterprises, after privatisation, have been making sincere and modest attempts in imparting professional training and development to their labour in order to get acquaint themselves with the changing environment. Sampson (1999: 227) substantiates in his study that the enterprise after its privatisation era doubled its efforts in training and development. Nonetheless, the results on domestic enterprises were far from satisfactory as this study find little efforts on training and developing their employees.

Factor for Retention

Retention of the labour is an important issue in management. This issue becomes more critical when the labour enforcement is found stronger in a country. Nonetheless, in the privatised business environment, the prevalence of "the survival of the fittest" atmosphere is much common, and as a result, the factor of efficiency is given much preference despite restrictions on the reduction of workers from the labour laws. In Ethiopia, Article 29 furnishes a few conditions for the reduction of the labour, the violation of which may invite unnecessary problems to the enterprise (GoE, 2004: 2462). Table 25 shows the trend, revealing the privatised enterprises' approach in retaining the labour.

Table 25
Factor for Retention

Privatised Enterprises	*Retention of Employees*			*Total*
	Labour law	*Efficiency*	*Indifferent*	
Domestic	12 (41.37)	14 (48.27)	03 (10.36)	29 (100.00)
Foreign	17 (18.88)	59 (65.56)	14 (15.56)	90 (100.00)
Total	29 (24.36)	73 (61.34)	17 (14.36)	118 (100.00)

Note: Figures in parentheses indicate the percentages to row total.
χ^2 value is 6.02 which is significant at 0.05 level.
Source: Primary data.

The result of the survey statement shows that a majority (61.34 per cent) of the respondents viewed their efficiency and talent as a factor for their retention in the enterprises, while 24.36 per cent of the respondents viewed the labour law as a protecting factor for their retention in the enterprise. The percentage of respondents that viewed their efficiency and talent as a factor for their retention was found more in foreign enterprises whereas the percentage of respondents that viewed the labour law, as a factor for their retention was found more in domestic enterprises. The chi-square test with a significant computed value rejects the null hypothesis, and therefore strongly affirms that there was a significant difference between domestic and foreign enterprises on this issue. It is important to note that the foreign privatised enterprises as expected give more preference to efficiency rather than simply a retention of the labour, bothering labour law.

The foregoing analyses of the approach of privatisation towards managerial issues come up with a somewhat different result as compared to that towards economic, political and macro labour issues. Privatisation slowed down production and sales, but raised the over all net profitability of the privatised enterprises. The study affirms this result thanks to the improved technical efficiency, coupled with the adoption of newer production techniques and innovative system. Fixed assets per person were also declined, showing their restructuring deliberation on the size of the labour. However, the technical efficiency was yet to reach the desired level because one-forth of its utilisation remained unexploited. The study cautions the privatised enterprises to see that their production capacity would be used to a great extent, otherwise, the observed ROI might become worse in due course of time.

The analyses over the qualitative issues of management observed that there was a tremendous development after privatisation. The management shifted its administration philosophy to either democratic or free-rein, ensuring the professional approach of the privatised enterprises. Work freedom, opportunities for training and development and relationship with management was relatively improved. However, the retention of the labour by the management was found no more adhering to labour laws, but efficiency was deemed the most important factor for their retention. This observation signals a wider use of hire and fire policy which is going to be a new trend in the Ethiopian labour market. On all these managerial issues, the foreign privatised enterprises were observed as better-doers as compared to the domestic privatised enterprises.

To conclude this chapter, it may be stated that privatisation brought a mixed result. Privatisation contributed positively to per capita income in spite of which the condition remained unimproved. It may be said that if privatisation were not implemented, the per capita income would have become worse than it was. Poverty reduced but insignificantly with no strong evidences of attributing to privatisation. General employment declined as this study observed that there was a substantial reduction in a number of employees in the aftermath of privatisation. It is more pathetic to observe that these reductions resulted in the most potential and larger enterprises which have been expected to increase the employment opportunities. However, privatisation showed a new way of managing the labour as well as organisation, resulting in an increase of profitability. The labour benefited but the effect was much limited to a few people who were retained after privatisation. It can, therefore, be summed up that the empirical evidences do not support privatisation, contributed positively to the macro socio-labour issues, but the evidences are sufficient enough to support privatisation on the micro labour and managerial issues.

REFERENCES

Abu Shair, O.J.A.R. (1997), *Privatisation and Development.* London: Mac Millan Press Ltd., p. 145.

Aharoni, Y. (1991), "On Measuring the Success of Privatisation", in Ramamurthi, R. and Vernon, R. (eds) *Privatisation and Control of State Owned Enterprises,* Washington, D.C.: World Bank, pp. 73-84.

Christiaensen, L., Lionel, D. and Paternostro, S. (2002), *"Growth, Distribution, Poverty in Africa: Messages from the 1990s",* Washington, D.C.: World Bank, pp. 21-7.

CSA (1999) Ethiopia: Statistical Abstract 1998, April, 1999, Addis Ababa, CSA, pp. 336-340.

CSA (2002) Ethiopia: Statistical Abstract 2001, March, 2002, Addis Ababa, CSA, p. 338.

CSA (2004) Ethiopia: Statistical Abstract 2003, June 2004, Addis Ababa, CSA, pp. 338, 334 & 335.

Decenzo, A.D. and Robbins, P.S. (2003), *Personnel/Human Resource Management.* New Delhi: Prentice-Hall of India Pvt. Ltd., pp. 398-99.

Dercon, S. (2002), *"The Impact of Economic Reforms on Rural Households in Ethiopia: A Study from 1989 to 1995",* Poverty Dynamics in Africa Series, Washington, D.C.: World Bank.

Edmonds, T.P., Edmonds, D.C. and Tsay, Bor-Yi (2000), *Fundamentals Managerial Accounting Concepts.* Boston: Irwin McGraw-Hill, pp. 534-35.

EPA (2002), "Data on Post Privatisation Performance of PSUs", Post-Privatisation Monitoring Department, Addis Ababa, EPA.

Fernando, R.E. (1999), "Privatising Bus Transport in Sri Lanka" in Prokopenko, J. (ed.) *Management for Privatisation: Lessons from Industry and Public Services.* Geneva: ILO, p. 243.

Gebeyehu, W. (2000), "Has Privatisation Promoted Efficiency in Ethiopia?: A Comparative Analysis of Privatised Industries vis-a -vis State Owned and Other Private Industrial Establishments", *Ethiopian Journal of Economics,* Vol. 9, No. 2, pp. 109-133.

GoE (1994), "Negarit Gazeta of the Transitional Government of Ethiopia: Budget Proclamation No. 80/1993", Addis Ababa, GoE, p. 166.

GoE (1995), "Negarit Gazeta of the Transitional Government of Ethiopia: Budget Proclamation No. 108/1994", Addis Ababa, GoE, p. 84.

GoE (1996), "Negarit Gazeta of the Transitional Government of Ethiopia: Budget Proclamation No. 13/1995", Addis Ababa, GoE, p. 204.

GoE (1997), "Negarit Gazeta of the Transitional Government of Ethiopia: Budget Proclamation No. 46/1996", Addis Ababa, GoE, p. 575.

GoE (1998), "Negarit Gazeta of the Transitional Government of Ethiopia: Budget Proclamation No. 80/1997", Addis Ababa, GoE, p. 812.

GoE (1998), "Negarit Gazeta of the Transitional Government of Ethiopia: Labour Proclamation No. 377/2003", Addis Ababa, GoE, pp. 2462 & 2470.

Gupta, A.S. (2005), *In Conversation with Rajiv Mehrotra, Interview on DD News India,* Watched on 12th June, 2005, IST 11.30 a.m-12.00 noon.

Hebdon, R. (1995), "Contracting Out in New York State: The Story the Louder Report Chose Not to Tell", *Labour Studies Journal,* Spring, pp. 3-29.

Hinds, B. (1999), "Privatising Telecommunications in Guyana" in Prokopenko, J. (ed.) *Management for Privatisation: Lessons from Industry and Public Services.* Geneva: ILO, p. 199.

Hoeven, Rolph van der and Sziraczki, G. (1998), "Privatisation and Labour Issues" in Hoeven, Rolph van der and Sziraczki, G. (eds.) *Lessons from Privatisation: Labour Issues in Developing and Transitional Countries.* Geneva: ILO, p. 8.

Jauch, H. (2002), *"The Big Privatisation Debate: African Experiences",* 13th November, Namibia, Labour Resource and Research Institute, pp. 1-5.

Khan, A.R. (2001), "Macroeconomic Policies and Poverty: An Analysis of the Exerience in Ten Asian Countries", in McKinely, T. (ed.)

Macroeconomic Policy, Growth and Poverty Reducation. New York: Palgrave, pp. 147-8.

Kühl, J. (1998), "Privatisation and its Labour Market Effects in Eastern Germany" in Hoeven, Rolph van der and Sziraczki, G. (eds.), pp. 134-35.

Park, Young-Bum (1998) "Privatisation and Employment in the Republic of Korea", in Hoeven, Rolph van der and Sziraczki, G. (eds), pp. 34 & 44.

Pendletin, A. (1997), "What Impact has Privatisation had on Pay and Employment: A Review of the UK Experience", *Industrial Relations,* Vol. 53, No. 3, pp. 554-79.

Prokopenko, J. (1999), "Future Management Strategies", in Prokopenko, J. (ed), pp. 280-81.

Ratnam, V.C.S. (1998), "Adjustment and Privatisation in India", in Hoeven, Rolph van der and Sziraczki, G. (eds), p. 60.

Sampson, C.I. (1999), "Privatising Banking Services in Jamaica" in Prokopenko, J. (ed), pp. 226 & 27.

The Hindu (2001), "Fact File: OECD Social Indicators-Educational Attainment", 12th, November, p. 20.

Thobani, M. (1994), "The Privatisation Experience of Latin America: Sell-off Helps Fiscal Stability" *Public Policy for the Private Sector,* December, 1994, pp. 9-12.

Tripathi, P.C. and Reddy, P.N. (2004), *Principles of Management.* New Delhi: Tata McGraw-Hill Publishing Co., pp.187 & 220.

UNDP (1998), Human Development Report, 1998, Oxford: Oxford University Press, p. 130.

UNDP (2003), *"Human Development Report: Millennium Development Goal Indicators"*, New York: UNDP, pp.199-25, 244.

Week, J. (2001), "Macroeconomic Policy for Growth with Reference to Africa South of the Sahara" in Mckinley, T. (ed.) Macroeconomic Policy, Growth and Poverty Reduction. New York: Palgrave Publishers Ltd., pp. 46-79.

Word Bank (2003), "Ethiopia: Letter of Intent, Memorandum of Economic and Financial Policies, and Technical Memorandum of Understanding", July, 2003, Washington, D.C.: World Bank, pp. 1-2.

World Bank (2004), "Ethiopia: Relations with the World Bank", January, 2004, Report No. 27753, Washington, D.C.: World Bank, pp. 1-5.

CHAPTER - 7

Findings, Conclusion and Suggestions

From the discussions and empirical analyses of the emergence of the Ethiopian economic reforms and privatisation (chapter III), processing issues and mechanisms (chapter IV), economic and political issues (chapter V) and socio-labour and managerial issues (chapter VI), this study furnishes following summary of findings, hypotheses testing, conclusion, suggestions and scope for further study. The findings are furnished in such a way to show that the objectives set forth for this study are hereby accomplished.

FINDINGS

Emergence of Economic Reforms and Privatisation

Economic Background and Emergence of Economic Reforms: Ethiopia is the third most populous country in Africa, and 9th in terms of geographical area in the whole of Africa. As far as the economic status is concerned, Ethiopia remained the poorest country with per capita income of USD100. The economic system during the Imperial government was a mixed economy, followed by the Derg Regime that adopted the system of socialism. The government that came after the Derg Regime, adopted again a mixed economy, but highly directed towards market led economy. It is so unique to find that these three changes in the economic system occurred within the past three decades.

Ethiopia was perhaps the first African country to prepare a comprehensive plan with "The First Five Year Development Plan

1957-61". Before the Derg Regime came into power, the three five-year plans were implemented which achieved annual growth rate of 3.2 per cent, 4.6 per cent and 4.0 per cent respectively.

The pattern of the economy moved from more or less outward economy to a rigid socialism during the Derg Regime which is otherwise called a Marxist Military government. Having ruled for 17 years between 1974/75-1990/91, the regime slowed down the growth rate of GDP to 1.9 per cent, falling considerably short of the population growth which recorded then 2.7 per cent. Furthermore the per capita income declined by 0.8 per cent, deteriorating the standard of living of the average Ethiopian. Hence, the dismaying state brought by the Derg Regime necessitated the successor to adopt economic reforms in 1991 for the recovery of economy.

The implementation of economic reforms on finance and trade brought money devaluation by 58.6 per cent in USD terms, reforms on export and imports particularly reduction of import tariff by 10 per cent, elimination of retail price control on fertilizer, entry of forex bureaus in commercial banks, foreign exchange retention, and liberalisation of interest rates. The trade sector was more advantages as the average import tariff rate was lowered by 3 per cent (the average import tariff rate was lowered from 24.5 per cent to 21.5 per cent) while the maximum tariff rate remained at 50 per cent. New enactments were made on investment, labours, and private sector development. The most important reform was that of the establishment of Ethiopian Privatisation agency 1994 which was meant to facilitate privatisation of the public sector undertakings.

Precedence to the study of the impact of privatisation, an analysis is made to review the performance of economic reforms. The study finds that the economic indicator during the post reform period was satisfactory as compared to the pre reform period. Agriculture and industrial output grew at the rate of 2.78 per cent and 7.3 per cent respectively which, in turn, raised GDP to 5.7 per cent as compared to 1.7 per cent in the pre-reform period. However, GDP and their component growth rates were found unstable with a higher degree of variation.

It is also found that during the reform period, inflation and consumer price index (CPI) were found normal but they too inflated highly in some of the fiscal years of post reform period. GNI per capita remained lower because it recorded only USD103 in the reform period. Budgetary, trade and current account balances were increased respectively from negative 10.96 per cent, 16.37 per cent, and 10.2 per cent to negative 15.3 per cent, 25.54 per cent, 13 per cent. However, indicators on export and gross private investment were found satisfactory as compared to pre privatisation. FDI grew insignificantly at an annual average rate of 0.27 per cent. The findings show that no satisfactory result was found on poverty and income inequality.

OLS model, which is applied to examine the impact of economic reforms on economic growth, reveals the positive growth of agricultural and industrial out put. The capital is positive but insignificant. However, the OLS model result surprisingly exhibits that the economic reforms played a negative role in the economic growth of the country, owing to its slowness and incompleteness in nature.

The institutional framework of PSUs operated during the imperial government was a free enterprise system with an open policy. The role of government was then mainly to encourage potential investors from within and outside the country to commit resources in industrial development. The PSUs showed faster growth and expansion. But under the Derg Regime these PSUs identified as basic industries, industries that produced essential goods, drugs, medicine, tobacco and beverages were nationalised through their socialistic economic policy.

It is found that during the Derg Regime the expansion of public ownership proved to be a failure, owing to mismanagement, over staffing, inappropriate investment, poor coverage and quality of services, high debt and physical losses and increased corruption. The other important reason for the failure of the public ownership was that many of the nationalised enterprises became obsolete to run and their number showed a declining trend.

The causal analysis made in this study exhibits no strong justification in retaining the PSU with the government. The analysis proved that production, profitability, liquidity, capacity utilisation, external debt of PSUs and other macro economic indicators such as budgetary deficit and external debt in general caused a major reason for privatisation. However, the study does not reject the role of external agencies behind the privatisation programme in the country.

For the reasons as proved in the causal analysis, privatisation was inducted as one among those economic reforms in 1994, targeting not only for alleviating the problems vested with PSUs, but also for other macro economic objectives such as reduction of alarming budget deficit and external debt, injection of openness and development of private sectors at macro level. The objectives for Ethiopian privatisation is found as same as that for privatisation in other LDCs.

Processing Mechanisms and Issues in Privatisation

Business Environment and Legal and Regulatory Framework Issues: Market condition, financial sector and conditions for export development improved significantly during the privatisation period. However, the imperfection and inadequate competition in the market existed. Availability of highly skilled human capital to match with an increase of technology was found to be questionable. Legal and regulatory issues, particularly the judiciary system, land tenure system, commercial framework, tax system, intellectual property rights, patent and copyright laws in the country was found unsatisfactory for the faster development of private sector.

Issues on the Privatisation Legal Framework: To carry out the privatisation, the Agency (EPA) was established in February 1994. The findings question the independence and autonomy of the Agency since the Agency was made directly accountable to the Prime Minister Office in all matters. Furthermore, the proclamation, which guides the Agency and privatisation programme, came late into operation in 1998, and hence ran the first phase of programme haphazardly.

Transformation Issues: Privatisation was carried out, using the case by case approach. There were three major steps found in the whole process of privatisation: first, pre-privatisation phasing that includes identification and sequencing of PSUs candidates and preparation of PSUs through restructuring and valuation. Second, privatisation implementation that consists of bidding and tendering, assessment and selection of bidders, selection of modalities and sale. Third, post privatisation phasing that is to carry out the monitoring of the privatised enterprises.

While selecting the candidates, the most strategic and viable candidates were retained with the state control and the rest, which included a few potentially viable, have been slated and sold to buyers.

It is found that Ethiopia followed bottom-top approach by privatising the small ones initially. Out of 124 enterprises privatised during the initial period of privatisation, 102 were small and petty enterprises. The sequencing was made not only based on the size of enterprise, but also to some extent based on their profitability. However, there were a few transactions in the initial period of privatisation gone on demand side.

The study finds that the Agency carried out two types of valuation: Asset valuation and Business valuation. Valuation was carried out with the clear cut guidelines. For the sake of confidentiality and to ensure a fair sale, the business valuation was not disclosed to the enterprise. It is also found that after re-structuring and valuation, the enterprises were transformed into a new share company—otherwise called as corporatisation—using internationally accepted methodologies. Nonetheless, the study affirms that the privatisation processing failed to look into the macro-economic conditions, particularly the fluctuations in the inflation and exchange during the valuation process.

The findings on tender convertibility shows that most of the enterprises were sold out in the first tender attempt itself and rest was gone even up to fourth attempt of tender. The study also finds that the higher indicative price was the major reason for the failure in converting these tenders into sale actions within one or two attempts of tender. The bidders were weighed in terms of three criteria. Price offered, business plan and technical and managerial expertise which shared the weight of 70 per cent, 20 per cent and 10 per cent respectively. These evaluation criteria were found as much same as internationally accepted ones.

As far as the response to privatisation, the study finds that the average number of the bidders to the slated enterprises was 1.79, indicating less than two bidders responded to each sale offer. No sector attracted more than three bidders for offering for each sale except a sale for mining. Buyers' response over the study period was found far from satisfactory.

Regarding the modalities, most of sale was performed in the country through the asset sale (73.18 per cent), and followed by MEBO (20.45). Restitution that occurred in a political change accounted for 6 per cent in the total number of transactions. The study also finds that there was one transaction each on joint venture and lease respectively. It is interesting to note that under asset sale modality, 124 transactions were made on a full sale, where as 33 transactions were done on a partial sale.

Size and Speed Issues: The size of privatisation in the country was very small. A sale over two hundred and twenty enterprises contributed only USD433.7 million to the country's exchequer. Regarding the phase of privatisation, the first phase (1994/95-1998/99) was considered lucrative, collecting 88 per cent of the total privatisation proceeds, whereas the second phase (1999/00-2003/04) showed the poorest performance. For this poor performance, the study finds reason not only in the weak business environment and legal framework, but also in the war broken out with Eritrea in 1998.

Retailing business dominated in the number of privatisation transaction which constituted 58.64 per cent in the total number of transactions, but contributed a meagre of 7.06 per cent in the total proceeds collected over the study period. Next to retailing, the farm and agriculture constituted 26 in the number of transactions, contributing 22 per cent in the total proceeds. Food and beverage stood third in the number as well as in the contribution.

Food and beverage with 22 transactions yielded USD74.06 million which accounted for 17.14 per cent of the total proceeds. It is also found that that hotel and tourism—an emerging sector in the country—with 21 transactions fetched up only 1.20 per cent of the total proceeds, where as the mining sector with one transaction contributed surprisingly 39.81 per cent of the total proceeds. Leathers, cement and chemicals, wood and furniture, textiles and pharmacy contributed 6.15 per cent, 3.46 per cent, 2.04 per cent, 0.96 per cent and 0.15 per cent respectively for the total privatisation proceeds.

Economic and Political Issues

Economic Growth and Development Issues: GDP grew at an annual average of 5.2 per cent in which agriculture grew at 3.1 per cent over the privatisation period. It is found that there was a significant variation in the economic performance, owing to the fluctuation in the agricultural output which accounted for an annual average of 46 per cent in the total output over the study period. Agriculture showed its poorest performance in the EFY1996/97, 2001/02 and 2002/03 because of the drought and war conditions. However, the soothing effect was industry and services which grew at an annual average growth rate of 5.52 per cent and 6.56 per cent respectively over the study period.

Nevertheless, this study finds little evidence on economic development as three things are found unsupportive: first, the industrialization in the country is absolutely slow in progress with a few agricultural products, particularly coffee and hide and skin—coffee's share in total export earnings as of 2003/04 fiscal year stood at 37.2 per cent; second, Ethiopia was a major importer even for the basic and necessary raw material for its industrial sector and finally, the technological advancement in Ethiopia was found poorer than any other Sub-Saharan African (SSA) countries.

Precedence to the OLS empirical analysis, a simple correlation analysis was conducted to measure the correlation between privatisation and the three major components of GDP. The result indicates that there is a negative correlation between privatisation and GDP growth (correlation coefficient is -0.308). The similar results are found for agriculture (correlation coefficient is -0.378) and industry (correlation coefficient is -0.320. Nonetheless, the correlation behaved differently for services, showing a positive correlation (correlation coefficient is 0.664).

Budget Deficit and External Debt Issues: No improvement was found on budgetary deficit, but fluctuated rapidly ($\sigma = 2.29$ per cent) over the study period. Budget deficit to GDP, which stood at 3.7 in the first fiscal year of the privatisation, 1994/95, was raised to 7.13 per cent in the last fiscal year of 2003/04, and grew at an annual average of 5.48 per cent over the period. The preliminary correlation that there is a weak correlation (correlation coefficient is -0.268) found between privatisation and budgetary deficit.

External debt to GDP moved down from 178.37 per cent in 1994/95 to 97.16 per cent in 2003/04 which results in the reduction of indebtedness of the country. However, a simple correlation analysis ruled out any major role of privatisation in this reduction (coefficient correlation is 0.382), but thanks to the waiving off USD4,321 million in the fiscal year 1998/99.

While analysing debt services, the indicators such as debt service to export and to debt showed a significant change. Debt service to export reduced substantially while debt service to debt increased. The results on these two debt variables left a notion that the condition on indebtedness may reverse to normal. This result is substantiated by the fact that external debt to export was reduced from of 1,275 per cent in 1994/95 to 574 per cent in 2003/04 over the privatisation period. Nonetheless, the findings eventually say that the country's present value of debt was in danger since it ran out of safe ratio.

International Trade and Current and Trade Account Deficits Issues: Openness improved, but was slow to reach the standard requirements. It recorded only an annual average of 20.9 per cent over the study period which is considered insufficient in this globalised business environment. A simple correlation analysis failed to show a correlation between privatisation and openness. Export to import, which stood at 59.54 per cent in the first year of privatisation, 1994/95, was reduced to 45.88 per cent in 2003/04. Import started to exceed export particularly after 2002/01. Nonetheless, export, predominantly with coffee, shows an increase over the period.

Trade deficit increased slowly over the period and so did the current deficit, but with a little fluctuations. This trend of increase in the export to GDP was expected to have smoothened the trade and current account balance over the period, but the analysis over export to import prevented the expectation from yielding positive effect on these balances. The study also finds that the current account balance (deficit) was increased, but not proportionately to the increase of trade account deficit, owing to an increase of the international reserve that the country held. Although there was an improvement in the openness, export orientation and current account deficits, attributing these developments to privatisation was highly questioned in this study because the major exporting commodity, coffee, was seldom handled in privatisation.

Investment: Private investment over the privatisation period grew at an annual average rate of 9.26 per cent, where as the public investment attained only 8.18 per cent. Although the difference of annual average rate between the public and private investment in per cent of GDP was too narrow—the difference between the private and public investment was only 1.8 percentage points, the successful achievement on the private investment was said to be satisfactory. FDI as a share of GDP increased, but insignificantly from 0.14 per cent to 0.21 per cent over the period. However, these achievements comparing to other Sub-Saharan Africa (SSA) was found far from satisfactory as the latter were able to achieve in an annual average of 13.5 per cent over the same period.

Heterodox based OLS model in examining the impact of privatisation on different economic variables prove that there is no visible effect on any economic variable taken for this study. The analysis reveals that privatisation is found insignificant for GDP growth despite a robust and positive result was found for agriculture growth. The OLS models on the budgetary deficit, external debt and export orientation also reveal that privatisation contributed insignificantly. The analysis also proves a failure of privatisation on investment with robustly negative in general, and on FDI in particular. This result on FDI reveals that privatisation is not an important element in the FDI decision.

Political Issues: On analysing the political issues vested in privatisation, against all odds, the issues such as anti-privatisation feelings among public and trade union's resistance were not observed in the privatisation scenario of the country. Resistance from labour unions was not observed against privatisation, but slightly against retrenchment. The externalities (external pressures) on privatisation of the country may not be ruled out since there have been evidences about the country's high dependency on external loan and aid. However, a simple correlation analysis ruled out the relationship between privatisation and externalities which is measured in terms of the SAL.

The analysis on foreign dominance shows that the foreigner bought 75 per cent of the total privatisation transactions in spite of acquiring a few number of enterprises. Foreign dominance was found much prevalent in the sectors like food and beverages, leathers, mining and farm-agro industries. The reason for the foreign dominance on these sectors is attributed not only to their growth prosperity, but also the highest indicative price fixed for their sale. Leathers and mining received 100 per cent of foreign dominance.

The study reveals that 91 per cent of the total foreign privatisation was dominated by Saudi nationalities through purchasing 23 large sized transactions. The second share went to Yemenis who held 6 per cent of the foreign privatisation with only one transaction. French, the only European, purchased a single transaction, holding 3 per cent in this value. The interesting note that the study leaves that a single person from the Saudi dominance held his share which accounted for 92.6 per cent—63.47 per cent in the total privatisation proceeds. Ownership distribution analysis reveals that 1,579 new owners were created out of 220 transactions over the study period. The analysis also reveals that in many fiscal years, the ownership-creation efficiency ratio was below one. However, the ratio stood at 7.17 over the study period, owing to the MEBO transactions.

Socio-labour and Managerial Issues

Social Issues: On social issues, the impact of privatisation on per capita income, education expenditure, health expenditure, road construction and social welfare expenditure was analysed. Per capita income over the study period declined from USD110 in 1994/95 to USD100 in 2003/04 despite the population grew only at 2.56 per cent. A simple correlation analysis shows that there is no correlation (correlation coefficient is 0.143) between these two variables.

On education, literacy rate and gross enrollment improved satisfactorily over the privatisation period. Relating privatisation to this improvement through a simple correlation analysis, however, rules out the effect of privatisation. On health, conditions became worse during the privatisation period because the expenditure declined by almost half the amount over the period. Nonetheless, a simple correlation analysis shows that there is a moderate correlation (correlation coefficient is 0.523) between privatisation and health expenditure.

On road construction and social welfare, the expenditure on road construction increased rapidly, where as the spending on social welfare declined over the study period. The study finds that Rc/GDP increased from 0.31 per cent to 1.90 per cent, establishing an annual average of 0.71 per cent over the study period. The annual average of Sw/GDP stood only at 0.031 per cent over the period. A simple correlation analyses on the variables of road construction and social spending reveal that there is a negative correlation (correlation coefficient is-0.508) observed with road construction, whereas a positive relationship (correlation coefficient is 0.469) with social welfare spending. Privatisation programme was linked to poverty reduction mission in the country. However, its impact on poverty reduction was found very little. The absolute poverty declined only by 4.26 per cent over the study period, but no improvement was observed on the UN definition of poverty.

OLS empirical analysis indicates that privatisation contributed significantly to per capita income, confirming the side by side effects of a steady increase in industrial sector coupled with a slow growth of population. Privatisation is found insignificant for health expenditure. On the variable of education, privatisation is significant, but contributed negatively, while showing insignificant and fragile coefficients to road construction and social welfare.

Labour Issues: For this study, the analysis on labour issues was segregated into micro and macro issues. Micro labour issues includes variables such as awareness and communication about privatisation, fear, wage and salary, incentive system, job security, working hours and load, adherence to labour law and total favourability after privatisation. Results on these issues reveal a satisfactory approach of privatisation. The issues such as the labours' right to know their transfer to another legal form of enterprise, and communication with labourers and unions were well handled by privatisation. Fear towards privatisation as expected was highly prevalent among labours, but it was surprisingly lower among those transferred to foreign enterprises.

Overall wage and salary structure and incentive plans after privatisation were relatively improved, but contrarily, the labours in domestic enterprises are more satisfied as compared to the labourers in foreign enterprises. Job security, the major job factor, was perceived to be uncertain since a little less than half the total number of labourers felt themselves unsecured in their jobs. As far as working hours and load are concerned, many viewed that there was an increase, particularly in the foreign enterprises.

The study also reveals that there was a less adherence to labour law, attributing to the failure in the enforcement, but the foreign enterprises were proved to be better ones as compared to the domestic enterprises. The most important finding is that no single labourer in both type of enterprises viewed their post-privatised working conditions bad. Rather many deemed it favourable.

The effects of privatisation on the macro issues are, however, negative since the number of labourers was reduced by 7.56 per cent in the name of re-structuring. The study underscores the fact that the most potential sectors recorded these reductions to a large extent. In the total retrenchment, the enterprises gone to foreign buyers shared more than two-third, signaling their intensive structural adjustment despite they shared the higher share in new job creation.

Managerial Issues: The approach of privatisation towards managerial issues comes up with somewhat a different result as compared to that towards economic, political and macro labour issues. Privatisation slowed down production and sales, but raised the over all net profitability of the privatised enterprises. The study affirms this result thanks to the improved technical efficiency, coupled with the adoption of newer production techniques and innovative system. Fixed assets per person were also declined, showing their restructuring deliberation on the size of labours. However, the technical efficiency was yet to reach the desired level because the one-forth of its utilisation remained unexploited. The study gives caution to the privatised enterprises to see that their production capacity would be used to a great extent, otherwise, the observed ROI might more become worse in the due course of time.

From the analyses over the qualitative issues of management, it is observed that there was a tremendous development after privatisation. The management shifted its administration philosophy to either democratic or free-rein, ensuring the professional approach of the privatised enterprises. Work freedom, opportunities for training and development and relationship with management was relatively improved. However, the retention of the labour by the management was found no more adhering to labour laws, but efficiency was deemed most important factor for their retention. This observation signals a wider use of hire and fire policy which is going to be a new trend in the Ethiopian labour market. On all these managerial issues, the foreign privatised enterprises were observed as better-doers as compared to the domestic privatised enterprises.

Hypotheses Tested

The following are the summary of hypotheses testing which are empirically performed in this study.

Hypothesis 1: Privatisation in Ethiopia is slow and absurd

This hypothesis is tested in chapter IV. Privatisation over the study period of ten years yielded only USD433.7 million with a receipt of USD24.5 million a year. The quantitative analysis done in this chapter, thus, proves it to be very slow. Privatisation proceeds expressed in terms of GDP accounted for an annual average of 0.21 per cent also authenticates this derived result. Regarding the speed, the chi-square approves a robust difference between the expected and the observed speed in privatisation. The chi-square's computed value (χ^2 473 > $\chi^2_{0.05}$ 16.9190) is significant at 5 per cent level. Hence, the hypothesis is proved to be accepted.

Hypothesis 2: Privatisation in Ethiopia as an economic reform has failed to bring a desired change in economic issues

This hypothesis is tested in chapter V. To prove the hypothesis on economic issues, seven economic variables are tested at 5 per cent or 1 per cent significance level. The details of t-statistics and explanatory power (R^2) of each hypothesis testing are given below:

> ***On the Economic Growth:*** *Privatisation is insignificant with t-value 0.808 at 0.05 significance level. The explanatory power (R^2) of the model is 0.992.*
>
> ***On Budgetary Deficit:*** *Privatisation is insignificant with t-value 0.599 at 0.05 significance level. The explanatory power (R^2) of the model is 0.733.*
>
> ***On External Debt:*** *Privatisation is insignificant with t-value 0.780 at 0.05 significance level. The explanatory power (R^2) of the model is 0.506.*
>
> ***On Import and Export:*** *Privatisation is insignificant respectively for import and export with t-value -0.695 and -0.686 at 0.05 significance level. The explanatory powers (R^2) of these models respectively for import and export are 0.620 and 0.729.*
>
> ***On Investment:*** *Privatisation is insignificant with t-value -2.607 at 0.01significance level. The explanatory power (R^2) of the model is 0.835.*
>
> ***On FDI:*** *Privatisation is insignificant with t-value -0.894 at 0.05 significance level. The explanatory power (R^2) of the model is 0.974.*

Hence, the resulting t-statistics arrived on all economic variables are found to be insignificant, proving the hypotheses as valid ones.

This result matches with the relationship between economic reforms and economic growth, the model of which is also statistically proved insignificant with t-value 0.835 at 0.05 significance level. The explanatory power (R^2) of the model is 0.982, the hypothesis of which is tested in chapter III.

Hypothesis 3: Privatisation in Ethiopia has failed to show any positive outcome in the social and labour conditions

This hypothesis is tested in chapter VI. To prove the hypotheses on social issues, the social variables are tested at 0.05 or 0.01 significance level. The details of t-statistics and explanatory power (R^2) of each hypothesis testing are given below:

> ***On Per Capita Income:*** *Privatisation is significant with t-value 3.359 at 0.05 significance level. The explanatory power (R^2) of the model is 0.865.*
>
> ***On Education:*** *Privatisation is significant with t-value -3.151 at 0.05 significance level. The explanatory power (R^2) of the model is 0.868.*
>
> ***On Health:*** *Privatisation is insignificant with t-value 2.089 at 0.01 significance level. The explanatory power (R^2) of the model is 0.429.*
>
> ***On Road Construction and Social Welfare:*** *Privatisation is insignificant with t-value -1.96 at 0.01 significance level. The explanatory power (R^2) of the model is 0.433, whereas being test at 0.05 level, privatisation shows an insignificant t-value of 0.339 with explanatory power (R^2) of a meager 0.078.*

Labour Issues: The statistical evidences on the labour issues have almost disapproved the hypothesis. The details of the statistical evidences are given below:

> *The surveyed labourers for this study reveal that the issues pertaining to them were handled in an effective manner and their work conditions and environment improved more significantly in their privatised enterprises as compared to their previous public sector undertakings. The chi-square which is applied to ascertain the difference between the domestic and foreign enterprises has strong statistical evidences that the foreign privatised enterprises were doing better than the domestic enterprises. The employment after privatisation resulted in a net loss of 1,506 jobs which got a share of 441 and 1,065 job losses respectively from the domestic and foreign enterprises. Thus, having these mixed*

results in social issues as well as in labour issues, the hypothesis may not be fully accepted.

Hypothesis 4: Privatisation in Ethiopia has not effected any betterment in productivity, profitability and management working environment in the privatised enterprises

This hypothesis is tested in chapter VI. The statistical evidences on productivity and sales show that they decreased respectively from 20.61 per cent and 23.63 per cent in the pre-privatisation period to 17.68 per cent and 17.57 per cent in the post privatisation period. However, the net profit ratio increased significantly by switching over from 0.087 in the pre-privatisation period to 2.79 in the post-privatisation period. The study considers it to be a significant achievement in the privatised enterprises. To add up to the positive evidence on managerial issues, the capacity utilisation increased from 58.62 per cent in the pre-privatisation period to 71 per cent in the post privatisation period.

The statistical evidences on managerial issues disapprove the hypothesis which is because of the reason that the managerial approach toward the organisation and labourers improved robustly in the privatised enterprises. The chi-square statistically proves that the foreign privatised enterprises were doing better than the domestic enterprises on most of the variables selected for the study. Therefore, this hypothesis in general cannot be fully validated.

CONCLUSION

Privatisation in Ethiopia exhibits a mixed result, revealing a negative impact of privatisation on macro economic, political and socio-labour issues, and a positive result on the micro labour and managerial issues. The result on per capita income is, however, a consoling effect on privatisation, owing to the controlled growth rate of population over the study period. The results on the micro labour and managerial issues are the indication of a mile-stone achievement of privatisation which occurred among the privatised enterprises. The scope and purview of this positive effect from the privatised enterprises is, however, very minimal because the beneficiaries are limited in number, and their contribution to the economic and social is not so imminent.

The partial failure in privatisation as revealed in this study does not mean that the private sector has failed in the country. Private sector development can be developed and made work well even without the privatisation programme through an effective policy of creating the private sector much parallel to the public sector undertakings. It can, therefore, be said that the initiative on the private sector development should continue, but with the critical examination of feed backs of privatisation in the country which, in turn, helps the privatisation programme to become successful in the near future.

SUGGESTIONS

Privatisation should be viewed, not as an end itself, but as part of a broader programme of reforms. If the reform measures fail, privatisation cannot stand alone to succeed. Hence, it can be said that a well tailored and user friendly reform policy with high clarity and transparency is a pre-requisite for making the privatisation programme successful. While setting the objectives for privatisation, it should be ensured that the objectives should be practically workable and achievable with the size of the privatisation programme. Imaginary and exaggeration in setting the objectives should be avoided.

On the flaws found in the processing issues, this study suggests that the privatisation agency should be as much independent as possible to ensure a fair service in privatisation. This study suggests the government to withdraw its unnecessary interference and influential representations from the Agency. Regarding the personnel in the Agency, this study recommends that the Agency should be well-equipped with the trained personnel and experts as the programme may ignite again at any time for the rest of the huge public sector.

Privatisation laws should be made in such a way that undue restrictions from the government in tying the Agency's hand can be avoided. The legal framework for privatisation should be flexible and comprehensive. A flexible legal framework enables the government or responsible agencies to adapt their approaches to changing circumstances. It is because of the reason that many changes to perfection in the laws of the LDCs like Ethiopia are natural and common.

The issues on valuation can be minimised if the most of the PSUs came under a systematic financial accounting. Professional accounting seemed to be emerging, but it has to be nourished to the extent that these enterprises cannot easily get away from the systematic examination of books of accounts by these accounting firms. The other suggestion is that the Agency to give as much time as possible to the buyers to contemplate and pool resources to buy the enterprise.

The privatisation programme aimed at even for poverty reduction was not properly directed and linked with the policy implications of poverty reduction. Setting realistic goals is important to developing appropriate procedures for privatisation if it targets indirect objectives like poverty reduction. The country is strongly perceived as the most poverty stricken and political chaotic in Africa. The political struggle and nationalisation during the Derg regime and the recent war with Eritrea have had a damaging message in building the goodwill of the country. This study finds that neither does this condition exist nor is imminent. The government should do enormous efforts through the Ministry of Foreign Affairs, Ministry of Trade and commerce, Chamber of Commerce to demonstrate the on-going private sector development initiatives to the rest of the world. In these goodwill promotion activities, the Ministry of Tourism may also play a vital role hand in hand with other ministries.

Privatisation is an important element in attracting investment despite the fact that causality runs each other. Privatisation cannot be carried out in an unsound investment climate. Hence, it is not too late to create a conducive climate since many PSUs are yet to be privatised. The sound investment climate includes a long-term macroeconomic stability, freedom entry and exist, well-tailored financial reforms, and adequate physical infrastructure.

For privatisation to be successful, the country needs to build its openness of the economy. The size of the economy does not matter to build this openness as many small sized economies have been proved successful on this issue through their systematic deregulation and liberalisation policies. Having more than a decade in the name of reforms, the country was found to be more static and inward oriented. Hence, this study recommends that the country should build its export capacity at the earliest, and at the same time, improve its production capability of the basic raw materials required for its industry.

Cost-structures, differential returns, market growth and the institutional characteristics of the country are the most important determinants in making privatisation effective, but they are yet to be lucrative in the country. Investors wishing to invest always look for a favourable trade and investment regimes, good infrastructure, property rights, political stability and an educated and committed workforce. Above all, the major investment incentives, particularly tax concessions need to be reformed to the extent that it should create business friendly conditions.

It should also be noted that among all types of investment flows, foreign investment through privatisation is considered an important input for the economic growth and it may play a significant role in generating a positive spill over effect, bringing new technologies and management and marketing skills contributing to the economic growth. But the empirical evidence in this study proves that FDI was little to flow. The study, therefore, recommends that foreign investors should be encouraged and handled diligently by creating a conducive-environment for FDI in the private sector development. The government should also facilitate domestic as well as foreign investors to get out of difficulties in the areas of technological information, support services and market information, particularly on the area of export and raw material market, and basic infra-structural facilities.

The judicial system seems to be an obstacle not only for private investors, but also for foreign investors. Foreign investors perceive the country so backward in its commercial judicial system which could be deemed as potential threat to their business. Hence, it is suggested that the judicial system should be injected with clear-cut commercial codes and judges who are expert in judging commercial suits.

In addition to a review of domestic laws and regulations, the country access and adherence to international laws should be enhanced. Although there have been a few treaties signed with some international organs, it has yet to be ratified and strengthened. For this, the government should make use of AU and NAPED for internationalising and harmonising the country's law system.

The confusions and uncertainties regarding land ownership of privatised enterprises presents a potential concern to any investor. The owners of the privatised enterprise were much frustrated about the land lease system in which the land does not appear in their balance sheet. Though it requires a time-consuming and complicated political process, there must be a bold decision from the government to transfer the ownership of land to the investors.

For a wider share ownership and a speedy transformation from the centralized to market economy, it should take necessary steps to sell the PSUs through the method of public offerings instead of sale of assets. This study suggests that the country should lay a foundation to establish a well-structured and informative capital market, followed by the security market. The lead time regarding to set up such markets is normally too long. The first step would be to develop basic security legislations, regulating issues and trade of shares and operation of financial intermediaries.

A properly functioning autonomous banking system is critical to the successful accomplishment of privatisation programme. Effective banking system is needed to allow the domestic investors to leverage their purchase and to enable local and foreign investors to finance future working capital requirements domestically. In addition, a broad range of financial sector laws including sureties (collateral), credit, leasing and insurance should be prepared to ensure the smooth flow of financial transactions and claims. Tax system and administration should be modified to the extent that it should encourage the investors to multiply their business in the country. More tax concessions needs to be announced to encourage the local and foreign investors. Furthermore, dual tax system with a view to give indirect and undue privileges to PSUs should be abolished.

Labour laws should be ensured to apply for the protection of basic rights of labour regarding retrenchment or severance pay or other compensation, but care should be taken to see that the law and its enforcement should never become an impediment to the investors.

This study suggests that the government should allocate a substantial portion of money from the budget for the development of education and health which ensures a highly skilled and healthy human resource in the near future. A highly talented and healthy human resource in a country is considered an important element in attracting private investment.

Having observed a severe retrenchment within this small sized privatisation, it is suggested that the employment issues should be seriously considered by the government. Although the employees safety net programme seemed to exist but it became ineffective in many circumstances, it is absolutely essential to revitalising this safety net to enhance their livelihood. As fear exists among the employees even after privatisation irrespective of domestic and foreign enterprises, the management should make all necessary efforts to speak to them for reducing unnecessary fear. They have to be clearly told that nothing except inefficiency or misbehavior or lethargy would threaten their jobs.

An inefficient and non-transparent bureaucratic system contributes to high transactions and business costs to investors. It is necessary to streamline the bureaucracy and increase transparency of rules in general and particularly those governing investment, labour, trade, the environment, land and taxation. It can, therefore, be said that a strong and bureaucratically free economic foundations to attract investment should a first-hand priority.

The financial sector reforms should be restructured at the earliest, and should go hand in hand with the reform measures. The creation of a sound financial system is crucial to transition and reconstruction, and to revising the living standard of the Ethiopian people. The financial reforms cannot be spared in the case of Ethiopia where the growth rate was not satisfactory.

The economic isolation—the common and chronic issue in Africa—of the county may also provide a strong explanation for the country's poor performance on privatisation and investment. The government should activate its participation in COMESA and AGOA. It is also suggested that the country should become a member in WTO in order to cope with the emerging gloablised trade.

SCOPE FOR FURTHER RESEARCH

This study suggests the following a few further researches to be carried out in connection with privatisation.

- A further research is urged to be carried in order to examine the relationship between privatisation and investment, particularly on government (public) investment.
- Although this study deals with some of the social issues of privatisation, the untouched issues such as the connectivity between privatisation and price level and the relationship between privatisation and accessibility to goods and services could be taken for further study.

- A fact-finding study on the impact of privatisation on the overall private sector development of the country could be done.
- A study that is to examine the effect of privatisation on market creation and competition is hereby recommended.
- A link was made between private sector development through privatisation and poverty reduction. It needs a detailed further probe.

Bibliography

Books

Abraham, K. (2001), *Ethiopia: The Dynamics of Economic Reforms (Economic Liberalisation and Political Transformation)*, Addis Ababa: EIIPD (Ethiopian International Instt. for Peace and Development).

Abu Shair, J.A.R.O. (1997), *Privatisation and Development.* London: MacMillan Press Ltd.

Agénor, P.R. and Montiel, P.J. (1999), *Macroeconomic Development.* New Jersey: Princeton University Press.

Ambrosio, D.C. (1976), *Principles of Modern Investment.* Chicago: Science Research Associates.

Bhatia, H.L. (1989), *History of Economic Thought.* New Delhi: Vikas Publishing House Pvt. Ltd.

Barro, R. and X. Sala-i-Martin (1995), *Economic Growth.* New York: McGraw-Hill.

Baumol, W.J. and Blinder, A.S. (1997), *Macro Economics: Principles and Policy.* Florida: Dryden Press.

Bolnick, B.R. (1987), *Economics of Development: Study Guide and Work Book.* New York: W.W. Norton & Co.

Buckley, J.W. (1976), *Research Methodology and Business Decisions.* New York: National Association of Accounts.

Carbaugh, R.J. (1995), *International Economics.* Ohio: South-Western College Publishing Co.

Christiaensen L., Lionel, Demery and Paterson, S. (2002), *Growth, Distribution and Poverty in Africa: Messages from the 1990s.* Washington, D.C.: World Bank/IBRD.

Decenzo, A.D. and Robbins, P.S. (2003), *Personnel/Human Resource Management.* New Delhi: Prentice-Hall of India Pvt. Ltd.

Dhameja, N. and Sastry, K.S. (1998) *Privatisation: Theory and Practice.* New Delhi: Wheeler Publishing & Co. Ltd.

Dornbusch, R. and Fischer, S. (1981) *Macro Economics.* New York: McGraw-Hill Book Company.

Ekelund and Tollison (1997), *Micro Economics: Private Markets and Public Choices.* New York: Addison-Wesley Publishing Company.

Edmonds, T.P., Edmonds, D.C., and Tsay, Bor-Yi (2000), *Fundamentals Managerial Accounting Concepts.* Boston: Irwin McGraw-Hill.

Gareth and Smith, C. (1998), *Economic Development.* New York: Palgrave.

Griffith, R.J. (1998), *"Developing World 1998/99: Political Economy and the Developing World",* Guildford (CT): Dushkin/McGraw-Hill.

Gómez-Ibáñez, J.A. and Meyer, J.R. (1993) Going Private: *The International Experience with Transport Privatisation.* Washington, D.C.: The Brookings Institution.

Hill, C.W.L. (1998) Global Business Today. Washington: Irwin/McGraw-Hill.

Hyman, D.N. (1997), Macroeconomics, Boston: Irwin.

Miller, R. Le Roy (1997), *Economic Today: A Micro View.* Boston: Addison-Wesley Educational Publisher.

Miller, R. Le Roy (1998), *Economic Today.* New York: Addison-Wesley Educational Publisher.

Nicholas, H. (2001), *Public Administration and Public Affairs.* New Delhi: Prentice Hall of India Pvt. Ltd.

Oxford (1996), *Dictionary of Business.* Oxford: Oxford Printing Press.

Pirie, M. (1988), *Privatisation.* England: Wildwood House Ltd.

Posner, M.V. and Woolf, S.J. (1967), *Italian Public Enterprise.* London: Gerald Duckworth and Co.

Reich, R.B. (1991), *The Work of Nations:* Preparing Ourselves for the 21st Century. New York: Alfred A. Knopf.

Schiller, B.R. (1991), *The Economy Today.* New York: McGraw-Hill, Inc. p. 693.

Stiglitz, J. (1997), *Economics.* London: W.M. Norton & Company Inc. pp. 162-3.

Taylor, J.B. (1995), *Principles of Macro Economics*. Boston: Houghton Mifflin Co. p. 661.

Thirwall, A.P. (2004), *Growth and Development: With Special Reference to Developing Economies*. London: Palgrave, pp. 561-640.

Timmorthy Tregarthen (1996), Macro Economics. New York: Worth Publishers, pp. 492-500.

Tripathi, P.C. and Reddy, P.N. (2004), Principles of Management. New Delhi: Tata McGraw-Hill Publishing Co., pp. 187 & 220.

Tucker, I.B. (1997), *Macroeconomics for Today*. New York: West Publishing Co., p. 122 & 338-427.

Edited Volume

Aharoni, Y. (1991), "On Measuring the Success of Privatisation", in Ramamurthi, R. and Vernon, R. (eds) *Privatisation and Control of State Owned Enterprises*. Washington, D.C.: World Bank.

Ahmed, M.U. (2000), "Privatisation in Bangladesh" in Gopal Joshi (ed.) *Privatisation in South Asia: Minimising Negative Social Effects through Restructuring*. New Delhi: ILO.

Alesina, A. (1998), "The Political Economy of High and Low Growth", in Pleskovic, B. and Stiglitz L. Joseph (eds) *The Annual World Bank Conference on Development Economics 1997, Washington*, D.C.: World Bank.

Befekadu Degefe (1994), "Strategies and Macroeconomic Policies for the Development of the Private Sector in Ethiopia" (ed.) *The Ethiopian Economy: Problems and Prospects of Private Sector Development-Proceedings of the Third Annual Conference of the Ethiopian Economy*. Addis Ababa: AAU Press.

Bhardhan, P. (1998), "Economies of Market Socialism and the Issue of Public Enterprise Reform in India", in Basu, K., Majumdhar, M. and Mitra, T. (eds.) *Capital, Investment and Development: Essays in Memory of Sukhamoy Chakravarthy*. New Delhi: Oxford Printing Press.

Bierstelley, T.J. (1997), "The Triumph of liberal economic ideas in the developing world", in Shephany Griffith Jones and Barbara Stallings (eds) *New Global Financial Trends Implications for Development*. Cambridge: Cambridge University Press.

Botelho, A. and Addis, C. (1988), "Privatisation of Telecommunications in Mexico" in Rolph Vander Hoeven and Gyorgy Sziraczki (eds) *Lessons from Privatisation: Labour Issues in Developing and Transitional Countries*. Geneva: ILO.

Bräutigam, D. (1998), "Comment on What can Developing Countries Learn from East Asia's Economic Growth? by Takatoshi Ito", in Pleskovic, Boris and Stiglitz L. Joseph (eds) *The Annual World Bank Conference on Development Economics 1997*, Washington, D.C.: World Bank.

Cook, P. (1998), "Privatisation in the UK: Policy and Performance", in Parker, D. (ed.) *Privatisation in the European Union: Theory and Policy Perspectives*. London: Routledge.

Eardley, R.F. (1999), "Privatising Bus Transport in Sri Lanka" in Prokopenko, J. (ed.) *Management for Privatisation*. Geneva: ILO.

Esser, J. (1998), "Privatisation in Germany: Symbolism in the Social Market Economy?", in Parker, D. (ed.) *Privatisation in the European Union: Theory and Policy Perspectives*. London: Routledge.

Fernando, R.E. (1999), "Privatising Bus Transport in Sri Lanka" in Prokopenko, J. (ed.) *Management for Privatisation: Lessons from Industry and Public Services*. Geneva: ILO.

Gopal Joshi (2000), "Privatisation in India" in Gopal Joshi (ed.) *Privatisation in South Asia: Minimising Negative Social Effects through Restructuring*. New Delhi: ILO.

Griffin, K. (2001), "Macroeconomic Reform and Employment: An Investment-led Strategy of Structural Adjustment in Sub-Saharan Africa" in Mclinely Terry (ed.) *Macro Economic Policy, Growth and Poverty Reduction*. New York: Palgrave.

Hinds, B. (1999), "Opportunities and Constraints of Privatisation" in Gormley, W.T. (ed.) *Privatisation and its Alternatives*. Oxford: Oxford University Press.

Hinds, B. (1999), "Privatising Telecommunications in Guyana" in Prokopenko, J. (ed.) *Management for Privatisation: Lessons from Industry and Public Services*. Geneva: ILO.

Hoeven, Rolph van der and Sziraczki, G. (1998), "Privatisation and Labour Issues" in Hoeven, Rolph van der and Sziraczki, G. (eds) *Lessons from Privatisation: Labour Issues in Developing and Transitional Countries*. Geneva: ILO, p. 8.

Hoody, N. and Young, S. (1999), "The United Kingdom", in Dunning, E.J. (ed.) *Governments, Globalisation, and International Business* Oxford: Oxford University Press.

Hyman, D.N. (1997), Macro Economics. Boston: The Mc Graw-Hill Company, Inc. p. 98.

ILO (1999) "Report of the Sub-Regional Workshop on Privatisation in South Asia", 24–26 November, Kathmandu, ILO.

Itoh, M. & Kiyono, K. (1988) "Foreign Trade and Direct Investment" in Kamiya, M. Okuno, M. & Suzumuru, K. (eds.) *Industrial Policy of Japan.* Tokyo: Academic Press.

Khan, A.R. (2001), "Macroeconomic Policies and Poverty: An Analysis of the Exerience in Ten Asian Countries", in McKinely, T. (ed.) *Macroeconomic Policy, Growth and Poverty Reducation.* New York: Palgrave.

Kibre Moges (1994), "The Role of the State and Private Sector under Economic Liberalisation -Theoretical Perspectives", in Getachew, Y., and Abdulhami, B., (eds.) *The Ethiopian Economy: Problems and Prospects of Private Sector Development-Proceedings of the Third Annual Conference of the Ethiopian Economy.* AAU Press: Addis Ababa.

Kühl, Jürgen (1998), "Privatisation and its Labour Market effect in Eastern Germany" in Rolph Vander Hoeven and Gyorgy Sziraczki (eds.) *Lessons from Privatisation: Labour Issues in Developing and Transitional Countries.* Geneva: ILO.

Lal, D. (2001), "International Capital Formation and Economic Development" in Scott, M. and Lal, D. (eds.) *Public Policy and Economic Development: Essays in Honor of Ian Little.* Oxford: Larendon Press.

László Neumann (1998), "Privatisation of Telecommunications in Hungary", in Rolph Van der Hoeven and Gyorgy Sziracközki (eds.) *Lessons from Privatisation: Labour Issues in Developing and Transitional Countries.* Geneva: ILO.

Meenakshi S. Rajan, A. (2003), "Globalisation and its Impacts on Social and Human Development in India- an Analysis" in Mukhopadhyay et al. (eds) *Globalisation and Challenges of Education: Focus on Equity and Equality,* New Delhi, Shipra Publications.

Mkandawire, T. and Soludo, C.C. (2003), "Towards the Broadening of Development Policy Dialogue for Africa" in Mkeandawire, T. and Soludo, C.C. (eds) *African Voices on Structural Adjustment.* New Jersey: African World Press.

Mujaju, A. (1990), "A Public Sector without a Public Philosophy: The Case of Uganda" in Chole, E., Mlay, W. and Oyugi, W. (eds.) *The Crisis of Development Strategies in Eastern Africa.* New Delhi: OSSERA.

Oyugi, W.O. (1990), "Privatisation in Africa: Promises and Prospects" in Chole, E., Mlay, W. & Oyugi, W.O. (eds.) *The Crisis of Development Strategies in Eastern Africa.* OSSERA (Organsiation for Social Science Research in Eastern Africa): New Delhi.

Park, Young-Bum (1998), "Privatisation and Employment in the Republic of Korea", in Hoeven, Rolph van der and Sziraczki, G. (eds.) *Lessons from Privatisation: Labour Issues in Developing and Transitional Countries.* Geneva: ILO.

Parker, D. (1998), "Privatisation in the European Union", in Parker, D. (ed.) *Privatisation in the European Union: Theory and Policy Perspectives.* London: Routledge.

Preper, U. and Taylor, L. (2000), "The Revival of the Liberal Creed: the IMF, the WB, and the Inequality in a globalised economy" in Dean Baker, Gerald Epstein and Robert Pollin (eds.) *Globalisation and Progressive Economic Policy.* Cambridge: Cambridge University Press.

Prokopenko, J. (1999), "Future Management Strategies", in Prokopenko, J. (ed.) *Management for Privatisation: Lessons from Industry and Public Services.* Geneva: ILO.

Ratnam, V.C.S. (1998), "Adjustment and Privatisation in India", in Hoeven, Rolph van der and Sziraczki, G. (eds.) *Lessons from Privatisation: Labour Issues in Developing and Transitional Countries.* Geneva: ILO.

Rondinelli, D.A. (1999), "Privatisation and Economic Transformation: The Management Challenge", in Prokopenko, J. (ed.) *Management for Privatisation: Lessons from Industry and Public Service,* Management Development Series No. 32. Geneva: ILO.

Sampson, C.I. (1999), "Privatising Banking Services in Jamaica" in Prokopenko, J. (ed.) *Management for Privatisation: Lessons from Industry and Public Services.* Geneva: ILO.

Savas, E.S. (1999), "Global perspectives on local Issues", in Yul Kwon, O. (ed.) *International Privatisation: Global Trends, Policies, Processes and Experiences.* Saskatchewan: Institute of Saskatchewan Enterprises.

Vácha, S. (1999), "Privatisation in Three Large Manufacturing Companies in the Czech Republic and Slovakia" in Prokopenko, J. (ed.) *Management for Privatisation:* Lessons from Industry and Public Services. Geneva: ILO.

Week, J. (2001), *"Macroeconomic Policy for Growth with Reference to Africa South of the Sahara"* in Mckinley, T. (ed.) *Macroeconomic Policy, Growth and Poverty Reduction.* New York: Palgrave Publishers Ltd.

Journals

Ajayi, I.S. (2001), "What Africa Needs to do to Benefit from Globalisation", *Finance & Development,* A Quarterly Publication of the International Monetary Fund, Vol. 38, No. 4.

Anderson, R. (2000), 'How Government Can Help Business in Poor Countries', *Journal of Economic Integration'*, Vol. 15, No. 1.

Bennet, T. and Johnson, M.H. (1979), *"Public Vs Private Provision of Collective Goods and Services: Garbage Collection Revitalised"*, Public Choice, No. 34.

Boardman and Vining (1989), "Ownership in Competitive Environments: A Comparison of the Performance of Mixed, Private and SOEs", *Journal of Law and Economics*, April, No. 32.

Bös, D. (1992), "Privatisation in Europe: A Comparison of Approaches", *Oxford Review of Economic Policy*, Vol. 9, No. 1.

Bös, D. (1987), "Privatisation of Public Enterprises", *European Economic Review*, Vol. 31, No. 1 & 2.

Caves, D.W. and Christensen, L. (1980), "The Relative Efficiency of Public and Private Firms in a Competitive Environment: The Case of Canadian Railroads", *Journal of Public Economy*, No. 88.

Cook, P. and Uchida, Y. (2003), "Privatisation and Economic Growth in Developing Countries", *The Journal of Development Studies*, Vol. 39, No. 9.

Earle, J.S. (1999), "Privatisation in Russia Offers Lessons for Others", *Economic Reform Today*-CIPE (Privatisation in the Digital Age), No. 2.

Eden, L. (1996), "Whither WIR?", *Transnational Corporation*, Vol. 5, No. 2.

Ernest ten Heuvelhof and Helen Stout (2000), "Sustainable Utilities: New Opportunities for Sustainability through Liberalization and Privatisation", *UNEP Industry and Environment*, Vol. 23, No. 1-2.

Fosu, A.K. (2003), "Political Instability and Export Performance in Sub-Saharan Africa", *Journal of African Economies*, Vol. 39, No. 4.

Gebeyehu, W. (2000), "Has Privatisation Promoted Efficiency in Ethiopia? : A Comparative Analysis of Privatised Industries vis- a-vis State Owned and Other Private Industrial Establishments", *Ethiopian Journal of Economics*, Vol. 9, No. 2.

Guo, K. and Yao, Y. (2005), "Causes of Privatisation in China: Testing Several Hypothesies", *The Economics of Transition*, Vol. 13, No. 2.

Hebdon, R. (1995), "Contracting Out in New York State: The Story the Louder Report Chose Not to Tell", *Labour Studies Journal*, Spring.

Leon Louw (1999), "What Would Make Privatisation Work in South Africa", *Economic Reform Today*-CIPE [Privatisation in the Digital Age], No. 2.

Lorrain Eden (1996), "Whither WIR?", *Transnational Corporation,* Vol. 5, No. 2.

Masood Ahmed, Timothy Lane, and Marianne Schulze-Ghattas (2001), 'Refocusing IMF Conditionality', *Finance & Development,* December, Vol. 38, No. 4.

Meenakshi S. Rajan, A., T. Iyappan and Selvam, J. (2005), "Impact of Economic Reforms on Economic Issues: A Study of Ethiopia", *African Development Review,* Vol. 17, No. 1.

Megginson, W.L., Nash, R.C. & van Randenborgh, M. (1994), "The Financial and Operating Performance of Newly Privatised Firms: An International Empirical Analysis", *Journal of Finance,* Vol. 49, No. 2.

Megginson, W.L. and Neller, J.M. (2001), "From State to Market: A Survey of Empirical Studies on Privatisation", *Journal of Economic Literature,* November, Vol. 39.

Megginson, L.M. (1998), "The Impact of Privatisation", *Economic Reform Today* (Centre for International Private Enterprises (CIPE)), No. 1.

Novak, M. (1991), "Transforming the Democratic Capitalistic Revolution", *International Journal of Value Based Management,* Vol. 4, No. 2.

Pendletin, A. (1997), "What Impact has Privatisation had on Pay and Employment: A Review of the UK Experience", *Industrial Relations,* Vol. 53, No. 3.

Plain, P. (1997), "Privatisation and Economic Growth: An Empirical Investigation from a Sample of Developing Market Economies", *Applied Economics,* Vol. 29, No. 2.

Rahn, R.W. (1999), "Money: The Ultimate Privatisation", Economic Reform Today, *Privatisation in the Digital Age,* No. 2.

Ramakrisha, G., Sivarama Krishanan, V., & Abdul Hamid Sukar (2003), "Impact of Globalisation on growth, poverty and income inequality: A Study of Ethiopia and India", *Asian Economic Review,* August, Vol. 45, No. 2.

Rangarajan, C. (2002), "Economic Reforms: An Assessment", *The Indian Economic Journal,* July-September, Vol. 49, No. 1.

Sastry, K.S. (1988), "Privatisation of Public Enterprises", *Productivity,* Vol. 28, No. 2.

Shirley, M.M. (1995), "Getting Bureaucrats Out of Business: Obstacles to State Enterprise Reform", *Economic Reform Today,* No. 4.

Sitikantha, P. and Sangita, M. (2003), "The Spectre of IMF Conditionality: Some Streamlining Option", *The Indian Economic Journal,* Vol. 50, No. 1.

Starr, P. (1989), "The Meaning of Privatisation", Yale Law and Policy Review, Vol. 6.

Voszka, E. (1999), "Privatisation in Hungary: Results and Open Issues", *Economic Reform Today-CIPE* [Privatisation in the Digital Age], No. 2.

Young, P. (1998), "The Lessons of Privatisation", *CIPE Economic Reform Today,* No. 1.

Reports and Gazettes

CSA (1999), Ethiopia: Statistical Abstract 1998, April, 1999, Addis Ababa, CSA.

CSA (2002), Ethiopia: Statistical Abstract 2001, March, 2002, Àddis Ababa, CSA.

CSA (2003), "Report on Large and Medium Scale Manufacturing and Electricity Industries Survey", Statistical Bulletin 281, October, (Central Statistical Authority), Addis Ababa: CSA.

CSA (2004a), Ethiopia: Statistical Abstract 2003, June 2004, Addis Ababa, CSA.

CSA (2004b), Ethiopia: Statistical Abstract, 2003, January, Addis Ababa: CSA.

EPA (2002a), "Data on Post Privatisation Performance of PSUs", Post-Privatisation Monitoring Department, Addis Ababa, EPA.

EPA (2002b), "Report on Post Privatisation Performance of PSUs", Post-Privatisation Monitoring Department, Addis Ababa, EPA.

EPA (2003), "Privatisation Proceeds", Dept. of Finance and Administration, Addis Ababa, EPA.

EPA (2004), "Ethiopian Privatisation Proceeds", Department of Finance and Administration, Addis Ababa: EPA.

GoE (1994a), "Negarit Gazeta of the Transitional Government of Ethiopia: Budget Proclamation No. 80/1993", Addis Ababa, GoE.

GoE (1994b), "Negarit Gazeta of the Transitional Government of Ethiopia: Ethiopian Privatisation Agency Establishment Proclamation No. 87/94", February, Addis Ababa: GoE.

GoE (1995), "Negarit Gazeta of the Transitional Government of Ethiopia: Budget Proclamation No. 108/1994", Addis Ababa, GoE.

GoE (1996), "Negarit Gazeta of the Transitional Government of Ethiopia: Budget Proclamation No. 13/1995", Addis Ababa, GoE.

GoE (1997a), "Negarit Gazeta of the Transitional Government of Ethiopia: Budget Proclamation No. 46/1996", Addis Ababa, GoE.

GoE (1997b), "Negarit Gazeta of the FDRE: Federal Rural Land Administration Proclamation No. 89/97", December, Addis Ababa: GoE.

GoE (1998a), "Negarit Gazeta of the Transitional Government of Ethiopia: Budget Proclamation No. 80/1997", Addis Ababa, GoE.

GoE (1998b), "Negarit Gazeta of the Transitional Government of Ethiopia: Labour Proclamation No. 377/2003", Addis Ababa, GoE.

GoE (1998c), "Privatisation of Public Enterprises Proclamation No. 146/ 1998", Federal Negarit Gazeta of the Federal Democratic Republic of Ethiopia, Addis Ababa, GoE.

Government of India (1997), "Disinvestment Commission Report V", November, New Delhi.

IEG (1968), "Third Five Year Development Plan-1968/73", Berhane Selam Hailai Selassie Imperial Printing Press: Addis Ababa.

MEDaC (1999), "Survey of the Ethiopian Economy: Review of Post Reform Developments (1992/93-1997-98)", June, Addis Ababa: MEDaC, pp. 1-35.

IFC/WB (2001), "Ethiopia: Foreign Investment Promotion Strategy Framework", World Bank, Washington, D.C., p. 16.

MoFED (2002a), "Development and Poverty Profile of Ethiopia (Analysis Based on the 1999/00 Household Income, Consumption and Expenditure and Welfare Monitoring Surveys)", March, Addis Ababa: MoFED.

MoFED (2002b), "Ethiopia: Sustainable Development and Poverty Reduction Program", July, Addis Ababa: MoFED.

MoFED (2003a), Economic Indicators, Department of Policy Analysis, Addis Ababa, MoFED.

MoFED (2003b), Economic Indicators, Department of National Accounts, Addis Ababa, MoFED.

MoFED (2003c), "Annual Report on Macroeconomic Development in Ethiopia, September, Addis Ababa, MoFED.

MoFED (2004a), "Annual Report on Macroeconomic Development in Ethiopia, 2003/04", September, Addis Ababa, MoFED.

MoFED (2004b), "Ethiopia: Private Sector Development Capacity Building Project", Report No. 30639, Addis Ababa: MoFED.

MoFED (2004c), Economic Indicators, Department of National Accounts, Addis Ababa: MoFED.

MoI (1992), "Industrial Restructuring in Ethiopia", Vol. I, August, Addis Ababa: MoI.

MoPED (1994), "Survey of Current Economic Conditions in Ethiopia", Vol. II, No. 1, February, Addis Ababa: MoPED.

MoPED (2003), Economic Indicators, Department of Policy Analysis Computation, MoPED: Addis Ababa.

NBE (2003), Annual Report, 2002/03, Addis Ababa, NBE.

NBE (2004), Annual Report, 2003/04, Addis Ababa, NBE.

TGE (1994), "Negarit Gazeta of the Transitional Government of Ethiopia: Ethiopian Privatisation Agency Establishment Proclamation No. 87/94", February, Addis Ababa: TGE.

Tefera, A.H. (1993), "Privatisation Initiative in Ethiopia", September 1993, Addis Ababa: Ministry of Industry.

World Bank (1995), "Structural and Sectoral Adjustment Lending: World Bank Experience (1980-1992)", Operation and Evaluation Department, Washington, D.C., World Bank.

World Bank (1995), "Congo-Privatisation and Capacity Building Project", Report No. T-6654-COB, July 25.

World Bank (1997), African Development Indicators, Washington, D.C.: World Bank.

World Bank (2001), "Ethiopia: Foreign Investment Promotion Strategy Framework", Foreign Investment Advisory Service (FIAS), Washington, D.C.: World Bank.

World Bank (2002a), Development Report 2000/01, Washington, D.C.: World Bank.

World Bank (2002b), African Development Indicators (Drawn from the World Bank Africa Data Base), Washington, D.C.: World Bank.

World Bank (2003a), "Global Development Finance: Striving for Stability in Development Finance (Summary and Country Table)", Washington, D.C., World Bank.

World Bank (2003b), "Ethiopia: Letter of Intent, Memorandum of Economic and Financial Policies, and Technical Memorandum of Understanding", July, 22, Washington, D.C., World Bank.

World Bank (2003c), "Implementation Completion Report on a Loan Credit/ Grant in the amount of USD120 Million to the Federal Democratic Republic of Ethiopia for an ESAC", Report No. 27570, December, 19, World Bank.

World Bank (2003d), World Development Indicators, Washington, D.C.: World Bank.

World Bank (2004a), African Development Indicators, Washington, D.C., World Bank.

World Bank (2004b), "Global Development Finance: Harnessing Cyclical Gains for Development (Summary and Country Table II)", Washington, D.C.: World Bank.

World Bank (2004c), "World Bank List of Economies", July, Washington, D.C., World Bank.

World Bank (2004d), "Ethiopia: Relations with the World Bank", January, 2004, Report No. 27753, Washington, D.C.: World Bank.

World Bank (2004e), "Structural Adjustment Credit: Private Sector Development", Washington, D.C., World Bank.

UNDP (1998), "Human Development Report, 1998, Oxford: Oxford University Press, p. 130.

UNDP (2003), "Human Development Report: Millennium Development Goal Indicators", New York, UNDP, p. 200.

Discussion and Policy Papers

Barnett, S. (2000), "*Evidence on the Fiscal and Macro Economic Impact of Privatisation*", IMF Working Paper, July, Washington, D.C.: IMF.

Bayliss, K. (2000) *"The World Bank and Privatisation: A Flawed Development Tool"*, November, London, Public Services International Research Unit, University of Greenwich.

Debebe, F. (1993), *"Privatisation in Sub-Saharan Africa: Origins, Trends, and Influences on Development Strategies"*, New Jersy: Centre for Economic Research on Africa.

Dercon, S. (2002) *"The Impact of Economic Reforms on Rural Households in Ethiopia: A Study from 1989 to 1995"*, Poverty Dynamics in Africa Series, Washington, D.C.: World Bank.

Donaldson, D. and Wagle, D.M. (1995) *"Privatisation: Principles and Practices"*, IFC Lessons of Experience Series No. 15007, September, Washington. D.C.: IFC.

Fekru, D. (1993), *"Privatisation in Sub-Saharan Africa: Origins, Trends, and Influences on Development Strategies"*, New Jersey: Centre for Economic Research on Africa (CERAF).

Fundanga, C.M. and Mwaba, A. (1997), *"Privatisation of Public Enterprises in Zambia: An Evaluation of the Policies, Procedures and Experiences"*, Economic Research Papers No. 35, African Development Bank.

Geeta, B. and Syed Mahmood (2003), *"Direct Support to Private Firms: Evidence on Effectiveness"*, World Bank Policy Research Working Paper 3170, November, IMF.

Gibbon, H. (1996), "A Guide for Divesting Government Owned Enterprises", How to Guide, No. 15. July.

GoE (1998), "Ethiopia: Economic Reforms for 1998/99-2000/01, The Policy Framework Paper", Prepared in Collaboration with the IMF and the WB), September 28, Addis Ababa: FGDRE.

Jauch, H. (2002), *"The Big Privatisation Debate: African Experiences"*, 13th November, Namibia, Labour Resource and Research Institute.

Mugerwa-Kayizzi, S. (2002), *"Privatisation in Sub-Saharan Africa: On Factors Affecting Implementation"*, Discussion Paper No. 2002/12, Helsinki: UNU/WIDER.

Nankani, H. (1988) *"Techniques of Privatisation of State Owned Enterprises"*, Vol. II, Selected Country Case Studies, World Bank Technical Paper No. 89, Washington, D.C.: IBRD/WB.

Nellis, J. (2003) *"Privatisation in Africa: What happened? What is to be done?"*, Working Paper No. 25, Centre for Global Development.

Parker, D. and Kirkpatrick, C. (2003), *"Privatisation in Developing Countries: A Review of the Evidence and the Policy Lessons"* Working Paper Series 55, Manchester: Institute for Development Policy and Management.

Pierre-Richard, A., Nihal, B. and Karine El, A. (2005), *"Roads out of Poverty? Assessing the Link between Aid, Public Investment, Growth and Privatisation"*, Policy Research Working Paper 3490, Washington, D.C.: World Bank.

Radomir Sabela, Terézia Hrnèíové and Josef Vais (1995), *"Process of Privatisation in Field of Industry and Trade in the Czech Republic"*, Study No. 5, June 1995, Institute of Economic Studies: Prague.

Sadar, F. (1995), *"Privatising Public Enterprises and Foreign Direct Investment in Developing Countries, 1988-93"*, Occasional Paper 5, Foreign Investment Advisory Service, Washington: IFC.

Shirley, M. and Nellis, J. (1991), *"Public Enterprise Reform: The Lessons of Experience,* Washington, D.C.: IBRD/World Bank.

TGE (1992), "Ethiopia: Transitional Government's Policy Framework Paper, 1992, 1992/3-1994/95", Addis Ababa: TGE.

UNDP (1989), *"A Study of the Experience with Privatisation of Public Enterprises in Developing Countries"*, November, New York: UNDP.

Vuylsteke, C. (1988), *"Techniques of Privatisation of State Owned Enterprise"*, Vol. I, Methods and Implementation, World Bank Technical Paper No. 88, Washington, D.C.: World Bank.

Welch, D. & Frémond, O. (1998), *"The Case-by-Case Approach to privatisation: Techniques and Examples"*, World Bank Technical Paper No. 43, Washington D.C.: World Bank.

Seminar and Conference Papers

Bulti, T. (1992), "Recent Trends in the Development of Manufactured Industries in Ethiopia" in Mekonen Taddesse (ed) *The Ethiopian Economy: Structure, Problems and Policy Issues,* (The Proceedings of the First Annual Conference on the Ethiopian Economy). Addis Ababa, pp. 139-156.

Girma, S. (1993), *"Ethiopia's Private Sector under Structural Adjustment Response to Foreign Trade Liberalisation and Exchange Rate Policy Reforms"*, A Paper Submitted for the Third Annual Conference on the Ethiopian Economy, The Department of Economics, AAU and EEA, December 3-6, 1993, Nazereth, Ethiopia.

Kebede, G. (1993), *"Privatisation of Public Enterprises: Modalities and Sequencing"*, A Paper Submitted for the Workshop on Public Enterprises Reforms and Privatisation in Ethiopia, July 1-3, Nazareth: EEA and USAID: (Ethiopia), pp. 1-30.

Mutebile, E.T. (1999), *"Better Public Sector Management: Capacity Building and Good Governance"*, in Wallace Laura (ed) AFRICA: Adjusting to the Challenges of Globalisation (Proceedings of a Seminar held in Paris, May 4-5, 1998). Washington, D.C.: IMF and Ministry of Finance of Japan, pp. 107-13.

Oumar Makalou (1999), *"Privatisation in Africa: A Critical Analysis"*, A paper presented on the 9th International Anti-Corruption Conference [IACC], 10-15 October 1999, Durban, South Africa, p. 10.

Sach, J.D. (1992), *"Accelerating Privatisation in Eastern Europe: The Case of Poland"*, The Proceedings of the World Bank Annual Conference on Development Economics 1991, Washington, D.C.: IBRD/WB, pp. 15-43.

Selvam, J., Iyappan, T. and Meenakshi S. Rajan, A. (2005), *"Ethiopian Privatisation Paradigm and its Effect on Investment"*, A Paper Presented at the Third International Conference on Ethiopian Economy, June, 2-4, 2005, UNECA Centre, Addis Ababa.

Newspapers and Magazines

Ahluwalia, M. (2003), 'Some of the criticism directed at the IMF is not valid', an exclusive interview, D+C [Development & Cooperation], September, Vol. 30.

Business Africa (2000), "A Long Way to Go: Special Report-Nigeria", *Business Africa,* Vol. 8, No. 9.

Chakravarthi, R. (2001), "The World Bank, Globalisation and Poverty", *Third World Economics: Trend and Analysis,* 1-15 December, No. 270.

Chandrasekhar, C.P. (2003), "Economic Perspectives: Privatisation on Hold", *Frontline,* October, Vol. 20, No. 20.

Economic Perspective (2001), "Focus Article: Privatisation in South Africa", *Economic Perspectives,* Fourth Quarter.

EPA (2002), *Privatisation News,* Published by the Public Relations Department of the EPA, Vol. 5, No.1.

Frontline (2003), "Disinvestment: Indian Oil Corporation Ltd. (IOCL), the next in line", , Vol. 20, No. 21.

George (2002), "Aid Listen", New African- IC Publication, Vol. 2002, No. 411.

John Winter (1999), "Taking Stock: Is Nigeria prepared to privatise?", *Africa Economic Digest,* 31 May.

Keefe, Joseph O'. (2003), "The Private Sector Drives Economic Growth", *Development Outreach,* March.

Mishra, R.K., Nandagopal and Lateef Syed, A. (1993), "Sale of Public Enterprise Shares: Frittering Away Nation's Wealth", *Economic and Political Weekly,* Vol. 28, No. 48.

Nellis, J. (1994), "Is Privatisation Necessary", *Public Policy for the Private Sector,* December.

New African (1999), "A Giant Step Forward", Special Report: Tunisia, October, No. 378.

Padmanaphan, B.S. (2003), "Towards Total Solutions" in Focus: MTNL-DELHI, *Frontline,* July, Vol. 20, No. 14.

Pamela Ann Smith (1999), "Gulf Privatisation Gathers Momentum", *The Middle East,* November.

Sheel, A. (1999), "The Privatisation Wheel", *The Economic Times,* 4 September, Vol. 39, No.177.

Sridhar, V. (2003), "Disinvestment: Airport for Sale", *Frontline,* October 24, Vol. 20, No. 21.

Tagama, H. (2002), "Who's for Privatisation", *New African,* July/August, No. 409.

Thobani, M. (1994), *"The Privatisation Experience of Latin America: Sell-off Helps Fiscal Stability",* Public Policy for the Private Sector, December, 1994.

The Hindu (2001), "Fact File: OECD Social Indicators-Educational Attainment", 12th, November.

The Hindu (2001), "Fact File: India and the World - Global Competitiveness", 22 October.

The Reporter (2003), "IMF Urged to Understand Privatisation Concerns", Vol. 5, No. 219, 16 February.

Theses and Encyclopedia

Balema, A.A. (2003), *"Economic Development and Democracy in Ethiopia"*, A Ph.D. Thesis Submitted to Erasmas University, Rotterdam, Rotterdam: Erasmas University.

Kidane, T. (1996), *"Challenges and Prospects of the Privatisation Process of the Public Enterprises in Eritrea"*, A Paper Submitted for the Partial Fulfillment of the Degree, March, University of Asmara, Asmara.

Microsoft (2004), "Microsoft Encarta Encyclopedia Standard 2004: Ethiopia", USA, Microsoft Corp.

Interviews

Diwan, I. (2004), *Interview with the Country Representative of the World Bank in Ethiopia,* Reporter, Vol. VIII, No. 399, pp. 14-5.

Gupta, A.S. (2005), *In Conversation with Rajiv Mehrotra, Interview on DD News India,* Watched on 12th June, 2005, IST 11.30 a.m-12.00 noon.

Sach, J.D. (2005), Interview with the Special Advisor to the Secretary General, UN, on Hard Talk, BBC World, Watched on 14th April, 2005, GMT 6.00 p.m.-6.30 p.m.

Websites

EPA (2003), "Privatisation", Viewed on 06/11/2003 in the EPA Website, *http://www.telecom.net.et/~epa/Privatise/index.html.*

Ram Mohan, T.T. (2004), "Privatisation in China: Softly, Softly Does it", viewed on 02/10/2004 at *http://www.iimahd.ernet.in/publications/public/Fulltext.jsp?wp-no=2004-09-04.*

Stifanos, H and Henk von Eije (2003) "The Impacts of Slow Privatisation in the Beverage and Textile Industry in Eritrea", Viewed on 12th January, 2005, http://som.rug.nl/

Wikipedia (2004), "Privatisation", Viewed on 18/02/05, *http://en.wikipedia.org/wiki/Privatisation*

World Bank (2002a), "Investment Climate Surveys in Ethiopia", Viewed on 12th March, 2005, *http://rru.worldbank.org/InvestmentClimate/Exploreeconomies/Snahshot.aspx?*

World Bank (2002b), "Investment Climate Surveys in Ethiopia", Viewed on 12/03/05, *http://rru.worldbank.org/InvestmentClimate/Exploreeconomies/Snahshot.aspx?*

World Bank (2003), World Development Indicators Database, August, Washington, D.C.: World Bank, (*http://www.devdata.worldbank.org/external/cppprofile*).

APPENDIX - I

Questionnaire

Dear Respondent,

I, Jesiah Selvam, hereby seek your kind cooperation to spare a few minutes for filling up this questionnaire, which is right now disseminated to you help my research objectives pertaining privatisation in Ethiopia. The information that you give is neither to criticise organization you work nor to bring up any adverse effect to you and your work environment, but rather to identify some of the labour issues of privatisation, which should not easily be undervalued. I assure you that the information given by you will be kept confidential, and will serve the genuine purpose of the research.

Thanking you,

1. Do you know whether your organization has been privatised?

   YES NO

2. How do you know that the organization you have been working is privatised?

By Media	By Your Managers	By Your Colleagues	If by other Means; Mention..............	Never Heard of

3. Have you ever been fearful of privatisation before it is taken place in your organization?

   YES NO

4. How do you rate your organization in general toward you after privatizing your organization?

Very Favourable	Somewhat Favourable	unfavour-able	Bad	No Change

5. Is there any shift in the management philosophy of the organization that you have had noticed after privatization?
   (a) You organization has shifted from Autocracy to Democracy
   (b) Your organization has shifted from Democracy to Autocracy
   (c) Your organization has shifted from Autocracy to Free-rein
   (d) Your organization has shifted from Democracy to Free-rein
6. How do your feel about work freedom be given to you after the change of ownership?

More Freedom	Moderate Freedom	Less Freedom	No Freedom at all	No Change

7. Do you see any positive change in your wage and salary structure after privatisation?

   YES NO

   If your answer is YES, by how much the increase is:

Less than 10 % of your salary	10% to 20%	More than 20%

8. Is there any performance-based incentives announced recently?

   YES NO

   (a) If YES, Mention what are those incentives? 1. ....

   2. ....

   3. ....

   (b) Are you satisfied with these newly announced incentives?

   YES NO
9. Is there any change in the work-hours and work load in your job after privatisation?

   YES NO

9.1 If your answer is YES, what kind of change is it?

Working hour and Work Load have increased	Working hour and work load have reduced

9.2 If there is an increase in the working-hours and work load, how do you see your ogranisation's adherence to the labour law especially on maximum working-hours a week, overtime and holidays?

High Adherent to Labour law	Somewhat Adherent to Labour laws	Less Adherent to Labour law	Not at all adherent to Labour law

10. How do you view the present relationship with your employer from the previous one?

Become Congenial/ Healthy	No Change at all (Same as it used to be)	Become Worse

11. Have your ever been oriented of the new environment that has arisen as a result of ownership change?

    YES NO

12. Have you undergone any professional training and development after privatization taken place in your organization?

    YES NO

12.1 If your answer is NO, do you think of being trained in near future by assessing the present management attitude?

    YES NO

13. Do you think that your job security is highly ensured in this organization after privatization?

    YES NO

14. What factor do you think or be told for your retention in the organization after privatization?

By the Labour Law	By my Efficiency and Talent	Indifferent

APPENDIX - II

Interview Schedule

Dear Respondent,

I, Jesiah Selvam, hereby seek your kind cooperation to spare a few minutes for filling up this questionnaire, which is right now disseminated to you help my research pertaining privatisation in Ethiopia. The information that you give is neither to criticise organization you work nor to bring up any adverse effect to you and your work environment, but rather to identify some of the policy issues in privatisation, which should not easily be underestimated. I assure you that the information given by you will be kept confidential, and will serve the genuine purpose of the research.

Thanking you,

1. What reasons do you attribute to the induction of privatisation programme in Ethiopia? (Enumerate in order of preference, e.g. rate your importance as 1,2,3 and so on)

   Increasing Budget Deficit and National Debt.................... = 1

   Poor Performance of SOEs.................... = 2

   Conditionalities of International Funding Agencies.................... = 3

   Others if any ________________________.................... = 4

2. Is the Privatisation Agency autonomous and independent? (Please encircle your answer)

   YES NO

2.1 If you say YES, how do you weigh the Agency's autonomy and independence? (Please indicate your answer using a scale of 1 (low) and 10 (high)

High									Low
10	9	8	7	6	5	4	3	2	1

If your answer is NO, what is the degree of interference that comes from the government, external agencies and other international donors?

High									Low
10	9	8	7	6	5	4	3	2	1

2.2a Whom do you think often interfere in the Agency's day-to-day affairs?

Government .... = 1

Politicians .... = 2

External Funding Agencies .... = 3

Donor Countries .... = 4

2.2b In which activity of the privatisation, does the government mostly interfere?

On the selection of SOE = 1

On the price of SOE = 2

On the selection of Buyers = 3

On the linkage between the Agency and External Funding Agencies = 4

Other activity if any

2.2c How do you rate the interference of government? {Please use the scale of 5(more interference) and 1 (less interference)}

High				Less
5	4	3	2	1

2.2d How do you perceive the interference of external funding agencies and countries?

High				Less
5	4	3	2	1

2.2e How do you perceive the interference of government?

More but supportive	More but destructive	Less but supportive	Less but destructive

3. Are you fully proficient in planning and execution of privatisation?

YES NO

3.1 If your answer is NO, how do you see the agency's dependency on others, such as foreign consultants and donor countries?

High				Less
5	4	3	2	1

4. Do you have any specific criteria for assessing the Buyers before selling the enterprise?

YES NO

4.1 If the answer is YES, mention those criteria (for example reputation, capital and efficiency of buyers):

....

....

5. What is the response of buyers in general to your sales offer from 1994/95 to 2003/04?

Increasing	Mixed	Declining

5.1 If the response trend is declining, what cause could you attribute to the declining trend?

Political Instability................. = 1

Ethiopia/Eritrea Border Conflict................. = 2

Corruption................. = 3

Non-conducive Government Policy and Legal Protection......... = 4

Size of the Domestic Market................. = 5

Difficulty in accessing to necessary raw materials................. = 6

Bureaucracy................. = 7

Tax Regulations and Heavy Custom Duties................. = 8

Lack of quality infrastructure................. = 9

Over valuation of assets................. = 10

Mention, if any other reasons.......................

5.1 If you give a considerable weight to Non-conducive Government Policy and Legal Protection for the declining trend of response to buy SOEs, could you please mention specifically those obstacles in respect to government policy?

....

....

....

6. How many work-hours (in average) do you need for the completion of a single privatisation activity (privatising a single SOE) particularly between the slating point and selling point?

Less than One Week	Between one and two weeks	Between two weeks and One month	More than one Month

6.1 How do you rate yourself in ensuring time efficiency of the process, which is asked in question 6?

Highly Efficient	Moderately Efficient	Less Efficient	In efficient

7. Are buyers satisfied with your processing time and assets valuation?

YES NO

8. What other complaints do you receive from the buyers?

....

....

....

9. What are the main reasons behind the returning of privatised enterprises once again to the agency?

....

....

....

10. How does the agency ensure that the labours' well-being is protected after privatisation?

Mention those measures:

(1) ....

(2) ....

(3) ....

11. What sectors of SOEs have attracted more private investors? Give reasons.

Sector	Reasons

12. How do you foresee the fate of the Ethiopian privatisation in near future?

More prospects of continuing	Completing soon	At Stake	Can't say

13. What are the reasons for some SOEs not being slated for privatisation?

More Strategic .... = 1

More Profitable .... = 2

Keep a balance between the private and public sector .... = 3

Any other reasons .... = 4

No perception .... = 0

14. During the post privatisation monitoring, are you satisfied with cooperation and transparency of those privatised ones towards your assessment?

Highly Satisfied	Satisfied	Less Satisfied	Not at all

14.1 If you answer is 'Less satisfied and not at all', could you mention the reasons for those privatised ones not being cooperative and transparent to the agency?

....

....

....

15. What problems do you face pertaining (methodological issues) the techniques and methods of privatisation?

....

....

....

16. What are the general problems you had have been facing toward the implementation privatisation in Ethiopia? (Indicate in the order of severity)

....

....

....

17. What kinds of quality control measure have you taken so far to improve the overall performance of privatization process of SOEs?

....

....

....

Interviewee's Name: ....

Dept./Organisation ....

Date of Interview: ....

Duration of the Interview: ....

APPENDIX - III

Interview Schedule

I, Jesiah Selvam, hereby seek your kind cooperation to spare a few minutes for filling up this interview schedule, which is right now given to you help my research pertaining privatization in Ethiopia. The information that you give is neither to criticise organization you work nor to bring up any adverse effect to you and your work environment, but rather to identify some of the policy issues in privatization, which should not easily be underestimated. I assure you that the information given by you will be kept confidential, and will serve the genuine purpose of the research.

Thanking you,

1. How long you have been working in the World Bank?

   ....

2. Are you satisfied with the overall structural adjustment programme in Ethiopia?

   YES NO

2(a) If your answer is 'NO', what cause do you think for such a poor show?

   ....

   ....

   ....

3. Are you satisfied with the overall performance of the privatization programme of the country?

   YES NO

3(a) If your answer is 'No', on what criteria or issue do they lag in privatizing the State owned enterprises? (Keep the criteria in the order of priority)

Regulatory Framework .... = 1

Public Enterprises reforms .... = 2

Modalities and Techniques .... = 3

Valuation of Assets .... = 4

Others if any................................. = 5

4. How do you see, from the bank point of view, the speed of SAP, particularly the Ethiopian privatization programme over the past eight years?

Very Fast	Fast	Slow	Very alow	Almost Stand still

5. What is the role of the Ethiopian privatization programme towards bank's announcement on the Ethiopian' HIPC initiative-completion point?

Highly Important Very Negligent

5	4	3	2	1

6. To what extent, the Ethiopian privatization programme is consistent with the bank conditionalities?

Highly Important Very Negligent

5	4	3	2	1

6(a) If your answer is 'between the scale 2 and 1', on what conditionalities of the bank are they (Government/Ethiopian Privatisation Agency) most inconsistent?

Please mention, in brief, those conditionalities:

....

....

....

6(b) To what level, the inconsistency of the government in general and EPA in particular has affected the bank's further funding to the overall structural adjustment programme, compared to that of other African nations?

Highly Affected	Less Affected	Not all Affected

7. How do you rate the bank's volume and nature of support for the Ethiopian privatization programme?

Highly Supportive	Moderately Supportive	Not all Supportive

7(a) If you answer is 'Not all Supportive', What has made the bank to adopt that unsupportive policy?

Give your reasons: ....

....

....

....

8. What suggestions from the bank point of view do you like to give to the Ethiopian Privatisation Agency for quality improvement of the programme?

....

....

....

Interviewee's Name: ....

Dept./Organisation ....

Date of Interview: ....

Duration of the Interview: ....

APPENDIX - IV

Issues Discussed through Focus Group Discussion (Among the Managerial Staff/Owner of the Privatised Enterprises)

Name of the Organisation	*Number of Persons*	*Issues for Discussion*
Fin Fine Furniture PLC.	2	Relationship with Owner, and Career Development
St. George Brewery PLC.	2	Relationship with Owner, and Career Development
Ethio Agri-CEFT PLC	1	Relationship with Owner, and Career Development
Universal Leathers Articles Factory	2	Relationship with Owner, and Career Development
Wush Wush Tea Plantation	4*	Relationship with Owner, and Career Development
Moha Soft Drinks PLC.	2	Relationship with Owner, and Career Development

Note: One among them is owner

APPENDIX - V

Valuation Guidelines Planning aid–A guide of the initial steps

INTRODUCTION

The purpose of this planning aid is to assist staff at the time of the preliminary review and in starting the assignment. It is not intended to be exhaustive, but rather to identify some of the issues which should be considered to ensure that the exercise is conducted as efficiently as possible

1. SUBJECT OF VALUATION?	REF
What is to be valued - shares or business - assets - non-cash purchase consideration?	
Are we valuing a company or unincorporated business?	
Are we valuing a minority, majority or controlling interest?	
Are particular assets to be valued separately, for example, property, pension fund?	
What type of valuation is required?	
What is point in time of the valuation?	
What form is the consideration (eg cash, shares, other assets)?	
Do we know where the subject is located? Arrange tour of business. Will we be working there or at some other location? Do we have the address, telephone and fax numbers?	
Have we recorded the names and titles of the people interviewed in the course of our preliminary review?	

1. SUBJECT OF VALUATION?	REF
How many individual units/locations does the subject have?	
What are the subject's activities? What is the size and extent of these activities?	
Have we obtained an understanding of the economic, commercial and social environment? Are there any environmental problems?	
Which employees will we have access to?	
Will we have access to the subject's premises and as counting records?	
Does the subject produce consolidated financial information? Is the financial information audited? What reconciliation's have been performed to show consistency with financial and other information?	
Will we have access to the subject's auditors and other advisers?	
Have the auditors and other advisers been briefed about our work and have they been authorized to communicate with us?	
Record general impressions of the business, management, organization, plant layout and products arising from preliminary review and tour of business.	
Summarise all items which may be a problem area in undertaking the valuation.	

VALUATION GUIDELINES

Planning aid–A guide to the initial steps

2. SCOPE OF OUR WORK	REF
Does the timetable provide us with sufficient time to complete the assignment and report?	
How many year's historical information do we need to obtain and use?	
Are we using forecasts or projections?	
How detailed is the work to be? What scope limitations are there?	
Have we been granted access to other advisers (eg auditors, legal etc)	
Have we been given unrestricted access to the enterprise and its management?	

3. OUTPUT EXPECTED	REF
What type of output is required from us – a long or short form report, opinion paragraph, more than one report and has this been agreed with the Board or review panel?	
How detailed should the output be?	

Contd....

3. OUTPUT EXPECTED	REF
Are we required to produce a single or range of values, or an opinion on the fairness and reasonableness of the proposed transaction?	
Will our conclusions be final and binding, or will they solely provide guidelines for negotiations?	
In what language is the original version of our output to be prepared? Will translations into other languages be required?	
Will any other parties have access to the output?	
What is the timetable for the draft and final versions of the output?	
Will the enterprise's management be shown a draft of our report to verify factual accuracy?	
Will the enterprise's management accept responsibility for any factual content include in any output?	
Are any 'by products' to the main output expected?	

VALUATION GUIDELINES

Planning aid – A guide to the initial steps

4. STAFFING AND THE USE OF OTHER SPECIALISTS	REF
What are the appropriate levels of staff for the assignment? Do we have the right mix?	
Do we need specific language skills?	
Has a competent translator been booked to translate instructions, our end report etc?	
Do we require the use of specialists? (lawyers/asset valuers, market specialists, industry experts)?	
Can we get staff with previous experience on this enterprise or nature of assignment? Is previous experience a necessity, merely advantageous or positively undesirable?	
Are the staff selected available to do the assignment: – Are they aware of the deadlines? – What overtime is expected? – Will they have to, and be able to, cancel porevious commitments?	
Has the whole team (including specialists) been properly briefed about the assignment including sensitivities, confidentiality requirements and security?	
Have instructions been drafted for the use of internal/external specialists?	
Has a manager been nominated to be our internal project co-ordinator?	

4. STAFFING AND THE USE OF OTHER SPECIALISTS	REF
What arrangements have been made to ensure adequate supervision of other departments/external resources?	
Has a satisfactory process been set up for sharing of issues arising from the work performed by all team members?	
Has management of the typing resource been considered (eg when, how much, arrangements for late work)?	
Do we require the use of any other staff- especially during out of office hours (eg photocopying services, etc)?	

VALUATION GUIDELINES

APPENDIX A–Planning aid–A guide to the initial steps

5. GETTING STARTED	REF
Check with EPA's central register for previous experience of valuations of similar entity, industrial sector, assets etc.	
Initiate searches for general background information on target and industry from public record, newspapers, accounts.	
Have outline work programmes been written? If not are staff fully aware of the type, scope, and details of the work to be performed and any specific tests which should be carried out?	
Have members of staff been set objectives for appraisal?	
What form should the working papers take and what should the file structure be?	
Are staff aware of the need to obtain any additional information during their visit to the business's premises in order to satisfy the requirements of any additional output that may be requested at a later stage?	
Have we adequately briefed the support staff (eg typists, etc.) and arranged for night typing/additional resources as necessary.	

VALUATION GUIDELINES

Contents of a typical "long-form" report

BACKGROUND

The form and content of the report will depend on the objectives of the assignment. Any report must always be tailored to meet the specific requirements of the agency. Whatever form the contents of the report take, it is important that they are concise and unambiguous.

The following headings provide a systematic approach to a valuation exercise to ensure that it is approached in a methodical manner. The headings are not, however, exclusive, or always essential, and valuations for different types of enterprises within different industries may require a refinement of the headings.

The contents of a typical long form report include.

1. Introduction
2. Executive summary
3. Brief description of the subject of the valuation
4. Description of the industry
5. Financial performance of the subject
6. Assets
7. Financial performance of the industry
8. Summary of SWOT analysis
9. Valuation calculations

INTRODUCTION	✓
Confirm understanding of the requirements of the assignment – Valuation requirement – Why? – Business/Asset to be valued – What? – Basis of Valuation/methodology – How? – Valuation date – When?	
Scope of work undertaken and responsibilities assumed; any limitations placed on the work (eg where there has been no access to the subject's officials, auditors or other advisers, or only limited access or and, particularly, if you have been instructed not to consider something)	
Confirmation that auditors reported without qualification on the financial statements or provide details of significant qualifications	
Summary of any major qualifications to financial data shown in valuation report; treatment of inflation/hyperinflation	
Sources of information and any restrictions as to scope	
Summary of major assumptions underlying forecast/projected financial data (if appropriate) and key sensitivities	
Conclusions and valuation (or valuation ranges)	
A statement as to whether [extracts/drafts] of report have been discussed with senior officials of the enterprise being valued in order to confirm matters of fact	
An acknowledgement of assistance received	

VALUATION GUIDELINES

Contents of a typical "long-form" report

EXECUTIVE SUMMARY

For particularly lengthy reports, it may be desirable to include an executive summary of findings.

INTRODUCTION	✓
Legal status	
Constitution	
Background and history	
Products, customers, suppliers and trading activity	
Operational structure	
Strategic alliances, dependence on related parties	
Management structure; key executives	
Management information systems	
Insurance cover	
Environmental factors	

DESCRIPTION OF THE INDUSTRY

INTRODUCTION	✓
History	
Competitors	
Environmental factors	
Future prospects	

FINANCIAL PERFORMANCE OF THE ENTERPRISE OF THE ENTERPRISE BEING VALUED

INTRODUCTION	✓
Accounting policies	
Trading record; effects of inflation and discretionary expenditure	
Extent of treasury/foreign exchange/hedging operations	
Actual performance against plan	
Taxation	
Dividend distribution history	
Future projections/prospects	

VALUATION GUIDELINES

Contents of a typical "long-form" report

ASSETS	✓
Operational assets; owned/leased	
Depreciation policy	
Intangible assets	
Contingent liabilities	
Non operational assets	

FINANCIAL PERFORMANCE OF THE INDUSTRY	✓
Financial performance of competitors	
Takeover of comparable companies	
Market ratings of comparable companies	

SUMMARY OF SWOT ANALYSIS	✓
Indicate factors which have been identified as strengths, weaknesses, opportunities and threats of the subject of the valuation.	

VALUATION CALCULATIONS	✓
Reasons for methodology selected	
Outline of methodology	
Summary of calculations (details in Appendices)	
Balancing of views on different calculation methods	
Final judgment on valuation	

Source: EPA (2004).

APPENDIX - VI

Ethopian Privatisation Agency information Checklist

This is a standard checklist of information required by the team. Please complete the checklist and where possible please enclose copies of documents required in a file,

	Information available and filed			
	Yes	*No*	*N/A*	*Comments/File reference*
Corporate and business ownership documents				
• Details of when, where and by whom the business was established.				
• Details of changes in ownership since inception.				
• Incorporation documents, proclamations and company's memorandum and Articles of Association				
• Composition of the Board of Directors and Board of Management Information available and filed Management				
• Minutes of Board of Management meetings for the last 5 years				
• Minutes of senior management committees' meetings for the last 3 years				
• Management organization chart.				
• Brief description of the age, experience and qualifications of management staff.				
• Details of management service agreements. Details of training/personnel policy for maintaining continuity of executive management and other key personnel.				

	Information available and filed			
	Yes	*No*	*N/A*	*Comments/File reference*
Employees				
• Number of employees and important changes in labour force during the five years prior to valuation date.				
• Key employees on whom earnings continuity depends and, more specifically, comments on whether replacements are readily available.				
• Details of salaries and wage rates and benefit plans for each category of employees.				
• Employment and incentive contracts with individual executives or employees.				
• Details of labour disputes (if any) in the last 5 years				
• Copies of present union agreements.				
• Pension fund accounts and latest actuarial valuations and details of any unfounded liabilities-past or present service-and plans for funding the same.				
Banking and insurance arrangements				
• Details of existing bank line of credit and security given for bank borrowings as at the valuation date.				
• Details of existing insurance cover as at the valuation date.				
Industry Information				
• List of major competitors, their history, their relative market shares, prices and pricing policies, production capacities, distribution channels, major customers and suppliers.				
• List of membership of trade associations, or similar industry associations.				
• Details of competition from imports and its effect on the pricing and volumes of the industry.				
• Any information which the company may have concerning takeovers of the companies in the industry or a related industry.				
• Any information which the company may have concerning takeovers of the companies in the industry or a related industry.				
• Financial statements of comparable companies (if available).				
• Reports on the industry and companies within the industry (if available)				

	Information available and filed			
	Yes	No	N/A	Comments/File reference
• Any relevant details of the outlook for the future of the industry e.g; press cuttings, industry magazines etc.				
Company Profile Market Strategy				
• Five year plans setting out goals, strategies, objectives, and policies of the company.				
• The company's marketing strategy plan & analysis of marketing costs e.g. into advertising, promotions etc.				
• Analysis of market trends and the historic and anticipated future trends or market share of the business and/or major product lines.				
• Details of any franchise, patents, distribution and royalty agreements e.g. expiry date of the current agreement, fees payable or receivable, key terms and conditions etc.				
• Agreements, if any, outside the normal course of business, and related party transactions (transactions with other SOE's) detailing the names of the related parties, the nature of the relationship with the related party and the volume of business carried out with the related party and terms of that business.				
• Brochures explaining company's products.				
Sales				
• Analysis of monthly/quarterly/half yearly* sales by volume and value for the last 3 years on a divisional basis as well as on a company basis (*as appropriate)				
• List of major customers (those accounting for more than 10% of total sales volume), and the type of products sold to them.				
• Details of sales promotion methods, export methods, distribution channels, etc.				
• Broad analysis of sales by product, by major customers and between home and export sales for the past five years.				
• Basis used in fixing selling prices, e.g. cost plus, competitor driven etc.				
• For major products, provide a profile of price increases over the past five years giving details of the date of each increase, the selling price after the increase and the % increase.				

	Information available and filed			
	Yes	*No*	*N/A*	*Comments/File reference*
• Details of inter-company and inter-divisional trading and the pricing policy used eg show the amount of purchases or sales to related companies and divisions in each of the past five years, whether the sales/purchases were made at the same prices available to third-party customers and, if not, the differences between these transfer prices and third-party prices				
• Details of any controls over selling prices exercised by Government departments, trade associations, etc.				
• Details of contracts with major customers.				
• Particulars of any major contracts unfulfilled at the valuation date.				
• List backlog of contracts at the valuation date stating type of contract and number of man-hours and costs involved.				
• Analysis of expected future profits/losses on major long-term contracts.				
• For commodity related companies and those relying on commodities as inputs, details of world prices for the grade of product being produced, for the past five years and likely trends for the future.				
Purchasing				
• List of major suppliers (those accounting for more than 10% of total cost of materials purchased), giving type of goods and services purchased.				
• Details of alternative sources of supply for materials and services critical to the continuing operations of the business.				
• Details of price movements (in US$) within the last 3 years for all purchases of raw materials				
• Details of any significant forward purchase commitments.				
• If significant amount of purchases are imported, rate of import duty and average delivery time.				
• Details of controls over raw material prices exercised by Government departments.				
• Details of contracts with major suppliers.				
• Nature and amount of work subcontracted to outside companies.				

	Information available and filed			
	Yes	No	N/A	Comments/File reference
Production				
• A brief description of the production process.				
• Details of estimated capacity of factory and current operating level; details of scope for increasing capacity, details of limiting factors of production.				
• Analysis of monthly production volumes for the last 3 years by product for each of the divisions and for the company as a whole				
• Details of the company's replacement plans for productive equipment				
• Details of the main operating parameters				
Research and development				
• Details of levels of expenditure over the last five years				
• Information on research and development programme including product research, facilities and past successes.				
Financial documents				
• The audited financial statements (consolidated and unconsolidated) of the company and its subsidiaries for the five years prior to the team visit (together with supporting schedules showing the a further breakdown of the figures appearing in the financial statements)				
• Management accounts for the company and for each of the divisions for the last three years				
• Details of debt or loan agreements				
• Correspondence with banks relating to trade financing arrangements.				
• Copies of income tax returns to all tax authorities with supporting schedules for the five years prior to the valuation date. Also information as to which years are open for assessment, major reassessments, if any, etc.				
Fixed assets				
• Categories fixed assets into the following categories giving details of cost, depreciation, net book values, depreciation rates and insurance cover for each of the following categories: land & Buildings, Motor vehicles, Plant and Machinery.				
• Itemise and list fixed assets detailing year of purchase, condition, cost and remaining useful life for the above categories. For Plant &				

	Information available and filed			
	Yes	*No*	*N/A*	*Comments/File reference*
Machinery, only list items whose cost is >5% of the total fixed asset costs. (Obtainable from fixed asset register if one exists)				
• Major capital commitments and capital expenditures anticipated or programmed at the valuation date indicating the source of financing these projects.				
• Schedule of major differences between book and tax values of fixed assets.				
• Summarise financing policy and schedule details of lease agreements or lease options.				
• Details of any outstanding purchase/sale options (equipment, land, etc) as at the valuation date.				
• List of asset valuations carried out in the past 3 years and copies of those reports.				
• Describe and list any redundant assets and give details of their book values.				
• List and describe non-core assets (assets which are not required for the operations of the business) e.g. excess cash, short term deposits, investments in marketable securities, and investments in excess land, buildings and equipment.				
Taxation				
• Details of any special agreements/tax exemptions applicable to the company				
• Copies of the company's corporate tax returns for the five years prior to the valuation date and assessments issued/ agreed by the tax department				
• Details of Sales Tax rates applicable to the company's sales				
• A breakdown of the amount owed to/from the Sales Tax department as at the last audited balance sheet date and the valuation date				
• A schedule summarizing any other duties applicable to the company's products or purchases eg Import Duty, excise duty and Sales Tax rates.				
• A schedule showing a breakdown of the amounts owed to the income tax department at the date of the last audited balance sheet and valuation date				

	Information available and filed			
	Yes	*No*	*N/A*	*Comments/File reference*
• Copies of any documents filed with the income tax department under the tax amnesty scheme.				
• Copies of correspondence with the tax authorities over the five years to the valuation date.				
Contingencies/Commitments/Guarantees				
• Details of any contingent liabilities existing at the valuation date e.g. outstanding lawsuits against the company, disputes with customers or suppliers etc.				
• Details of any commitments existing at the valuation date e.g. product warranties, sale or return commitments etc.				
• Details of any outstanding guarantees given by the company as the valuation date e.g. guarantees to banks for borrowing by related group companies etc.				
General economic factors				
• List and describe the economic factors that most impact the overall profitability of the industry e.g. exchange rates, etc.				
• List of government or other statistics used by the company, and sources of these statistics.				
Political factors				
• Any known or expected government pronouncements and intentions affecting the industry or company specifically.				
• Any public enquiry and other specialist governmental projects affecting the industry or company specifically.				
• Environmental reports affecting the industry or company specifically.				
Social factors				
• Details of any market research and attitude surveys relevant to the company.				
• Details of any census information or studies relevant to the company eg studies or statistics relating to demographic shifts.				
Other				
• Copies of share and/or business valuation reports previously commissioned by the company within the past five years.				
• Letters of inquiry or formal offers from prospective purchasers during the five years immediately preceding the valuation date.				

	Information available and filed			
	Yes	*No*	*N/A*	*Comments/File reference*
• Details of share transactions involving the company or any of its subsidiaries during the five years immediately preceding the valuation date.				
Future projections and prospects				
• Forecast of expected operating results and cash flows to the end of the current financial year.				
• Detailed budget of operating results and cash flows for the next financial year.				
• Projections of operating results and cash flows for at least five years subsequent to the valuation date.				
• Describe key assumptions made in compiling the budgets and forecasts in respect of the items below.				
– economic environment e.g. exchange, inflation and interest rates				
– sales and pricing policies				
– expenditure plans e.g. increased promotional expenditure, etc.				
– capital replacement plans (compared to previous years).				
– Financing assumptions for working capital and long term growth.				

APPENDIX - VII

FORM OF BID SUBMISSION

THE GENERAL MANAGER
ETHIOPIAN PRIVATISATION AGENCY
P.O.BOX 11835, ADDIS ABABA

Re: Proposal for the partial or total acquisition of the Government owned Shares in ....Share Company.

1. Having read and understood the Bid Documents for Notice No. 002/ 2001-2002 and fully complying or agreeing to comply with the conditions and requirements in the Bid Documents, I or we the undersigned, offer

   Birr .... /USD .... per share for .... shares of the Company (payable in USD for foreign investors) Total price for .... Shares in Birr .... /USD

2. I/we have furnished a Bid Bond in the amount of Birr /USD .... /in the form of ....

3. I/we also agree to start the implementation of the proposed Business Plan as soon as the transfer of the shares is finalized I/we agree to abide by my/our Bid for a period of 120 days from the bid opening date.

4. Until the transfer is finished, the bid Document, this proposal and other documents related to these documents shall constitute a binding contract.

5. I/we understand that you are not bound to accept the most responsive or any bid you may receive.

   Dated this .... days of 2002

   Signed by ....

   (Print name) Signature

   Duly authorized to sign this proposal for and on behalf of .... (In block letters)

Source: EPA (2004)

APPENDIX - VIII

Post-Privatising Monitoring Form

1. Company Details

Name of Company ....

Location Region ....Wereda.............Kebele............City............

Economic Sector ....

Products /Services of the Company ....

....

....

....

Branches of the company

Distribution center ....

Retails outlets ....

Current Legal Status ....

Chief Executive officer...

Telephone Number...........................Fax Number................................

Postal Address ....

E-Mail ....

2. Production

2.1 Production in Quantity

S/N	Major Products	Unit	Actual Production in quantity			
			2001	2002	2003	2004
1						
2						
3						

2.2 Actual Production in Value (Birr)

S/N	Major Products	2001	2002	2003	2004
1					
2					
3					
4					

3. PROFIT AND LOSS ACCOUNT

- Please provide a copy of the audited accounts for the last 3 years. (After Privatisation)
- Please complete the following table

		2001	2002	2003	2004
3.1	Net sales				
	• Local				
	• Export				
3.2	Profit/(Loss) Before Taxation				
3.3	Taxation				
3.4	Profit/(Loss) After Taxation				
3.5	Dividends				
3.6	Retained Profit				

4. TAXES PAID/PAYABLE (After Privatisation)

		2001	2002	2003	2004
4.1	profit tax				
4.2	sales tax				
4.3	employees tax				
4.4	excise tax				
4.5	import duties				
4.6	others (specify)				

5. BALANCE SHEET

Please provide a summary of the balance sheets (Birr)

		2001	2002	2003	2004
5.1	Fixed Assets				
5.2	Current Assets				
5.3	Current Liabilities				
5.4	Net Current Assets (liabilities)				
5.5	Long Term Liabilities				
5.6	Net Assets				
	Financed By:				
5.7	Share Capital				
5.8	Reserves				
5.9	Share holders' interest				

6. HUMAN RESOURCES

No.	Details	2001	2002	2003	2004
		Number	Number	Number	Number
6.1	Regular full-time employees				
	• Female				
	• Male				
6.1.1	Regular full-time production employees				

No.	Details	2001	2002	2003	2004
		Number	Number	Number	Number
6.1.1	Regular full-time Administrative employees				
6.1.3	Regular full-time New employees joins				
6.1.4	Regular full-time employees				
6.1.5	Regular full-time employees dismissed				
6.1.6	Regular full-time expatriate				
6.1.7	Professionals*				
6.1.8	Semi-Professionals**				
6.1.9	Others***				

* *Professionals:-* are those workers who are holders of Bachelor Degree or above

** *Semi-Professionals:-* are those worker who are Diploma holders

*** *Others:-* refers to workers other than mentioned above.

Please provide the range of monthly salaries and wages of employees

Range (Birr)	2001	2002	2003	2004
	Number	Number	Number	Number
100-200				
201-500				
501-1000				
1001-1500				
1501-2000				
2001-2500				
2501-3000				
>3001				

7. Do you employ seasonal labour? Yes/No.... If yes, please indicate below

		2001	2002	2003	2004
7.1	Number of Seasonal Labor employed				

7.2 Total Employment cost (salaries and wages) (Birr)

	Employment	2001	2002	2003	2004
7.2	Number of Seasonal Labor employed				

8. Training (and Cost)

	2001		2002		2003		2004	
	Number	Birr	Number	Birr	Number	Birr	Number	Birr
8.1 Managers								
8.2 Skilled								
8.3 Unskilled								
8.4 Total								

9. Investments and Disposals

Please indicate your expenditure on fixed assets (Capital Equipment including Land and Buildings) since privatization and also state the main purpose of investments: Replacement, Modernization, Expansion:

PLANT & MACHINERY (Birr)

		2001	2002	2003	2004
9.1	Replacement				
9.2	Modernization				
9.3	Expansion				

LAND & BUILDING (Birr)

		2001	2002	2003	2004
9.1	Replacement				
9.2	Modernization				
9.3	Expansion				

11. Please indicate your new investment in working capital since Privatization if any?

(Birr)

	2001	2002	2003	2004
11.1 Working Capital				

12. Please indicate your disposal of fixed assets since Privatization if any?

PLANT & MACHINERY (Birr)

	2001	2002	2003	2004
12.1 Excess Capacity				
12.2 Obsolete				
12.3 Other (specify)				

LAND & BUILDING (Birr)

	2001	2002	2003	2004
12.1 Excess Capacity				
12.2 Obsolete				
12.3 Other (specify)				

13. Please indicate export sales revenue and import substitution if any?

(Birr)

	2001	2002	2003	2004
12.1 Export Turnover (Net sales)				
12.2 Import Sub.				

14. New Products Introduced

If you have introduced new products to your production line since Privatization, please state the sales turnover per annum by product/ service type.

	2001 Turnover (Birr)	2002 Turnover (Birr)	2003 Turnover (Birr)	2004 Turnover (Birr)
13.1 Product 1 ( )				
13.2 Product 2 ( )				
13.4 Product 3 ( )				
13.5 Product 4 ( )				
13.5 Product 5 ( )				

15. What are the difficulties your company has faced as a result of structural reforms, investment and taxation policies:

....

....

....

....

16. Please suggest what government may do to enhance the development of the private sector:

....

....

....

....

17. Any Other Comments

....

....

....

....

....

Note: Use additional pages if necessary.

Source: Post Privatising Dept, EPA (2004)